Strangers in This World

Strangers in This World

Multireligious Reflections on Immigration

Allen G. Jorgenson, Hussam S. Timani, and
Alexander Y. Hwang

Fortress Press
Minneapolis

STRANGERS IN THIS WORLD

Multireligious Reflections on Immigration

Cover image: Street market in Mulberry Street, Lower East Side, New York City/
Peter Newark American Pictures/Bridgeman Images.

Cover design: Laurie Ingram

Library of Congress Cataloging-in-Publication Data

Print ISBN: 978-1-4514-7297-4

eBook ISBN: 978-1-5064-0034-1

The paper used in this publication meets the minimum requirements of American
National Standard for Information Sciences — Permanence of Paper for Printed
Library Materials, ANSI Z329.48-1984.

Manufactured in the U.S.A.

This book was produced using PressBooks.com, and PDF rendering was done by
PrinceXML.

Contents

Foreword

Strangers in This World: Multireligious Reflections on Immigration began as a project undertaken by several fellows of the American Academy of Religion/Luce Foundation Summer Seminars on Comparative Theology and Theologies of Religious Pluralism, cohort II (2010–2011). The editors wish to thank the Seminar for providing the inspiration and opportunity to develop the idea into the present volume, and we also wish to acknowledge the American Academy of Religion's support of this project by providing a place in the Annual Meetings to work on this project. John Thatamanil, the Director of the Seminars, deserves much credit for not only organizing and leading the seminars, but also in encouraging the project from the beginning. The Teaching Team and other fellows of the Seminar provided insightful feedback and were invaluable conversation partners.

Alexander Y. Hwang, Hussam S. Timani, and Allen J. Jorgenson

Introduction

Alexander Y. Hwang

Strangers in This World: Multi-Religious Reflections on Immigration is a contribution to the ongoing discussions on The Immigration Question. While scholars have long reflected on the spiritual and religious meanings and significance of human pilgrimage and resettlement, it is especially timely in our Age of Migration.[1] The collection of essays in this volume represents some of the ways that various religious and faith traditions interpret the theme of immigration. The rich diversity of perspectives presented here speaks to the different meanings of immigration, yet there is a common understanding of the important, if not essential, role that immigration plays in each of these faith traditions.

The diversity of cultures, religion, and faiths that is the result of the unprecedented movements of peoples—some by choice and others by degrees of force or necessity—have brought challenges as well as opportunities to our sense of individual, communal, national,

---

1. The standard study on the global movements of people is *The Age of Migration: International Population Movements in the Modern World*, 5th ed., ed. Stephen Castles et al. (Basingstoke, UK: Palgrave Macmillian, 2013).

and religious identities. The question of "who is my neighbor?" is especially appropriate in light of the ever-increasing religious diversity of our communities. Though the question is specifically drawn from the Judeo-Christian-Muslim tradition, it is a question that other religious traditions have expressed in their own ways. Our nation, our communities, our workplaces, and even our families have witnessed the presence of "new" neighbors, who are "different" from "us." They are "strangers" to us, most often because of their appearance, language, culture, and religion. Increasingly, the identity of "my neighbor" is someone who looks, speaks, and believes differently from us—they are strangers to us.

These strangers have been the subject of political, social, and economic reflections and debates, but less so in terms of religion.[2] What does our religious traditions and beliefs teach us about the stranger? This collection of multi-religious reflections seeks to answer this question and in doing so, reminds us that we are all strangers in this world. Moreover, these reflections also challenges and inspires us to consider our shared concern for universal human flourishing and the hope that we can and should become good neighbors to all. This hope is expressed in our sacred greetings to

---

2. The addition of religious perspectives to the immigration debate are becoming more numerous, systematic, and organized. Leading the way, Roman Catholic scholars have a deep and long tradition of concern for immigrants, particularly to the most vulnerable and the poor among them. For a review of the recent growth of the Christian—primarily Roman Catholic—theological literature on immigration, see Gioacchino Campese, "The Irruption of Migrants: Theology of Migration in the 21st Century," *Theological Studies* 73/1 (February 2012): 3-32. An excellent collection of essays by some of the leading Roman Catholic theologians, including Peter Phan and Gustavo Gutiérrez, are in *A Promised Land, a Perilous Journey: Theological Perspectives on Migration*, eds. Daniel G. Groody and Gioacchino Campese (Notre Dame: University of Notre Dame Press, 2008). In 2013, Palgrave Macmillian launched the Religion and Migration Book Series, and several volumes are in print with more expected. Recent scholarly attention to immigration is also evidenced in the American Academy of Religion's *Religion and Migration Group*, as well as the *Interreligious Reflections on Immigration Seminar*.

strangers: *shalom, peace, as-salamu alaykum,* and *namaste,* among many others.

The complexity and dynamism of the subject precludes any one answer to The Immigration Question. Theologies and faith perspectives on immigration as a formal topic of discourse are still in the process of development and refinement. Whatever the answer or answers may emerge, it must reflect the diversity and richness of the various religious and faith traditions—it must be ecumenical, inter-religious, and inter-disciplinary. There is much work to be done, both within our own respective faith traditions and in dialogue and engagement with others traditions and perspectives. Only with a "comprehensive" religious reform of our understanding of immigration can we move toward the answers to the question of our time, and must be included in any discussion on comprehensive immigration reform.

***

The chapters in this volume reflect both the diversity and universality of religious interpretations of the phenomenon of immigration. We hope these chapters will contribute not only to the advancement of the academic study of immigration, but also to the current debate on immigration, about which religion and faith have much to declare, clarify, and critique. The sections and the chapters are arranged topically with a concern for chronology, but the diversity of religious traditions and perspectives does not easily lend itself to a well-organized and coherent presentation. In a way, the resistance to neat and clearly defined boundaries of organization and groupings reflects something of the immigrant experience and reflection. The editors made the necessary choices of the order of presentation and its divisions into sections knowing that the order and divisions are far less important than their inclusion in this single volume.

Section One contains chapters from the perspective of the Hindu and Buddhist traditions, and begins with Reid Locklin's chapter, "Migration and Spiritual Conquest: Emplacing Contemporary Comparative Theology in a Hindu Theology of the 'Quarters' (*dik*)." Locklin explores the Chinmaya Mission's creative theological responses to the North American Hindu diaspora, and the problems created by the physical distance from India. In Chapter Two, John Thompson presents a Buddhist interpretation of immigration by noting its presence in early texts, its prominent theme in two Buddhist teachings: *bodhisattvas* and the "Pure Lands," and interpreting *nirvana* as immigration from physical and spiritual suffering. Karma Lekshe Tsomo's "Choices and Challenges: Tradition and Adaptation among Immigrant Buddhist Populations in North America" traces some of the history and adaptations of immigrant Buddhist communities in America. The section ends with Jonathan Seitz's "Missionary and Immigrants, Missionaries as Immigrants," written from the under-explored perspective of the missionary as the immigrant, and the challenges and opportunities for the missionary immigrant's religion and faith in relation to the new home.

In Section Two, "The Abrahamic Traditions," Jewish, Muslim, and Christian perspectives are presented. Daniel Moaz begins this section with a reevaluation of and challenges to the traditional views of Israel, God, and exile in the context of the Promise Land. In the next chapter, "Immigration Theology in Islam," Muhammad Shafiq introduces the Islamic understanding of immigration, drawing upon the Qur'an and the initial development of the Muslim theology of immigration in the Golden Age of Islam. Continuing on the theme of *hijra*, Hussam Timani's "The Islamic Doctrine of *Hijra* (Migration): Theological Implications" develops a doctrine of *hijra*, noting that the Prophet Muhammad was an immigrant. Timani locates the immigrant journey as a point of contact between the divine and the human, and relates it to the Islamic doctrine of *tawhid* ("oneness or unity of God or Being").

Craig Davis, "Gothic 'Immigrants' in the Roman Empire," traces the migration of the Goths into the Roman Empire and the subsequent development of the distinctive adoption and interpretation of the Christian faith among the various Germanic-speaking immigrants. In chapter nine, "White Protestant Efforts to Convert Italian Immigrants: The Case of Constantine Panunzio," Linda Mercadante examines the earnest, but largely unsuccessful, Protestant attempts to convert the mass of Roman Catholic-Italian immigrants who arrived in America at the end of the nineteenth and the beginning of the twentieth centuries. The complexity of this long-forgotten episode in American history is highlighted by the well-documented case of Constantine Panunzio. This section ends with Kristine Suna-Koro's chapter, "Journeying Before God with a Divided Heart: The Colonial and Postcolonial Migrations of Latvian Lutherans," which explores some of the challenges of global migration through the history of Latvian Lutherans immigrants to North America, and offers a constructive reflection on migration.

Section Three, "Native Americans and the First Strangers," reminds us of the relative and ironic nature of the current North American immigration debate. Often neglected in the current debate has been the perspectives and history of the relationship between indigenous peoples of North America and the "First Strangers." This section contains reflections on the white strangers (Europeans) and the native peoples of North America who received them with generosity and hospitality. Randy Woodley begins this section with a chapter on "Welcoming the Stranger: Native American Hospitality," which highlights the generous hospitality offered to the first white immigrants. Woodley points out the deep-seated concern for the stranger and the native people's tradition of hospitality to the stranger, which echoes the Jewish and Christian scriptures' call to welcome the stranger long before they were introduced to European religion. In chapter twelve, "A Shared Narrative," Ray Aldred advocates for the need of a shared narrative that will foster a shared identity for all Canadians. Aldred points to the tradition of the Treaty relationship, spiritually based, that could ultimately lead to proper relationships between First Nations, settlers, and new comers. In the last chapter of this section, "Immigration: From Borders to Boundaries under First Nations Tutelage," Allen Jorgenson reflects on his own relationship to the land once occupied by the First Nations, and proposes that Christians can learn from the First Nations' understanding of space and place which can lead to a reimagining of borders as boundaries.

The last section addresses issues related to traditional views on immigration. One reaction to the Age of Migration has been the focus on protecting and enforcing boundaries and borders, which the stranger's presence challenges. The presence and movements of immigrants challenges the purpose and legitimacy of borders and boundaries. Yet at the same time, boundaries and borders rightly conceived and interpreted are also necessary for human flourishing. This is true of political and physical borders and boundaries, as well as our spiritual, emotional, and psychological boundaries. Laura Alexander begins this section with "Lutheran Thought, Civil Disobedience, and the New Sanctuary Movement," which examines the New Sanctuary Movement in light of the Lutheran tradition. Alexander highlights and reminds us of the moral dilemma faced by morally conscious people who are "breaking" the law and those who support undocumented immigrants. While the Lutheran tradition emphasizes obedience to the secular law, Alexander posits that the thoughts of Luther and Bonhoeffer, taken together, sheds light on the discussion of the movement's shared concern for meeting all of our moral obligations—including the economic and political. Chapter fifteen, "The Morning After: The Role of Faith-Based Groups Post-Immigration Reform," deals with the role of faith-based groups in the context of the eventual passage of the proposed "Comprehensive Immigration Reform" legislation. Aja suggests new and bold steps that inter-faith organizations and groups can take, that will help address the economic, social, and political injustices suffered by millions of migrants. Joseph Bracken and Marc Pugliese introduce Whitehead's metaphysics to the immigration debate in "Blending Past and Future: Whitehead's Metaphysics and Immigration Reform." In this chapter, Bracken and Pugliese posit that the value of change, viewed negatively by both classical metaphysics and those opposed to undocumented and legal immigration, must be reformed to reflect reality that is defined by change. Changes, caused by immigration, are not to be feared, but appreciated as an expression of what Whitehead called Creativity, which provides hope for positive changes to our present societal forms, including reified borders and boundaries, that resist change. The final chapter is by Ronald Baard, who explores mental illness as a type of immigration, when one also becomes a "stranger in this world." Baard details the immigration, physical and psychological, of his immigrant grandfather. "Immigration as/and Mental Illness: More than Metaphor" presents immigration as a rich metaphor for the experiences suffered by those afflicted with mental illness, and the various responses to that immigration in society and in religion.

PART I

Hindu and Buddhist Perspectives and Encounters

1

Migration and Spiritual Conquest

*Emplacing Contemporary Comparative Theology in a
Hindu Theology of the "Quarters" (dik)*

Reid B. Locklin

As a formal discipline, comparative theology is the creature of a
distinctively modern and distinctively European scholarly
imagination, with its regard directed to other "places"—to persons,
traditions, and geographies conceived of as lying outside the
boundaries of Christendom. This is certainly true of the "old"
comparative theology, as the fruit of missionary encounters and
colonial conquest.[1] But it is arguably retained in the "new"

---

1. See Tomoko Masuzawa, *The Invention of World Religions: Or, How European Universalism Was
Preserved in the Language of Pluralism* (Chicago/London: University of Chicago Press, 2005), esp.
72–104; Francis X. Clooney, S.J., *Comparative Theology: Deep Learning across Religious Borders*
(Malden, MA: Wiley-Blackwell, 2010), 24–40; and Peter Henrici, "The Concept of Religion
from Cicero to Schleiermacher: Origins, History, and Problems with the Term," in *Catholic
Engagement with World Religions: A Comprehensive Study*, ed. Karl Josef Becker and Ilaria Morali
(Maryknoll, NY: Orbis, 2010), 1–20.

comparative theology articulated by Keith Ward, Francis X. Clooney, Robert Neville, James Fredericks, and their students. As just one example, the well-respected scholar of Hinduism and comparative theologian Francis Clooney writes frequently of his experiences of travel and study in India, and his comparative method privileges a model of personal transformation, in which the comparativist immerses herself in the texts and practices of another tradition so as to reinterpret texts and practices of her home tradition with new eyes.[2] Though this model need not involve literal travel, it is nevertheless most easily imagined in a geographical idiom of pilgrimage across the territorial boundaries of Hindu and Christian traditions. The comparativist departs from one place of social and religious identity, immerses herself in another, and returns home, ideally transformed.

It is worth noting that both Christian comparativists and theologians of religions frequently speak of globalization and new experiences of religious diversity in late modernity as the context for their work: the religious diversity that might once have existed "out there," has become an intrinsic feature of the cities and academic circles in which most theologians find themselves, "here" and "now," and thus demands our scholarly attention.[3] One important element of such a globalized context, at least in North America, is the new religious landscape created by the loosening of restrictions on immigrants from various parts of Asia in the United States and

2. See, for example, the accounts in Francis X. Clooney, S.J., "The Transformation of the Scholar as a Factor in Hindu-Christian Studies," *Journal of Hindu-Christian Studies* 3 (1990): 1–6; idem., *Theology after Vedānta: An Experiment in Comparative Theology* (Albany: State University of New York Press, 1993), esp. 33–35, 153–208; and idem., *Beyond Compare: St. Francis de Sales and Śrī Vedānta Deśika on Loving Surrender to God* (Washington, DC: Georgetown University Press, 2008), esp. 132–41, 202–12.

3. E.g., Clooney, *Comparative Theology*, 3–9; Michael Barnes, S.J., *Theology and the Dialogue of Religions* (Cambridge: Cambridge University Press, 2002), 3–28; Paul F. Knitter, *Introducing Theologies of Religions* (Maryknoll, NY: Orbis, 2002), 3–13.

Canada from the 1960s to the present. The infusion of significantly larger numbers of Hindus and Buddhists—among others—into the North American tapestry and, with it, the creation of new forms of North American Hinduism and Buddhism offer new opportunities and incentives for Hindu-Christian encounters. From a survey administered throughout Canada in the mid-1980s, for example, David J. Goa noted that particular initiatives in Hindu-Christian dialogue could often be traced to a desire among new Hindu communities for "support on a range of social and cultural issues."[4] So too a recently established national Hindu-Catholic dialogue initiated by the Canadian bishops identified pragmatic questions related to the formation of youth and fostering social cohesion as shared concerns for both communities.[5]

As these examples suggest, the new proximity of Christians, Hindus, and many religious others in major urban centers of North America and Europe offers a rich field for interreligious dialogue and encounters, and it does indeed call for the development of new pastoral and theological responses. At the same time, claims that such an experience is entirely new in the late twentieth and early twenty-first centuries, or that Western cities like New York, London, and Toronto stand out as uniquely pluralistic vis-à-vis the longer histories of diversity in many parts of Asia, can and should be contested.[6] More

4. David J. Goa, "Hindu-Christian Dialogue in Canada," in *Hindu-Christian Dialogue: Perspectives and Encounters*, ed. Harold Coward (Delhi: Motilal Banarsidass, 1993), 136.

5. See Michael Swan, "Catholic-Hindu Dialogue Opens," *Catholic Register*, 10 February 2013, accessed 28 April 2014, http://www.catholicregister.org/home/canada/item/15823-catholic-hindu-dialogue-opens.

6. Despite Diana Eck's oft-repeated claim that the United States has become the world's "most religiously diverse country," a recent Pew Survey gave it a rather modest religious diversity score, particularly vis-à-vis such Asian states as Singapore and Taiwan; see Diana L. Eck, *A New Religious America: How a "Christian Country" Has Now Become the World's Most Religiously Diverse Nation* (San Francisco: HarperSanFrancisco, 2001), and Pew Research Center, "Global Religious Diversity: Half of the Most Religiously Diverse Countries Are in Asia-Pacific Region," *Pew Research Religion and Public Life Project*, 4 April 2014, accessed 12 May 2014, http://www.pewforum.org/2014/04/04/global-religious-diversity/.

importantly for my purposes in this essay, the increasing presence of distinctively North American forms of Hinduism also complicates any easy vision of "departure" and "return" for contemporary comparative theology. What kind of departure is effected when the "other" text or tradition is nearer to hand than the geographic center(s) of one's own "home" tradition? The impact of questions such as these on the shape of the discipline has yet to be explored in a sustained way.[7] As Raymond Williams wrote at the end of the last century, "Hindu-Christian dialogue in the United States has become a trialogue of American Christians, Indian Hindus, and American Hindus, with the latter a silent partner."[8]

Of course, the most significant impact on contemporary comparative theology from the North American Hindu diaspora will be the construction of comparative theologies by North American Hindus, and this important work is underway.[9] But Christian

7. There are, of course, welcome exceptions. Kristin Johnston Largen refers directly to the experience of the diaspora Hindu community in the construction of her comparative theological reflections, and Mara Brecht has recently drawn on the ethnographic study of a North American interreligious dialogue group to inform her work in the theology of religions. See Kristin Johnston Largen, *Baby Krishna, Infant Christ: A Comparative Theology of Salvation* (Maryknoll, NY: Orbis, 2011); and Mara Brecht, *Virtue in Dialogue: Belief, Religious Diversity, and Women's Interreligious Encounter* (Eugene, OR: Pickwick, 2014), esp. 61–88.

8. Raymond B. Williams, "Immigrants from India in North America and Hindu-Christian Study and Dialogue," *Journal of Hindu-Christian Studies* 11 (1998): 24.

9. See, for example, Parimal G. Patil, "A Hindu Theologian's Response: A Prolegomenon to 'Christian God, Hindu God,'" in *Hindu God, Christian God: How Reason Helps Break Down the Boundaries between Religions*, ed. Francis X. Clooney, S.J. (Oxford/New York: Oxford University Press, 2001), 185–95; Jeffery D. Long, *A Vision for Hinduism: Beyond Hindu Nationalism* (London: I. B. Tauris, 2007); idem., "(Tentatively) Putting the Pieces Together: Comparative Theology in the Tradition of Sri Ramakrishna," in *The New Comparative Theology: Interreligious Insights from the Next Generation* (London/New York: T. & T. Clark, 2010), 151–70; Steven J. Rosen, *Christ and Krishna: Where the Jordan Meets the Ganges* (Nyack, NY: Folk, 2011); Madhuri Yadlapati, *Against Dogmatism: Dwelling in Faith and Doubt* (Champaign: University of Illinois Press, 2014); and many works of Anantanand Rambachan, including particularly "Hinduism," in *The Hope of Liberation in World Religions*, ed. Miguel A. De La Torre (Waco, TX: Baylor University Press, 2008), 113–29. A more polemical, but still engaged and constructive approach to Hindu-Christian theology can be found in Rajiv Malhotra, *Being Different: An Indian Challenge to Western Universalism* (New Delhi: HarperCollins India, 2011).

comparativists can also seek out paths to engage diasporic and transnational Hindu traditions as resources for Christian theological reflection. Thus, in this essay, I briefly explore the transformation of *place* in the theological imagination of immigrant Hindu traditions, particularly as this project has been taken up in the theology of the contemporary Chinmaya Mission. One oft-cited example of such transformation is Pittsburgh's Śri Veṅkateśwara Temple, where the sacred geography of southern India has been symbolically transposed to the similar landscape of western Pennsylvania and the Penn Hills.[10] In the case of the Chinmaya Mission, the transposition from place to place is not so literal, as the tradition's theology functions both to displace the physical geography of India and to re-place this geography itself within a longer narrative arc of religious evolution and historical transformation. At the center of this creative reinterpretation is a retelling of the great eighth-century C.E. Advaita teacher Śaṅkara's legendary "conquest of the quarters" (*dig-vijaya*) by the movement's founder Swami Chinmayananda (1916–1993) and his early collaborators.

My argument proceeds in three steps. First, I offer an overview of the distinctive history and teachings of the Chinmaya Mission, particularly as illustrated by Swami Chinmayananda's short text, *A Manual of Self-Enfoldment* (1975). Second, I turn to another short text from the same period, *Śaṅkara the Missionary* (1978), and its creative rearticulation of the traditional four "quarters" (*dik*) of the Indian subcontinent in the Śaṅkara hagiographies to construct a

---

10. See e.g., Eck, *A New Religious America*, 123–27; Vasudha Narayanan, "Creating the South Indian 'Hindu' Experience in the United States," in *A Sacred Thread: Modern Transmission of Hindu Traditions in India and Abroad*, ed. Raymond Brady Williams (New York: Columbia University Press, 1992, 1996), 147–76; and especially Vasudha Narayanan, "Sacred Land, Sacred Service: Hindu Adaptations to the American Landscape," in *A Nation of Religions: The Politics of Pluralism in Multireligious America*, ed. Stephen Prothero (Chapel Hill: University of North Carolina Press, 2006), 139–59.

new, transnational identity for the Chinmaya Mission. Finally, I offer a few reflections on how this Hindu tradition might affect the way that Christians consider the place of *place* in the Christian imagination. Once emplaced in this Hindu theology of the quarters, the dynamism of comparative theology may be sought less in its apparent departure from the stable place of the home tradition than in a renewed appropriation of that place, made possible by its displacement.

A Religion of No-Place: A Manual of Self-Unfoldment (1975)

The Chinmaya Mission is one of several guru-based Hindu movements that emerged in the mid to late twentieth-century in India, North America, and Europe.[11] Swami Chinmayananda claimed to stand in the tradition of the earlier, pioneering work of Swami Vivekananda (1863–1902) and the international Ramakrishna Mission at the turn of the century: in his inaugural address for the movement, he set as his goal the formation of "thousands of Śaṅkaras, hundreds of Buddhas, and dozens of Vivekanandas."[12] He received his formation and rite of renunciation from Swami Sivananda (1887–1963) of the popular Divine Life Society. Like the Ramakrishna Mission and the Divine Life Society, the Chinmaya

---

11. For an overview of this broader movement, see Carl S. Jackson, *Vedanta for the West: The Ramakrishna Movement in the United States* (Bloomington/Indianapolis: Indiana University Press, 1994); Karen Pechilis, ed., *The Graceful Guru: Hindu Female Gurus in India and the United States* (Oxford: Oxford University Press, 2004); Sarah Strauss, *Positioning Yoga: Balancing Acts Across Cultures* (Oxford: Berg, 2005); Maya Warrier, *Hindu Selves in a Modern World: Guru Faith in the Mata Amritanandamayi Mission* (London: RoutledgeCurzon, 2005); Thomas A. Forsthoefel and Cynthia Ann Humes, eds., *Gurus in America* (Albany: State University of New York Press, 2005); Michael Bergunder, ed., *Westliche Formen des Hinduismus in Deutschland* (Halle: Verlag der franckeschen Stiftungen zu Halle, 2006), and Srinivas Aravamudan, *Guru English: South Asian Religion in a Cosmopolitan Language* (Princeton: Princeton University Press, 2006).

12. Swami Chinmayananda, "Let Us Be Hindus!," reprinted in *He Did It: Swami Chinmayananda, a Legacy*, ed. Margaret Dukes et al. (Piercy, CA: Chinmaya Publications, 2011), 85.

Mission stands in the tradition of nondualist Hinduism, or Advaita Vedānta. A distinctive focus of the movement, however, at least in its self-understanding, has been to democratize the study of Hindu scriptures. In a trope one hears frequently in the movement, Chinmayananda "ended the monopoly of orthodox priests over Vedānta, handing the priceless knowledge of the scriptures to the masses of India and the world."[13] Beginning with his first public lectures in Pune, India in 1951, this has taken two primary institutional forms: Jñāna Yagñas, signature week- or fortnight-long discourses on the Upaniṣads and Bhagavad-Gīta; and the formation of small lay-directed study discussion groups whose shared scriptural study follows a well-defined "scheme of study."[14]

As already noted, Swami Chinmayananda understood the core teaching of Hindu tradition as the nondual vision of *advaita*, proclaiming the ultimate identity of the divine reality of *Brahman* and the innermost self of each individual. Himself a journalist and independence activist prior to entering monastic life, he often interpreted this teaching in nationalistic terms, as a "renaissance" of the Indian state.[15] Indeed, in 1964 he became one of the cofounders of the Hindu nationalist Vishwa Hindu Parishad (VHP).[16]

---

13. Dukes et al., eds., *He Did It*, 3.

14. See Margaret Dukes et al., eds., *Vedānta: Swami Chinmayananda, His Words, His Legacy* (Piercy, CA: Chinmaya Publications, 2011), esp. 95–107; and Anita Raina Thapan, ed., *Scripture: A Mirror: The Chinmaya Study Group* (Piercy, CA: Chinmaya Publications, 2013).

15. See, e.g., Dukes et al., eds., *He Did It*, 23–35, 83–86, 212–25, quotation at 224.

16. See the discussion in Chetan Bhatt, *Hindu Nationalism: Origins, Ideologies and Modern Myths* (Oxford: Berg, 2001), 180–83; Lise McKean, *Divine Enterprise: Gurus and the Hindu Nationalist Movement* (Chicago: University of Chicago Press, 1996), 101–2, 177–79; and Peter van der Veer, *Religious Nationalism: Hindus and Muslims in India* (Berkeley, Los Angeles, and London: University of California Press, 1999), 130–37. According to sources within the movement, Chinmayananda envisioned the VHP as a Hindu correlate to the World Council of Churches. In their authorized history of the movement, Swami Chidananda and Rukmani Ramani contend that Chinmayananda perceived this initiative as a response to disciples in foreign countries alerting him that the immigrants there lacked exposure to India's heritage. However, as the VHP became increasingly politicized, the Chinmaya Mission dissociated itself from it.

Yet, Chinmayananda also understood the scope of the movement to be universal. In one of his calls for renewal, for example, he wrote:

> In this vision we shall not limit our field to the Hindus only, nor is it only for India. Our vision shall comprehend all mankind, all nations, societies and communities. Man is our theme of devotion, and he is our main field of worship.[17]

In 1965, with the assistance of lay devotees, Chinmayananda launched the first of several world tours. Though members of the movement drew explicit parallels to Swami Vivekananda's famous missionary journey to the 1893 World's Parliament of Religions in Chicago, Chinmayananda's primary goal was to revive and purify the practice of Hindus in the diaspora.[18] He did teach the scriptures to a wider public, attracted a significant number of Western disciples, and eventually founded Chinmaya Mission West in California in 1975, as well as similar centers throughout Europe, East Asia, and Africa.[19] Nevertheless, the primary focus of the movement was and remains a work of internal mission, to "convert Hindus to Hinduism"[20]—albeit in the new, transnational context created by global patterns of migration.

A good example of Swami Chinmayananda's universalization of the teaching of Advaita for a global community can be found in a significant work from 1975, titled *A Manual of Self-Unfoldment*.[21] The preface to this work was penned in Cambridge, Massachusetts, in the shadow of Harvard and MIT, and Chinmayananda describes its audience as "modern university educated [and] scientific minded."[22]

See their *Call of the Conch: The History of the Chinmaya Movement* (Mumbai: Central Chinmaya Mission Trust, 2001), 38.

17. Quoted in Dukes et al., eds., *He Did It*, 224.

18. Ibid., 234.

19. See ibid., 233–90.

20. Ibid., 86.

21. Swami Chinmayananda, *A Manual of Self-Unfoldment* (Mumbai: Central Chinmaya Mission Trust, 1975).

Perhaps unsurprisingly, given this intended audience, Chinmayananda describes the teaching of Advaita unfolded therein as an objective and universal "Science of Reality," similar to the natural sciences, but distinguished by its inward focus.[23] This theme runs throughout the entire *Manual*. Chinmayananda first offers a portrait of true religion as a "great science," and the ancient Rishis, correspondingly, as "scientists of the spirit" and "glorious depth-psychologists."[24] He then turns, in subsequent chapters, to a systematic analysis of human experience in terms of five "sheaths" and the *vāsanās*, or mental impressions, which obscure the divine, innermost self of each and every conscious being.[25] From this foundation, he proceeds to outline preparatory ethical disciplines for cleansing the mind, practices for the conservation of energy and elimination of *vāsanās*, and, in the final chapters, detailed consideration of the threefold *sādhana* to release our mental power, including scriptural study, the disciplined repetition of mantras, and techniques for deeper meditation.[26]

Intriguingly, Swami Chinmayananda's explicit discussion of Hindu culture and religion, though implied throughout *The Manual of Self-Unfoldment*, arises only late in the work, in chapter 10, long after the initial account of human experience and identification of the "Divine-Principle" as the singular goal "advocated by all Religions."[27] This brief account of the Hindu history and scriptural traditions, in turn, leads into yet another broader, more philosophical question-and-answer about the "Composition of Man."[28] The religious culture of India is thus skillfully introduced and re-inscribed into a more

22. Ibid., ii.
23. Ibid., i.
24. Ibid., 4–5.
25. Ibid., esp. 53–87.
26. For this threefold scheme, see ibid., 117–18.
27. Ibid., 75–79, 157–70.
28. Ibid., 170–79.

universal and interior understanding of religion and an easily transportable series of meditative practices. The work, appropriately, concludes with a discussion of the formation and maintenance of study groups, mentioned above, as a form of religious practice replicable anywhere in the world.[29]

In the *Manual of Self-Unfoldment*, it seems, Swami Chinmayananda's vision of Vedānta is deliberately and specifically abstracted from any particular physical, cultural, or religious geography. Chinmayananda wrote to a Western disciple in 1968: "In the Eternal Heart, there are no continents, there are no peoples, there is only love."[30] So also, in the *Manual*, he redefines the place of the teaching less in terms of "continents" or "peoples" than in terms of cognitive, interior structures, as revealed especially in the so-called "BMI Chart." This distinctive visual diagram, presented twice in the *Manual*[31] and employed often by Chinmayananda in his public teaching, traces the origin of phenomenal experience—the body-mind-intellect (B-M-I) of the perceiver, with its corresponding objects, emotions, and thoughts (O-E-T)—to the obscuring power of *vāsanās* and, behind them, the divine Reality of *oṃ*, sometimes symbolized by an X.[32] "After listening intently to Gurudev's explanation of the BMI chart," one devotee reports, "I realized that this was a uniquely simple, yet comprehensive, way to explain all that is, both Real and relative."[33] To the degree that the *Manual* locates the teaching of Vedānta in a particular geography at all, then, it is not a physical landscape, but an interior geography of "all that is," schematized by abstract signifiers like B-M-I, O-E-T, and X.

29. Ibid., 180–89.
30. Quoted in Dukes et al., eds., *He Did It*, 246–47.
31. Chinmayananda, *Manual*, 76, 173.
32. See Dukes et al., eds., *He Did It*, 101, and Dukes et al., eds., *Vedānta*, 15–21.
33. Dukes et al., eds., *Vedānta*, 19–20.

A Religion of New-Place: Śankara the Missionary (1978)[34]

From one point of view, the vision of the *Manual of Self-Unfoldment* and the placelessness of a cognitive map like the BMI Chart seem ideally suited to reimagining this particular Hindu movement as a transnational, global tradition. Yet, even in the U.S. and Europe, Swami Chinmayananda and the Chinmaya Mission have also consistently advocated a form of cultural nationalism, rooted in the Indian land and culture. Given this, it would not be sufficient to divest the teaching of Advaita entirely of its geographical particularity; instead, ideally, this geography itself would need to be universalized. Hence, the importance of a second work produced by the Mission a few years after the *Manual*: *Śankara the Missionary*.[35]

As indicated in the prefaces of both editions,[36] *Śankara the Missionary* originated in 1978 as a souvenir volume to honor Swami Chinmayananda's 267th Jñāna Yagña. Twenty years later, and five years after Swami Chinmayananda's death, the work was thoroughly reorganized: much material was removed and several appendices integrated into the main narrative. Its authors identify as their primary source the *dig-vijaya* or "conquest of the quarters" of one Mādhava,[37] traditionally identified with the prominent fourteenth-century sage Vidyāraṇya.[38] This work, like many other *vijayas* dedicated to Śankara and other great teacher-renouncers, narrates

---

34. The discussion in this section depends and draws upon the more extensive analysis in Reid Locklin and Julia Lauwers, "Rewriting the Sacred Geography of Advaita: Swami Chinmayānanda and the *Śankara-dig-vijaya*," *The Journal of Hindu Studies* 2 (2009): 179–208, esp. 191–99.

35. Except where otherwise noted, all references to this work are taken from the 1998 revised edition: *Śankara the Missionary*, rev. ed. (Mumbai: Central Chinmaya Mission Trust, 1998).

36. Ibid., iii; *Śankara the Missionary* (Bombay: Central Chinmaya Mission Trust, 1978), xiii.

37. *Sankara the Missionary* [1978], xiii, 6; *Śankara the Missionary*, 4. Two English translations of this work are available: Swami Tapasyananda, trans., *Sankara-Dig-Vijaya: The Traditional Life of Sri Sankaracarya, by Madhava Vidyaranya* (Madras: Sri Ramakrishna Math, 1978), hereafter ŚDV; and K. Padmanaban, trans., *Srimad Sankara Digvijayam by Vidyaranya*, 2 vols. (Madras: K. Padmanaban, 1985–86), which includes both Sanskrit text and English translation.

its hero's pilgrimage throughout the Indian subcontinent, defeating scholars from rival schools and reestablishing *dharma* in terms specific to the particular teaching tradition.[39]

In *Śaṅkara the Missionary*, however, this traditional narrative is significantly transformed. Mādhava's text begins in the heavens, where a court of celestial devas requests that the god Śiva take human form to defeat Buddhists and other rivals and reestablish the *dharma* that such rivals have corrupted; *Śaṅkara the Missionary* instead begins with a historicized account of the evolution of Hinduism from its origins in the Vedic period to Śaṅkara's era in the eighth-century ce.[40] In Mādhava's conclusion, after Śaṅkara ascends a "throne of omniscience" in the sacred Himalayas as a symbol of his victory over the whole land, he travels to the holy site of Kedara, manifests his divine form as Śiva, and reascends to his divine abode.[41] *Śaṅkara the Missionary* here shifts the focus to Śaṅkara's institutionalization of the tradition. After traveling to Kedara, Śaṅkara organizes his disciples to preside over the tradition at four great *maṭha*s at Jagannātha Purī in the north, Śṛṅgeri in the south, Dvārakā in the west, and Jyotirdhāma in the east, writes a code of discipline, and then merges into "his own

38. Both the traditional ascription of the *Śaṅkara-dig-vijaya* to Vidyāraṇya and its early date have been challenged on philological and historical grounds, due to its apparent literary dependence upon three other hagiographies, especially the *Śaṅkaravijaya* of Vyāsācala, the *Śaṅkarābhyudaya* of Rājacūḍāmaṇi-Dīkṣita, and the *Śaṅkarācāryacarita* of Govindanātha. See the discussion in Bader, *Conquest of the Quarters*, 17–70.

39. See Phyllis Granoff, "Holy Warriors: A Preliminary Study of Some Biographies of Saints and Kings in the Classical Indian Tradition," *Journal of Indian Philosophy* 12 (1984): 291–303; William S. Sax, "Conquering the Quarters: Religion and Politics in Hinduism," *International Journal of Hindu Studies* 4 (2000): 39–60; and Jonathan Bader, *The Conquest of the Four Quarters: Traditional Accounts of the Life of Śaṅkara* (New Delhi: Aditya Prakashan, 2000).

40. See ŚDV 1.1–26; *Śaṅkara the Missionary*, 11–12.

41. ŚDV 16.81–92, 100–107. For further discussions of this central feature of the *Śaṅkara-dig-vijaya* and of many popular images of Śaṅkara, see Bader, *Conquest of the Four Quarters*, 76–77, 100–35; David N. Lorenzen, "The Life of Sankaracarya," in *The Biographical Process*, ed. Frank E. Reynolds and Donald Capps (Paris: Mouton & Co., 1976), 87–103; and Yoshitsugu Sawai, *The Faith of Ascetics and Lay Smārtas: A Study of the Śaṅkaran Tradition of Śṛṅgeri* (Vienna: Institut für Indologie der Universität Wien, 1992), 83–116.

supreme state of perfect Bliss."[42] These two alterations to the fabric of the *Śaṅkara-dig-vijaya*, one at the story's beginning and the other at its end, function to shift the focus from the heavens to the specific culture and geography of eighth-century India. They also reinscribe this specific culture and geography within a longer historical arc, and one that extends well beyond the "quarters" of India envisioned by Mādhava and other hagiographers in the tradition.

Nowhere does *Śaṅkara the Missionary* speak explicitly of extending Śaṅkara's conquest to include North America or Europe. Instead, its authors read universalist themes strategically into the traditional narrative itself. Building on the famous episode of Śaṅkara's meeting with Śiva in the form of an outcaste, for example, they characterize Śaṅkara as a person "whose heart throbbed with compassion and sympathy for all men and beings irrespective of whether they were rich or poor, learned or illiterate, *brahmaṇa* or *cāṇḍala*."[43] More significantly, in their retelling of the *dig-vijaya*, they draw special attention to its place within the progressive universalization of the tradition over time. When the teaching of the Upaniṣads is first introduced in chapter 1 of *Śaṅkara the Missionary*, the authors note that it could initially "only be the religion of the few" due to its inherent difficulty and individualist message.[44] They then go on to describe the initial rise of Buddhism as a kind of "second renaissance" of Hindu tradition and observe that, through the emergence of Śaiva and Vaiṣṇava devotional sects, the teachings of the Upaniṣads actually

---

42. *Śaṅkara the Missionary*, 53–54. In distinction from some of the other Śaṅkara hagiographies, Mādhava's *Śaṅkara-dig-vijaya* never explicitly mentions the four *maṭha*s. Given the work's widespread popularity and close association with the Śṛṅgerī *maṭha* in particular, its restraint on this score seems remarkable. See Bader, *Conquest of the Four Quarters*, 232–44; Vidyasankar Sundaresan, "Conflicting Hagiographies and History: The Place of Śaṅkaravijaya Texts in Advaita Tradition," *International Journal of Hindu Studies* 4 (2000): 147–48; Matthew Clark, *The Daśanāmī-Saṃnyāsīs: The Integration of Ascetic Lineages into an Order* (Leiden and Boston: Brill, 2006), 150–51.

43. *Śaṅkara the Missionary*, 30, 55–56 (quotation).

44. Ibid., 12.

became simplified and thereby gained wider acceptance among "the common people."[45] Śaṅkara's conquest, when it finally arrives, can therefore be read not only as arresting the decline of *dharma*, as in the traditional *dig-vijayas*, but also as consolidating and further extending a dynamic movement already underway, whereby the Advaita teachings reach beyond the few to the whole nation and even to the world.

So far, we have been examining the narrative strategy of *Śaṅkara the Missionary* as an alternative to the placeless, schematic vision of the *Manual of Self-Unfoldment* and the BMI Chart. The two are, however, very closely connected. This emerges very clearly in chapter 7, titled "The Philosophy of Śaṅkara." This chapter begins with the programmatic announcement that Advaita "commands the admiration of the whole world," due in no small part to Śaṅkara's "scientific exposition of the *Upaniṣadik* philosophy."[46] After a brief précis of major Advaita teachings, the authors of *Śaṅkara the Missionary* return to this scientific motif:

> Ours is an Age of Science, wherein we are trained to live and think with a spirit of enquiry. The modern scientists, by their wondrous discoveries in the world outside, have contributed much to usher in the Age of Enquiry. Their achievements deserve praise; but the scientists and the thinkers of the present generation have another role to play. They must deliver their brethren from an Age of Enquiry to an Era of Contemplation. . . . Their enquiry and research have so far been in "the outer world," and now they must shift their field of enquiry from the world of the "object" to the "subject," that is, the enquirer himself. The enquiry into the "subject" cannot be done in any laboratory. Subjective enquiry should be pursued in one's own within. And, therefore, it is an enquiry with a difference: an enquiry which we choose to call "contemplation."[47]

45. Ibid., 14, 16.
46. Ibid., 102.
47. Ibid., 104–5.

On the one hand, this interpretation of Vedānta as a "science of the mind" appears only as an appendix in the original 1978 edition. On the other, by invoking a historical transition from the "Age of Science" to an "Era of Contemplation," Chinmayananda and his collaborators invite the reader to interpret this transition as the logical terminus of the historical trajectory established earlier in their narrative. The esoteric teaching of the Upaniṣads, initially communicated only to the few in the late Vedic period, spread more widely through the rise of Buddhism and *bhakti* and eventually, by means of Śaṅkara's eighth-century tour, became the spiritual and cultural basis of India. Then, through Śaṅkara's systematization, this same teaching now emerges as a powerful force to set science and the world itself on a more deeply contemplative foundation.

Strictly speaking, of course, the scientific reinterpretation of the *Upaniṣads* is not the work of Śaṅkara or even of his medieval hagiographers: it is the work of Swami Chinmayananda and other modern Vedāntins. Indeed, the section of *Śaṅkara the Missionary* from which I have drawn the above quotation is titled "Self-Unfoldment," and, as it turns out, it is actually a lightly edited excerpt from the *Manual of Self-Unfoldment*.[48] Even more intriguingly, the authors of *Śaṅkara the Missionary*, precisely as in the *Manual*, conclude their discussion of humankind's progressive evolution toward the Era of Contemplation with a presentation of the BMI Chart. It is revealing, perhaps, that in its 1978 edition, *Śaṅkara the Missionary*'s frontispiece displayed a map of Śaṅkara's India and its fifth-to-last page carried an image of the BMI Chart. Taken as a whole, this work enacts a narrative and cognitive shift from one map to the other.

Mādhava's *Śaṅkara-dig-vijaya* may begin and end in the heavens, but it strategically draws together the four "quarters" of the Indian

48. Chinmayananda, *Manual of Self-Unfoldment*, 75–76; *Śaṅkara the Missionary*, 104–6.

subcontinent in its narrative of conquest. The new narrative offered by Chinmayananda and his collaborators begins and reaches its climax in India; but its narrative strategically extends these quarters outward to all humankind, precisely by moving the inquiry inward to the body, mind, and intellect at the base of all human experience. Śaṅkara's conquest can now reach North America and indeed the entire world by means of a cluster of disciplines and practices symbolized by the BMI Chart and oriented toward the inner, psychological geography of each and every human mind.

Conclusion: Emplacing Comparative Theology

In his introductory volume, *Place: A Short Introduction*, the social and cultural geographer Tim Cresswell notes that "place" never refers merely to physical landscapes, but always includes an inextricable element of human construction, self-definition, and not infrequently exclusion.[49] He writes:

> The idea of being "out-of-place" or "in-place" is admittedly a simple one, but one that nonetheless conveys a sense of the way segments of the geographical world are meaningful and how those meanings both produce and are reproduced by people and their practices. A saying from Sri Lanka states: "The fish don't talk about the water." What this means is that we rarely explicitly become aware of and talk about that which we take for granted.[50]

In the context of this passage, Cresswell is referring to the threat and opportunities posed by alternative sexualities to covert, heteronormative constructions of place and practice. But the experience of migration in a religious tradition is no less disruptive to settled, unnoticed grammars of place and no less fruitful for their reappropriation. Thus, a work like *Śaṅkara the Missionary* can be

49. Tim Cresswell, *Place: A Short Introduction* (Malden, MA: Blackwell, 2004).
50. Ibid., 108–9.

read as destabilizing settled, previously unnoticed understandings of Hindu tradition and the "quarters" of the traditional hagiographies. It can also, and perhaps more consistently in the light of Swami Chinmayananda's explicit interest in the diaspora Indian community, be read as a bold, imaginative reassertion of this geography in and out of the already-destabilizing experience of the tradition's migration, diffusion, and universalization. Both dynamics—destabilization and reappropriation—inevitably arise and belong together, in the same moment of creative (re)interpretation.

And what might this mean for the contemporary comparative theologian, and the Christian comparativist in particular? At one level, one can search Christian tradition for comparable reinterpretations and creative reappropriations of sacred place. In his influential 1987 work, *To Take Place*, for example, Jonathan Z. Smith traces the ritual re-placement of the sacred sites of Jerusalem by their transposition into sacred moments of Christian liturgy and spiritual practice, culminating in their full interiorization by Ignatius of Loyola in his *Spiritual Exercises*.[51] A similar process of transposition and interiorization can perhaps be located in a work like Edith Stein's short reflection, "On the History and Spirit of Carmel."[52] In his study of a Cuban shrine in Miami, Our Lady of Charity, Thomas Tweed identifies a more complex pattern of transformation, one that transcends the dualism of "*locative*" and "*supralocative*" religion to construct a new religious identity he describes as "*translocative*."[53]

51. Jonathan Z. Smith, *To Take Place: Toward Theory in Ritual* (Chicago: University of Chicago Press, 1987), esp. 85–95, 116–17.

52. Edith Stein, "On the History and Spirit of Carmel," in *The Hidden Life: Hagiographic Essays, Meditations, Spiritual Texts*, Collected Works of Edith Stein 4, ed. L. Gelber and Michael Linssen, O.C.D., trans. Waltraut Stein (Washington, DC: ICS, 1992), 1–6.

53. Thomas Tweed, *Our Lady of the Exile: Diasporic Religion at a Cuban Catholic Shrine in Miami* (New York: Oxford University Press, 1997), 91–98. Cf. Locklin and Lauwers, "Rewriting," 186–87, and Tweed's own extension of this insight in *Crossing and Dwelling: A Theory of Religion* (Cambridge, MA: Harvard University Press, 2006).

In this translocative pattern, attention shifts from correspondences constructed by immigrant communities between "homeland" and "new land" to the dynamic movement back and forth that such correspondences may enable for those who participate in them.[54]

Arguably, of course, Christian identity itself is already translocative in its own self-understanding. In a recent bibliographic survey of the Christian "theology of migration" in the last half-century, Gioacchino Campese notes that:

> The true Christian is the person who acknowledges in every moment the fact of being on a journey, of being a pilgrim of the reign of God, for this is the final goal of those who believe in the God revealed by Jesus Christ. . . . In this perspective the migrant becomes, with his or her simple and "naked" presence, the living witness of the human pilgrimage toward God as a response to a God who has "pilgrimed" toward humanity.[55]

If this is true for Christian identity in general, it is true *a fortiori* of the comparative theological project, which takes as its specific focus dynamic tensions between self and other, between home traditions and new traditions, between the comparativist's artful transgression and the particular, globalized social and religious contexts such transgressive practices are intended to negotiate.[56]

At a deeper level, then, a comparative inquiry into a work like *Śaṅkara the Missionary* will look to it as embodying a distinctively Advaita theology of migration, diffusion and, in its own idiom, *vijaya* or "conquest." A Hindu-Christian comparative theology of the quarters would locate itself neither in the imagined India of Śaṅkara's

---

54. Tweed, *Our Lady of the Exile*, 94–95.

55. Gioacchino Campese, C.S., "The Irruption of Migrants: Theology of Migration in the 21st Century," *Theological Studies* 73 (2012): 22–23.

56. On the latter point, see the discussion in Clooney, *Comparative Theology*, 157–62; and Terrence W. Tilley et al., *Religious Diversity and the American Experience: A Theological Approach* (New York: Continuum, 2007), 12–46, 186–89.

vijaya nor in its symbolic re-placement by an image like the BMI Chart. It would emplace itself, instead, in the dynamic movement between them. No doubt, this larger inquiry would at some point need to wrestle with the implicit imperialism of Chinmayananda's vision and indeed of the comparative project itself.[57] But it could do so in confidence that these particular Hindu and Christian traditions—as migrant, pilgrim traditions emplaced within broader visions of journey and transformation—presume their own thorough transcendence, as a condition of self-discovery. The immigrant comparativist, no less than the pilgrim *vijayin*, comes to know herself firmly in the home tradition only in and through a process of creative dis-placement.

---

57. See, e.g., Hugh Nicholson, "The New Comparative Theology and the Problem of Theological Hegemonism," in Francis X. Clooney ed., *The New Comparative Theology: Interreligious Insights from the Next Generation* (London/New York: T. & T. Clark, 2010), 43-62.

2

Seeking the "Farther Shore"

Buddhism as Spiritual Immigration

John Thompson

"May all embodied creatures,
Who throughout the universe
Experience hellish realms,
Come to enjoy the bliss of Sukhāvatī"
–Śantideva

The connection between Buddhism and immigration runs deep. Although it arose in India, Buddhism rather quickly spread through much of Asia, mainly due to immigrants bringing the Dharma ("teachings") with them as they settled among other peoples. In fact, as a tradition originating among *śramaṇas* ("strivers") seeking liberation, Buddhism focuses on moving toward a better life, the heart of any immigrant story. After examining images of "travel" in early Buddhism, I turn to the concepts of *bodhisattvas*, "wisdom beings" who aspire to help others attain Buddhahood, and "Pure Lands," paradisiacal realms where the faithful are reborn after this life. Such ideas encourage us to see Buddhist life as "spiritual immigration," an idea that can sensitize us to connections between immigration and religious life in general. Hopefully these insights can guide us toward a more humane approach to issues surrounding immigration in our world today.[1]

"Travel" and "Immigration" in Early Buddhism

Immigration involves travel from one place to another, and metaphors of travel continually turn up in Buddhism.[2] In fact, Buddhist cosmology centers on travel. The traditional Indian cosmos is a vast process powered by karma ("action"), a cosmic-moral force propelling beings through countless lives in a perpetual cycle known as *saṃsāra* ("wandering through"). Based upon their karmic trajectories, beings are reborn in one of six realms (*gatis*, "courses"): hells, *pretas* ("hungry ghosts"), beasts, humans, *asuras* ("titans"), and *devas* ("gods").[3] As a continuous movement through various states, *saṃsāra* is painful, and beings bound to it inevitably experience anxiety and frustration, a condition known as *duhkha* ("suffering"),

---

1. There is an important distinction between emigration and immigration. To emigrate means to leave a country or region (usually one's native place) to settle in another; to immigrate means to come to a country or region where one is not native, usually to settle permanently. While I may at times conflate these terms, in "good Buddhist fashion" I note that these terms define each other; when one *emigrates* one becomes an immigrant (at least aspirationally), and all immigrants have necessarily emigrated from elsewhere.

2. For example, in a famous parable, the Buddha likens the Dharma to a raft that will take one across a dangerous river (*saṃsāra*) to the safety of the far bank (*nirvana*). See Bhikku Nanamoli and Bhikku Bodhi, trans., *The Middle Length Discourses of the Buddha: A Translation of the Majjhima-Nikāya* (Boston: Wisdom, 1995), 134–35. Similarly, the Sanskrit/Pali noun *yāna* ("vehicle") forms the root term for two of the main branches of Buddhism, Mahāyāna and Vajrayāna ("Great Vehicle" and "Thunderbolt Vehicle" respectively).

3. For details, see "Karma and the Six Realms of Rebirth," in *The Experience of Buddhism: Sources and Interpretations*, 2nd edition, ed. John S. Strong (Belmont, CA: Wadsworth Group, 2002), 28–31.

since any action just creates more karma to push them into yet another life.

However, this is not the full story. Ancient "seers" (*ṛṣis*) realized that careful attention to our actions enables us to direct our karmic path to minimize negative effects, typically by acting morally, performing rituals honoring ancestors, *devas*, etc. Moreover, these seers realized that we could achieve liberation (*mokṣa*) from *saṃsāra* by destroying the desires and attachments that motivate karmic actions. This is an inward process of attaining insight into reality, disciplining and detaching from passions, and practicing austerities (yoga, meditation) to shed karmic layers built up over many lifetimes. Such a momentous reorientation, however, requires a major life change. Paradoxically, to end the "wandering" of *saṃsāra*, we need to leave home and "wander" in this world. That is, pursuing liberation means choosing to shape our destiny by moving elsewhere toward a better future, the quintessential immigrant story.

By the time of the Buddha (sixth century B.C.E.), various *śramanas* were wandering throughout India, living on alms. Such people were truly liminal figures, neither fully in nor outside of society. Ironically, while pursuing liberation from *saṃsāra* required leaving home, many *śramanas* congregated in settled communities, *aśramas* ("places of spiritual striving") established in secluded places around particular teachers. Thus seeking liberation did not entail perpetual wandering so much as a change in location. Spiritual life became an "immigration" to a place designed to foster ultimate liberation from ordinary existence.

The historical Buddha, Siddhartha Gautama, was one of these "spiritual immigrants," following the *śramana* path to reach *nirvana*, the "farther shore" beyond *saṃsāra*, and after attaining Awakening, his compassion motivated him to help others reach the same destination. Among the Buddha's insights was that intention is the key to overcoming suffering. Indeed, in one sermon he explicitly stresses that karma is intentionally willed action, hence cultivating right intention is central to following the eightfold path.[4] This inward focus, combined with meditative training, gives Buddhism a psychological orientation that encourages careful attention to oneself and the world rather than escapism. The Buddha did not reject society but offered an alternative for those seeking liberation: they could "leave home" and join his order, ritually repeating the Buddha's own renunciation.[5]

As with other *śramana* movements, so in Buddhism "leaving home" eventually became a matter of settling in a new home established for religious training. Such was the origin of institutionalized monasticism, a "middle way" between wandering and householder life, and during his lifetime, the Buddha established specific places where he and his disciples spent much of their time.[6] These first monasteries served various purposes: residences for monks and nuns, places of study and meditation, and temples for worship. Many monasteries became major sites of contact between clergy and laity, evolving into places of pilgrimage for travelers the world over. For most Buddhists, these are brief visits, but even the most settled householder often has a sense that such worldly trips are but one stage on the journey to *nirvana*. If not now, then perhaps in the next life, the devotee will leave his or her earthly home to dwell in such a place, becoming a "spiritual immigrant."

4. See "The Nibbedhika Sūtta," trans. Thannisaro Bhikku, accessed 10 Feb. 2014, http://www.accesstoinsight.org/tipitaka/an/an06/an06.063.than.html#part-5.
5. In Theravādin ordination ceremonies, the ordinand may dress in royal attire and ride a horse in imitation of Siddhartha's "great renunciation." See Donald K. Swearer, *Buddhism and Society in Southeast Asia* (Chambersburg, PA: Anima Books, 1981), 23–28.
6. These sites originated in the practice of the Buddha and his followers of settling in one place for the monsoon season, when roads were impassable. For a discussion, see John S. Strong, *The Buddha: A Short Biography* (Oxford: Oneworld, 2001), 101–5.

This notion of Buddhism as a type of immigration even informs the most basic Buddhist ceremony, "taking refuge," a formal profession of faith in the Three Jewels (Buddha, Dharma, and *Sangha*). At its simplest, this rite involves reciting the formula: "I take refuge in the Buddha; I take refuge in the Dharma; I take refuge in the *Sangha*." "Taking refuge" reinforces the view of Buddhist life as spiritual immigration, highlighting just how urgent this choice is. The *Dhammapada* ("Verses on Dhamma"), a popular early Buddhist text, emphasizes that "taking refuge" offers the only true security, saying: "that's the secure refuge/that, the supreme refuge/that is the refuge/having gone to which/you gain release/from all suffering and stress."[7] To enter the Buddhist path is thus to become a "refugee," yet while ordinary refugees may have little choice in their status (many are fleeing for their lives), refugees in the Three Jewels are intentionally choosing to overcome the sufferings of *saṃsāra*. At the very least, "taking refuge" demonstrates that one aspires to a better place and this marks a major shift in one's karmic trajectory: from now on, you are setting out for the "farther shore." Spiritually, one who "takes refuge" has become an immigrant.

As we can see, Buddhism as a way of life centers on images of travel, and immigration. However, these are not inevitable features of existence that we must passively accept. To be a Buddhist is to strive actively toward a state beyond suffering, sometimes by literally moving to a different place or, more importantly, moving to a different state of mind. This notion of Buddhism as "spiritual immigration" becomes more pronounced over time.

---

7. Thanissaro Bhikku, trans., *The Dhammapada: A Translation*, verses 188–92, accessed 10 Feb. 2014, http://www.accesstoinsight.org/tipitaka/kn/dhp/dhp.14.than.html.

The Bodhisattva—Immigrant for Others

Near the start of the Common Era, various changes were taking place within Buddhism that led to the formation of the Mahāyāna, although the details are sketchy. New texts claiming to be "Buddha Word" were circulating, stressing the supremacy of the Buddha while also advocating the universal pursuit of Buddhahood, but there was no united movement. Originally a small minority, followers of this "Great Vehicle" gradually came to see themselves as a distinct group following a superior way to those who failed to appreciate their lofty goals. Regardless, Mahāyāna now dominates East Asia and much of the Himalayan region.[8]

The hallmark of Mahāyāna is the *bodhisattva*, someone who vows to become Buddha out of compassion for others, even postponing her own entry into *nirvana* to remain in *saṃsāra* until all beings Awaken. We can find the notion of a *bodhisattva* in early Buddhism (e.g., the *Jataka Tales*, stories of Siddhartha's previous lives) but Mahāyāna expands upon it. Moved by the sufferings of those caught within *saṃsāra*, *bodhisattvas* draw on their store of *punya* ("merit") to teach and comfort all beings. According to tradition, highly advanced *bodhisattvas* may be reborn in heavenly realms from whence they can give aid to any who call upon them, much like saints in Christianity. At such advanced levels, *bodhisattvas* are virtually indistinguishable from Buddhas in that both *bodhisattvas* and Buddhas bestow grace upon faithful devotees.

The *bodhisattva* stands opposed to the *arhat* ("worthy one"), the earlier ideal. According to Mahāyānists, *arhats* limit their attainments by selfishly focusing on their own liberation rather than relieving the suffering of others. In contrast, Mahāyāna encourages all Buddhists

---

8. For a summary of the scholarship, see Paul Williams, *Mahayana Buddhism: The Doctrinal Foundations*, 2nd ed. (New York: Routledge, 2009), 21–44.

(male or female, monastic or lay), to take *bodhisattva* vows, typically during a ritual in which the aspirant formally vows both to become Buddha and to strive actively to help alleviate the suffering of others. In practice, this means living as devoutly as possible in the understanding that one will eventually be reborn in a heavenly realm, from which one can transfer merit to others. However, a *bodhisattva* may be reborn on earth (or a lower realm) if that would help diminish other beings' suffering. This type of "spiritual immigration," it seems, entails remaining within *saṃsāra*, even "immigrating" to different realms to help others reach better states.

Taking *bodhisattva* vows means dedicating oneself to a spiritual journey that may require many lifetimes. This is a path motivated by *mahākaruṇā* ("great compassion"), and can be taken by anyone who wishes to share her "merit" with others. Once more, intention plays a key role, particularly when it comes to generating *bodhicitta* ("Awakening Mind"). Usually an aspirant does this by vowing three times to attain Awakening *for the sake of all living beings*. One of the best statements of *bodhicitta* comes from the *Bodhicaryāvatāra* ("Guide to the Bodhisattva's Way of Life") by the eighth-century poet Śāntideva:

> May I be a guard for those who are protectorless,
> A guide for those who journey on the road.
> For those who wish to go across the water,
> May I be a boat, a raft, a bridge.
>
> May I be an isle for those who yearn for landfall,
> And a lamp for those who long for light;
> For those who need a resting place, a bed;
> For all who need a servant, may I be their slave.
>
> May I be the wishing jewel, the vase of plenty,
> A word of power and the supreme healing;

May I be the tree of miracles,
And for every being the abundant cow.[9]

Śāntideva helps to deepen our understanding of the *bodhisattva* and the notion of "spiritual immigration." Such a person is committed to helping others become immigrants, and serving them along their way. A *bodhisattva* as immigrant is a guide, facilitator, even a vehicle (or beast of burden), and a source for provisions for the journey to Awakening. Such a person is deeply engaged with those on the journey, so much so that they are virtually inseparable for the entire voyage. Interestingly, as Mahāyāna develops, the idea that all beings are destined to attain Buddhahood increasingly comes to the fore. An example of this proclamation of universal Buddhahood is in the *Lotus Sūtra*, when the Buddha compares himself to a great cloud, raining the Dharma down everywhere: "Those who have not yet been saved will be saved; those who have not been set free will be set free; those who have had no rest will have rest; those who have not yet attained nirvana will attain nirvana."[10] Essentially the Buddha declares that we are all *bodhisattvas* destined to attain full Awakening. It seems that each of us, then, is engaged in "spiritual immigration."

According to the earliest Mahāyāna texts, the *Prajñāpāramitā Sūtras* ("Perfection of Wisdom Sūtras"), *bodhisattvas* must cultivate various virtues (e.g., *dāna*, "generosity"; *śīla*, "morality"; *kṣānti*, "patience"; etc.) culminating in "transcendent wisdom" (*prajñā*), which enables them to practice all virtues "perfectly" with no selfish motive. Over time, Mahāyāna thinkers composed other texts such as the *Daśabhūmika Sūtra* ("*Sūtra* on the Ten Stages") that divided the *bodhisattva* path into "Ten Stages of Attainment." These stages are

9. Padmakara Translation Group, trans., *Shantideva: The Way of the Bodhisattva*, foreword by the Dalai Lama (Boston and London: Shambhala, 1997), 51.
10. Gene Reeves, trans., *The Lotus Sutra: A Contemporary Translation of a Buddhist Classic* (Boston: Wisdom, 2008), 160.

metaphorical rather than literal places (although advancing through them may entail traveling to various locations), with those in the higher stages earning the title *mahasattva* ("Great Being"). Progressing through all Ten Stages is truly admirable, but the general understanding is that *bodhisattvas* will need the aid of celestial Buddhas and *mahasattvas* to reach Awakening.

Because of the popularity of the *bodhisattva* ideal and the necessity for those traveling the path to be helped along their quest, various Buddhas and *mahasattvas* have become the focus of devotional cults. Of these, several are especially important, and they provide some interesting spins on this notion of Mahāyāna Buddhism as "spiritual immigration." One of the earliest *bodhisattva-mahasattvas* is Maitreya (the "Friendly One"), the next Buddha of our world, and his cult is one of the oldest and most widespread in the Buddhist world. Currently, Maitreya resides in the *Tuṣita* heaven, awaiting the time when the Dharma needs renewal. He will then be reborn here to teach the Dharma anew.[11] Some Buddhists pray to Maitreya to hasten his arrival or to be reborn when he comes. Another celestial *bodhisattva* is Kṣitagarbha ("Earth Store"), a *mahasattva* who vows to be reborn continually to liberate all beings in the six realms until Maitreya's new age. By the power of his compassion and merit, Kṣitagarbha pulls anyone who recites the name of a Buddha or a verse from a *sūtra* from the very brink of hell. Known in China as Dizang (Japanese, Jizo), he guides the departed in the afterlife and, as the "*bodhisattva* of the hell realms," is often the subject of devotional paintings.[12]

11. Williams, *Mahayana Buddhism*, 218–21. *Tuṣita* is the closest heavenly realm to earth, making Maitreya more accessible than other deities.
12. For details on Kṣitagarbha, see Buddhist Text Translation Society, trans., *Sutra of the Past Vows of Earth Store Bodhisattva* (Talmage, CA: Dharma Realm Buddhist University, 1982).

The most popular *bodhisattva*, however, is Avalokiteśvara (the "Lord Who Looks Down [from Above]"), the personification of *mahākaruṇā*, and a focus of devotion throughout the Buddhist world. He is a prominent figure in many texts and his image is found in artworks throughout the Buddhist world, from the caves of Ajanta, India to the temple complex of Borobudur, Indonesia. As devotion to Avalokiteśvara spread, interesting things happened, notably in China, where Avalokiteśvara took on female form, becoming Guanyin ("Regarder of the Cries of the World"). As Guanyin, this *bodhisattva* appears throughout East Asia, and is particularly favored by women seeking children or who have had children die in infancy.

We find one of the best descriptions of Avalokiteśvara's deeds in the *Lotus Sūtra*:

> Good son, if living beings in any land need someone in the body of a Buddha in order to be saved, Regarder of the Cries of the World Bodhisattva appears as a buddha and teaches the Dharma for them. . . .
>
> For those who need someone in the body of a Brahma king in order to be saved, he appears as a Brahma king and teaches the Dharma for them. . . .
>
> For those who need someone in the body of a lesser king in order to be saved, he appears as a lesser king and teaches the Dharma for them. . . .
>
> For those who need someone in the body of an ordinary citizen in order to be saved, he appears as an ordinary citizen and teaches the Dharma for them. . . .
>
> For those who need someone in the body of a monk, nun, layman, or laywoman in order to be saved, he appears as a monk, nun, layman, or laywoman and teaches the Dharma for them. . . .
>
> For those who need someone in the body of a heavenly being, dragon, satyr, centaur, asura, griffin, chimera, python, human, or non-human to be saved, he appears in such a body and teaches the Dharma for them. . . .[13]

---

13. Reeves, *The Lotus Sutra*, 373–74.

This *mahasattva* takes on multiple forms, appearing in the form best suited to the situation at hand, and may even have multiple manifestations at the same time. Avalokiteśvara also manifests on earth as the Dalai Lama, the religious and political leader of Tibet since the sixteenth century. Avalokiteśvara willingly immigrates to all *saṃsāric* realms, moved by the plight of all, yet is untouched by any sense of his/her own personal suffering. Not surprisingly, this *bodhisattva-mahasattva* remains *the* model, which all followers of Mahāyāna should emulate.

With the rise of the *bodhisattva* ideal, Mahāyāna spread among the general populace in Asia far more effectively than earlier "Hīnayāna" ("Small Vehicle") sects. As I suggest, *bodhisattvas* are spiritual immigrants for the sake of others, committing themselves to a series of immigrations to realms within *saṃsāra*. In addition to great compassion, *bodhisattvas* develop deep insight into reality, coming to see *nirvana* not as a distinct "place" so much as a realization that there is no ultimate separation between "self" and "other." Thus, in helping others overcome suffering, *bodhisattvas* teach us to overcome selfish thinking, and awaken to the Truth of our thoroughly interdependent existence. It is this realization that marks the attainment of Buddhahood. In keeping with the Dharma's strong psychological focus, the transformative insight attained along the *bodhisattva* path means that the "spiritual immigration" of Mahāyāna is more a change of mind rather than a literal change in cosmic location.

"Pure Land"—A Promised Land beyond *Sa?sāra*

Arguably, the development of the *bodhisattva* ideal culminates in the so-called "Pure Land" movement, a devotional style of Buddhism deeply rooted in Indian culture and Mahāyāna teachings. As Mahāyāna spread among India's population, some followers developed intense devotion to various *bodhisattvas*. One theme arising in these cults was that certain *bodhisattvas* and/or celestial Buddhas could create paradisiacal realms where their devotees would be reborn after this life.

The idea of a "Pure Land" derives from the basic Indian cosmology where our world (with its numerous inhabitants, heavens, hells, etc.) resides in the midst of many other worlds spread out across vast stretches of space-time and populated by all manner of sentient beings. Yet, scattered throughout this multiverse are countless *buddhakṣetras* ("Buddha Lands"), each with its own Buddha; in this view, a Buddha's primary duty is to maintain and aid all beings within his "Buddha Land." Interestingly, Buddhism's cosmological expansion correlates with the Dharma's expansion into more far-flung geographic regions. As Buddhists immigrated to other lands, settling in new places and meeting new peoples, so their cosmological horizons expanded to include new *buddhakṣetras* founded and inhabited by new Buddhas and *bodhisattvas*.

Essentially a *buddhakṣetra* is a Buddha's sphere of influence, a typically vast region governed by his spiritual authority and compassionate activity. Mahāyāna texts speak of different types of *buddhakṣetras* (pure, impure, mixed) but most focus on pure ones. These realms resemble "heavens" (*svarga*) or "*deva* realms" (*deva loka*) albeit with one crucial difference: a pure "Buddha Land" does not reside within *saṃsāra*; it is not karmically formed but arises from the purifying compassion of a Buddha. It is thus an abode in which devotees are reborn by the grace of Buddha rather than personal merit. Those beings residing in such a *buddhakṣetra* are always in the presence of a Buddha and so practice Dharma correctly, free from suffering, and eventually attain Awakening.

The most well-known *buddhakṣetra* is Sukāvatī ("supreme joy"), the Pure Land established by the Buddha Amitābha/Amitāyus ("Infinite Light/Life") for the sake of those who have faith in His Limitless Compassion. This radiant Land resides far to the "West," billions of "Buddha Lands" beyond our world.[14] In one *sūtra* the Buddha vividly describes Sukāvatī to his disciple Śāriputra:

> Śāriputra, Sukāvatī is adorned and enclosed by seven railings, seven rows of palm trees and strings of bells. And it is beautiful and embellished with four kinds of precious materials: gold, silver, lapis lazuli, and crystal . . . there are lotus pools there made of seven precious materials: gold, silver, lapis lazuli, crystal, red pearls, diamonds and coral. They are filled with water endowed with eight good qualities . . . and they are strewn with sand of gold. And going down into these lotus pools, from all four sides, are four flights of steps, beautiful and embellished, with four precious materials, . . . and all around the lotus pools jewel-trees are growing beautiful, and embellished with seven precious materials. . . . And in those lotus pools, lotuses are growing: various kinds of blue ones, and various kinds of yellow ones, and various kinds of red ones, and various kinds of white ones, beautiful, beautifully colored, beautifully resplendent, beautiful to look at, and as big around as the wheel of a cart . . .[15]

The Buddha explains how in this Land, divine music plays, the earth is "pleasant and golden," and showered daily by heavenly blossoms accompanied by a magnificent chorus of geese, peacocks, and other exotic birds. There are no beasts, hungry ghosts, or hell beings (the "three bad realms of rebirth") here, and its inhabitants are free from sorrow.[16] Best of all, faithful devotees reborn there dwell in the presence of a living Buddha, learning Dharma firsthand. In short,

---

14. The light imagery associated with Sukāvatī (including the name of its Buddha, Amitāyus, "Infinite Light") as well as its location in the "West" may suggest influence from ancient Persia and its native faith of Zoroastrianism.
15. From "Sukāvatīvyuha [samksiptamatrka]," quoted in Strong, ed., *The Experience of Buddhism*, 187.
16. Ibid.

this is a true Buddhist paradise in which all our needs are fulfilled, the perfect setting for worship and Dharma practice. Who would *not* wish to become an immigrant to such a wondrous place?

Pure Land texts say that Sukāvatī's creation is due to the *bodhisattva* Dharmākara, a young prince who lived eons ago and who, through diligent practice, became Amitābha. Dharmākara made forty-eight vows when aspiring to become enlightened, one of which was to establish a wondrous Pure Land of unsurpassed beauty and virtue. Now, all who trust in him and call on his name will be reborn there, fully established on the path, never to be reborn in a lower realm. Sukāvatī arises solely from Amitābha's merit and compassion, and this power sustains His devotees as they go on to attain *nirvana*.[17]

Descriptions of Sukāvatī contrast strikingly with descriptions of the Sahā world ("a place where suffering is endured"; our world of pain and decay) we find in other texts. Sukāvatī seems the archetypal "Promised Land," similar to Israel (Canaan/Zion, the land "flowing with milk and honey") in the Hebrew Scriptures. Pure Land Buddhism is a "salvation faith" much like the Abrahamic faiths, and it explicitly depicts religious life as a type of immigration. The heart of Pure Land faith is hope for a better future wherein we join others in a place where all can realize our full potential. Pure Land *sūtras* also speak directly to views that people in this current age are incapable of attaining Awakening on their own, offering instead an "easy path" requiring only that we have faith that Amitābha will fulfill his vows to bring us into his wondrous Land.

While Pure Land *sūtras* focus on Sukāvatī, other texts such as the *Lotus Sūtra* speak of other *buddhakṣetras*. In fact, since according to Mahāyāna *all* Buddhas have their own realms, innumerable

---

17. For a good example of a Pure Land text, see Luis O. Gomez, trans., *The Land of Bliss: The Paradise of the Buddha of Measureless Light* (Honolulu: University of Hawaii Press, 1996).

buddhakṣetras are scattered throughout the multiverse. The cosmic Buddha Akṣobhya ("Immovable One"), for instance, presides over Abhirati ("The Joyous"), a Pure Land far to the "East." Conditions for rebirth in Abhirati, however, require great moral effort and thus differ markedly from those governing rebirth in Sukāvatī:

> Do no injury to living beings,
> Hold firmly to all rules of restraint,
> Accept the Buddha's exquisite teaching,
> And you will be born in Akṣobhya's Land . . .
> Be the same as all the bodhisattvas,
> Always free from evil utterances,
> So that men will gladly hear what you say,
> And you will be born in Akṣobhya's Land . . .
>
> Dig good wells beside roads in the desert,
> Plant and cultivate orchards of fruit trees,
> Always give nourishment to mendicants,
> And you will be born in Akṣobhya's Land . . .
>
> If you can give charity to the sick,
> Even if it is just a piece of fruit,
> And giving them a pleasant, cheering glance,
> Then you will be born in Akṣobhya's Land . . .
>
> If you are able to listen, write down,
> Receive, and remember and read and recite
> All the Buddha's reservoir of secrets,
> Then you will be born in Akṣobhya's Land.[18]

Here seeking rebirth in Abhirati is essentially the same as venturing along the *bodhisattva* path, a matter of great effort as well as faith. Interestingly, this text enjoins those seeking rebirth in Abhirati to also establish their *own* Pure Lands to help others.[19] The faithful,

---

18. From the *Mahāparinirvāṇa sutra*, quoted in Strong, ed., *The Experience of Buddhism*, 191–92.
19. Jan Nattier, "The Realm of Akṣobhya: A Missing Piece of the History of Pure Land Buddhism," *Journal of the International Association of Buddhist Studies* 23 (2000): 71–102.

in other words, are to imitate Akṣobhya or Amitābha in their own spiritual pursuits. Such notions add a distinct twist to the immigration metaphor: Buddhas and *bodhisattvas* who have proceeded might be "Dharma pioneers" who have ventured ahead to set up camp and make the necessary preparations for our arrival in the future. Taking this analogy further (and borrowing a term from sociology), the Pure Land in such a view seems to be a spiritual "immigrant enclave," a temporary place of residence where newcomers initially congregate in "an inexpensive and congenial setting," but from which they move on to integrate into the larger society.[20]

Another facet of Pure Land faith adds an interesting wrinkle to the notion of "spiritual immigration." Devotees can, in fact, journey to these Buddha realms *in this life* to get a preview of their future destination. Typically such journeys occur by means of detailed visions attained only by diligent effort and practice. One text, the *Amitāyurdhyāna Sūtra* ("Amitāyus Meditation *Sūtra*"), instructs practitioners to begin by contemplating the setting sun and from there gradually visualize various aspects of Sukāvatī (jeweled trees, water, etc.), leading up to the magnificent lotus throne and the glorious Body of Amitābha.[21] Learning such practices involves intense effort, sometimes as part of a group with all participants vowing to be reborn in a Pure Land together. The resulting visions are transformative, virtually guaranteeing that the visionaries will reach their goal. Like postcards (or Skype exchanges) from the Buddha (or those who have preceded us to the Pure Land), such glimpses are powerful motivators, the spiritualized counterparts of "real-life" visits to monasteries and temples.

20. John R. Logan, Richard D. Alba, and Wenquan Zhang, "Immigrant Enclaves in Ethnic Communities in New York and Los Angeles," *American Sociological Review* 67, no. 2 (April 2002): 299–322.
21. For an English translation, see Junjiro Takakusu, "Meditation on Buddha Amitāyus," in *Buddhist Mahāyāna Texts*, ed. E. B. Cowell (Oxford: Clarendon, 1894), 161–201.

The most powerful passages in Buddhist writings take the injunctions about visualizing and working to establish Pure Lands even further, suggesting a fundamental identity of mind and place within the cosmos. In a scene from the *Vimalakīrtinirdeśa Sūtra* ("*Sūtra* of the Instruction of Vimalakīrti"), Śāriputra asks the Buddha why the Sahā world seems filled with decay and impurities. In response the Buddha presses his toe into the ground, suddenly transforming the scene into a dazzling jeweled paradise of indescribable beauty in which all beings are seated on magnificent lotus thrones. The Buddha explains that his realm is always pure; it is just that living beings experience it according to the purity of their own minds.[22] The Pure Land is a pure mind. Buddhist scholar Roger Corless notes that the deeper message of Pure Land Buddhism is that the devotee's mind and the mind of the "Other Power" (Amitābha) are "discovered to be nondual, as are (according to Mahāyāna teaching) *saṃsāra* and nirvana."[23] These points suggest that "rebirth in a Pure Land" (or even visualizing such a place) may ultimately be more a matter of *knowing* the truth of the here-and-now rather than *going* to a far-off place in the future. Once again, it seems that the Dharma enjoins "spiritual immigration," an immigration of mind rather than geo-cosmic location.

Conclusions

All told, we have come quite far in these reflections on Buddhism as "spiritual immigration," coming to see the centrality of ideas and images of travel and immigration within Buddhist tradition. Through it all, though, we find a deep paradox: Buddhist religious

22. Robert A. F. Thurman, trans., *The Holy Teaching of Vimalakīrti: A Mahāyāna Scripture* (University Park: Pennsylvania State University Press, 1976), 18–19.
23. Roger J. Corless, "Pure Land Piety," in *Buddhist Spirituality I: Indian, Southeast Asian, Tibetan, Early Chinese,* ed. Takeuchi Yoshinori et al. (New York: Crossroad, 1993), 248.

life involves almost continual travel while remaining at home in this world. Taking refuge as a Buddhist is not escaping responsibility in mindless wandering but committing to a more intentional existence. This path of intentional striving, marked by compassion and wisdom, should aim for the betterment of self and other. Such a life may entail literal travel and immigration in this world but even more so, it requires cultivating an "immigrant mindset" in which we aspire to something better for ourselves and others, and seek to make this a reality. Buddhas and *bodhisattvas* are models of perseverance and transcendence not as *escape from life* but as beings *committed to life*. For the *bodhisattva*, the challenge of the Dharma is to see, and to help others see, that this world is a "Pure Land." Such, then, is true *bodhicitta*. Acting upon this aspiration opens up the possibility for embracing life as a collective spiritual immigration leading to the Awakening of *all* beings.

As noted earlier, many great lights of Buddhism have been immigrants, and even a partial list is impressive: Mahinda and Sanghamittā (third century B.C.E.), brother and sister monastics who brought the Dharma to Sri Lanka and converted the whole country; Kumārajīva (344–413 ce), a scholar-monk whose translation work was instrumental in establishing Buddhism in China and throughout East Asia; Suzuki Shunryu (1904–1971), a Japanese Sōtō Zen master who founded the influential San Francisco Zen Center; Thich Nhat Hanh (1926–), Vietnamese Thiên (Zen) master and founder of the "Order of Interbeing," a global organization of Engaged Buddhists working for peace; Tenzin Gyatso (1935–), the current Dalai Lama, a Nobel laureate who fled Tibet in 1959 but is now perhaps the most famous Buddhist in history. These are inspiring figures whose examples resonate deeply even with those who, while not literal immigrants, nonetheless recognize their own status as "spiritual immigrants."

While this discussion may seem overly academic, these reflections on Buddhism as "spiritual immigration" can hopefully guide our thinking about immigration today. Currently in the U.S., "immigration reform" is a highly charged political topic demanding urgent attention, yet our leaders seem loath to deal with it. Meanwhile we are seeing increasing movements of populations around the world; more people are immigrants these days, pulling up stakes and relocating in unfamiliar areas, often with little choice. This fact presents many problems: Can host societies accommodate incoming populations given limited resources (housing, food and water, jobs, etc.)? Should we limit how many immigrants are admitted? If so, on what basis should we decide? How can newcomers make new lives for themselves? Must they leave behind their former customs and identities? These issues are particularly acute in the West, where immigrants from developing nations are radically changing the cultural landscape.

Justin Whitaker, a Buddhist blogger, makes some interesting observations in a 2013 post titled "Towards a Buddhist Policy on Immigration Reform":

> What would a Buddhist immigration policy look like for the US (or UK)? Obviously such notions as generosity (*dana*) and nonviolence (*ahimsa*) should come to mind. Or perhaps we should look to Shantideva's simile of the hand and the foot: urging us to reach out and help others because we are all ultimately interconnected. People may also like to stretch analogies regarding the Buddha as one who broke down barriers such as caste and gender, teaching openly to all and proclaiming the same spiritual potential in all beings.[24]

Whitaker goes on to note difficulties in acting on such ideals, particularly given growing backlash against immigrants in the West,

24. Justin Whitaker, "Towards a Buddhist Policy on Immigration Reform," accessed 20 Feb. 2014, http://www.patheos.com/blogs/americanbuddhist/2013/06/toward-a-buddhist-policy-on-immigration-reform.html.

where many natives see newcomers as threats. Yet he observes that such hostility is rooted in greed and attachment to material goods at the expense of others, adding, "To me one of the greatest American values has been the value of opportunity for everyone here. The opportunity to make something of their lives, to create new community, and to pass that forward to the next generation. Perhaps, contra Buddhism, that value has been translated into commercialism and greed. But it could also be translated into deeper opportunities for service, for realizing our interconnectedness, for overcoming ignorance."[25]

Indeed. Buddhism teaches that spiritual attainment cannot be divorced from daily life. To cultivate the Buddha Way is to set out on a path to a new state, a state of mind and being where we awaken to the interdependence of "self" and "other." Buddhism is a type of immigration from the world of suffering to *nirvana*. It is the way of the *bodhisattva* who sets out to help all beings enter the mythical "Pure Lands" established by Amitābha, Akṣobhya, and the myriad Buddhas of the ten directions. The trick is realizing that this "Pure Land" is here and now. We are all immigrants who, paradoxically, are seeking to find the land in which we already dwell. Such ideas should resonate particularly with Americans, who often pride themselves on their immigrant heritage and speak of America as a land that offers opportunities for a better life. Perhaps the Dharma can remind us of these aspects of American identity and prompt us to make this a better place for those currently here and those who wish to come. This would be a good step toward a wiser and more compassionate approach to the complexities surrounding immigration, something we need both in the U.S. and elsewhere.

25. Ibid.

3

———

Choices and Challenges

The North American Buddhist Immigrant Experience

Karma Lekshe Tsomo

Bells clang, gongs sound, the congregation chants, and children play—it's a typical day at a Buddhist temple in North America. Yet, the selection of a single temple to represent the whole of Buddhist populations is an impossible task. Thus any discussion about the experience of North American Buddhist immigrants must begin with the disclosure that there is no such thing as *the* North American Buddhist immigrant experience. Instead, each of the innumerable Buddhist immigrants in North America has a different experience. It would be far easier to describe the experiences of one specific North American Buddhist community, such as the Lao Buddhist laywomen in San Diego or the Japanese American *"Jodo Shinshu"* (married clerics) in Calgary or the Korean Buddhist nuns in New York, than describe Buddhist immigrants overall. In this chapter, I simply attempt to trace the outlines and note some patterns of tradition and adaptation among these ethnically and religiously diverse communities. I include some illustrations in hopes of opening a dialogue about the North American Buddhist immigrant experience.

Even after roughly 150 years of Buddhist immigration, research on Buddhism in North America is still preliminary. Setting aside the claim that Chinese Buddhist monks reached the West Coast of the New World in the early years of the seventh century, Buddhism is still relatively new to North America.[1] Many publications focus largely on the experience of non-Asian, nonimmigrant Buddhists[2] despite the fact that both the earliest and the largest American Buddhist populations are of Asian descent. On one hand, this appears to be a simple case of bias; on the other hand, given the complexity of the Buddhist immigrant experience, it is not surprising that many North American researchers have focused primarily on populations whose experiences most closely resemble their own. A number of these publications discuss the experiences of women, specifically non-Asian women.[3] However, there are a few studies of Asian Buddhist

1. A number of studies document the history and development of Buddhism in North America, including Rick Fields, *How the Swans Came to the Lake* (Boston: Shambhala, 1992); Richard Hughes Seager, *Buddhism in America* (New York: Columbia University Press, 2012); Charles S. Prebish and Martin Baumann, eds., *Westward Dharma: Buddhism Beyond Asia* (Berkeley: University of California Press, 2006); Charles S. Prebish and Kenneth K. Tanaka, eds., *The Faces of Buddhism in America* (Berkeley: University of California Press, 1998); Christopher Queen and Duncan Ryūken Williams, eds., *American Buddhism: Methods and Findings in Recent Scholarship* (Abingdon, UK: Routledge, 1999); Gary Storhoff and John Whalen-Bridge, eds., *American Buddhism as a Way of Life* (Albany: State University of New York Press, 2010); and Thomas A. Tweed, *American Encounter with Buddhism, 1844-1912: Victorian Culture and the Limits of Dissent* (Chapel Hill: University of North Carolina Press, 2010).
2. Studies in this genre include Michael Downing, *Shoes outside the Door: Desire, Devotion, and Excess at San Francisco Zen Center* (Washington, DC: Counterpoint, 2001); Helen Tworkov and Natalie Goldberg, *Zen in America: Five Teachers and the Search for an American Buddhism* (New York: Kodansha America, 1994).
3. Examples include Marianne Dresser, *Buddhist Women on the Edge: Contemporary Perspectives from the Western Frontier* (Berkeley: North Atlantic Books, 1996); Lenore Friedman, *Meetings with Remarkable Buddhist Women* (Boston: Shambhala, 2000); Sharon Suh, *Being Buddhist in a Christian World: Gender and Community in a Korean American Temple* (Seattle: University of

temples that do address the experiences of Buddhist immigrants to North America,[4] including a few written by immigrant Buddhists themselves.[5]

The challenges immigrant Buddhists experience mirror those of other immigrants in many ways. Adjusting to life in a new country involves adjusting to language difficulties, cultural differences, racial discrimination, and stereotyping. On a personal level, immigrants often face financial difficulties, family separations, homesickness, unemployment, generation gaps, social dislocation, trauma and stress-related disorders, substance abuse, gambling addictions, domestic violence, and other problems. Buddhist temples can provide new immigrants with not only a safe haven and sense of community, but also translation assistance and advice about how to navigate the medical system, political system, and social services agencies.

Buddhist immigrants began arriving in California and Hawai'i in the mid-1800s, mostly as migrant workers for the railways, mines,

Washington Press, 2007); Peter Gregory and Susanne Mrozik, eds., *Women Practicing Buddhism: American Experiences* (Boston: Wisdom, 2007); and Karma Lekshe Tsomo, "Global Exchange: Women in the Transmission and Transformation of Buddhism," in *TransBuddhism: Transmission, Translation, and Transformation*, ed. Nalini Bhushan, Jay Garfield, and Abraham Zablocki (Amherst: University of Massachusetts Press, 2009), 209–36.

4. Kenneth Kenichi Tanaka documents the experience of the oldest and largest immigrant Buddhist population in North America in *Ocean: An Introduction to Jodo-Shinshu Buddhism in America* (Berkeley: Wisdomocean, 1997). Two studies that are especially useful for understanding the experience of immigrants from Southeast Asia as they work to maintain their religious identities in new social environments are Wendy Cadge, *Heartwood: The First Generation of Theravada Buddhism in America* (Chicago/London: University of Chicago Press, 2005); and Paul David Numrich, *Old Wisdom in the New World: Americanization in Two Immigrant Theravada Buddhist Temples* (Knoxville: University of Tennessee Press, 1996). One of the few book-length studies of an immigrant Buddhist community is Suh, *Being Buddhist in a Christian World*. Janet McLellan compares the experiences of diverse Canadian Buddhist communities in *Many Petals of the Lotus: Five Asian Buddhist Communities in Toronto* (Toronto: University of Toronto Press, 1999); and Janet McLellan, "Social Capital and Identity Politics among Asian Buddhists in Toronto," *Journal of International Migration and Integration* 6, no. 2 (2005): 235–53.

5. Bhante Henepola Gunaratana and Jeanne Malmgren, *Journey to Mindfulness: The Autobiography of Bhante G.* (Somerville, MA: Wisdom, 2003); and Bhante Walpola Piyananda, *The Bodhi Tree Grows in L.A.: Tales of a Buddhist Monk in America* (Boston: Shambhala, 2008).

and pineapple and sugar plantations.[6] North American Buddhists today include immigrants from countries such as Korea, Vietnam, Burma, Laos, Cambodia, Taiwan, Thailand, Tibet, Sri Lanka, and, most recently, China, as well as Chinese and Japanese Americans who are fifth-, sixth-, and even seventh-generation Americans. Buddhist immigration from Asia is a continual process, as successive waves of new immigrants arrive and are gradually absorbed into existing communities.

Buddhists in these ethnically, linguistically, religiously, economically, and educationally diverse communities experience the adjustment to American life in different ways, and receive varying degrees of assistance from the government, family, friends, churches, and temples. They all understand and interpret Buddhism differently, as viewed through their own cultural lenses. The reality of these differences cannot be underestimated; when using labels such as Chinese Buddhism, Vietnamese Buddhism, and so on, it is important to acknowledge that each of these groups includes adherents of many different Buddhist schools who are from diverse educational, geographic, and socioeconomic backgrounds. It is also important to recognize that not all Buddhist immigrants remain Buddhist. Some convert to Christianity, for example, out of a sense of indebtedness or gratitude for assistance received in relocating and obtaining immigration papers. Some convert because, although they are imbued with practical Buddhist values such as compassion, they have little knowledge about the tenets of Buddhist philosophy.[7]

---

6. To get a feeling for the immigrants' experiences, from the beginning to the present day, see Dorothy and Thomas Hoobler, *The Chinese American Family Album* (New York: Oxford University Press, 1994) and *The Japanese American Family Album* (New York: Oxford University Press, 1995). These readable accounts include historical overviews, firsthand narratives, letters, documents, recruiting handouts, memoir selections, and photos.

7. Aihwa Ong takes up the topic of conversion in *Buddha Is Hiding: Refugees, Citizenship, the New America* (Berkeley: University of California Press, 2003), 195–202.

Buddhist religious leaders have played and continue to play major roles in assisting immigrants to North America by providing them with religious services, counseling, connections with others in the community who have expertise in various fields, and retention of a sense of cultural cohesion. In the temples, women contribute by cooking, cleaning, fundraising, caring for monks, translating, organizing, and counseling, and they carry out other supportive tasks that are essential to running Buddhist temples and monasteries that double as a cultural hubs and community centers. In some Buddhist temples, such as Jodo Shinshu, Zen, and Tendai, women serve as ordained clergy. Some Buddhist temples, especially in the Vietnamese community, provide classes for children, teaching the heritage language, history, and culture. Among the new wave of Asian immigrants who began arriving in the 1970s from Cambodia, China, Laos, Taiwan, Thailand, and Vietnam, community leaders have directed considerable energy to preserving their cultural identity by building temples, organizing Buddhist celebrations and merit-making activities, inviting monks for chanting ceremonies, and educating children. These activities also aim to provide wholesome options and traditional Buddhist values; unfortunately, however, some young people feel estranged from what they view as an old-fashioned way of life and join gangs and engage in risky behaviors instead. The language gap that exists between the older generation of monastics and the American-educated youth limits the usefulness of temple outreach programs for them.

Buddhists have immigrated to North America at different historical junctures and for a variety of reasons. For example, in the late nineteenth century, many Chinese and Japanese peasants emigrated to escape poverty and seek economic opportunity, which they found in limited measure by working on plantations, farms, and railway lines. The twentieth century subsequently saw successive waves of immigrants who were refugees escaping political and economic problems in Burma, China, Japan, Laos, Taiwan, Tibet, Vietnam, and other countries. Once they arrived in the United States, many immigrants experienced serious challenges related to their transplantation and adaptation to a new social, cultural, and religious environment. Basic survival and attempts at acculturation in their adopted homeland required new arrivals to make many unfamiliar, often difficult choices. Many found safe haven, as well as practical assistance and spiritual solace, at Buddhist temples. For the following discussion, I have surveyed a few immigrant communities to better understand the religious dimension of Buddhist immigration. To illustrate the experience of Theravada Buddhist immigrants, I describe a Lao temple community, and to illustrate the experience of Mahayana Buddhist immigrants, I use examples from the Korean, Vietnamese, and Tibetan communities.

Theravada Buddhist Communities

Theravada Buddhism is amply represented in North America today, with migration from South and Southeast Asia and a subsequent proliferation of Bangladeshi, Burmese, Cambodian, Lao, Thai, and Sri Lankan temples. Lao immigration to the United States began primarily after 1975, following the victory of the Pathet Lao and widespread trepidation about what was in store under the new socialist government. Over the next few years, thousands of refugees arrived in the United States, many traumatized by the catastrophic effects of the 200 million tons of U.S. bombs that had been dropped on their country.

Although Laos is ethnically diverse and animist beliefs are quite prevalent, the majority of lowland Lao are Buddhist. Many Lao immigrants quite proudly and devoutly continue their religious traditions, recognizing Buddhism as the heart of their culture, despite decades of French rule and Catholic missions.[8] Under the guidance of monks, temple communities gradually emerged that helped immigrants reaffirm their religious and cultural identity. The temples are spaces where new arrivals can create social connections and seek guidance to help them through the process of adapting to life in a new country. In the temple, Lao Buddhists feel comfortable wearing traditional dress and speaking Lao; the temples thus serve as cultural hubs as well as religious centers. The temple provides a sense of security and safety where Lao Buddhists can overcome their loneliness and sense of alienation, by being in an environment with others who remember their Buddhist homeland and share their cultural values.

Members of the Lao community have had to make many accommodations to their new living environment. For example, whereas traditional Lao temple services are typically held on full moon and new moon days, immigrant communities in North America generally schedule services on the weekends, because most people work on weekdays. And, since women have less time for labor-intensive food preparation, offerings to the monks increasingly include store-bought rather than homemade snacks. In place of the monks' traditional daily alms round, families sign up to prepare a meal for the monks on a rotating basis. Despite these adaptations, in many ways the temples consciously strive to maintain their cultural traditions and, in some ways, such as dress, often appear more traditional than temples in Laos today.

8. Catholic complicity in French colonial rule in Southeast Asia is well documented. See, for example, James P. Daughton's "Recasting Pigneau de Béhaine: Missionaries and the Politics of French Colonial History, 1894-1914," in *Viet Nam: Borderless Histories*, ed. Nhung Tuyet Tran and Anthony Reid (Madison: University of Wisconsin Press, 2006), 290–323. With approval from the French government, a young French Catholic priest and missionary by the name of Pigneau de Béhaine led a military expedition in Vietnam that began in 1787 and lasted until 1802. Although Pigneau was widely eulogized as a "warrior of the church" and "a national hero," Daughton argues that his motivation was primarily religious: to deflect Protestant influence.

On festival days at temples in large cities, such as Wat Lao Boupharam in San Diego, California, several hundred people gather at the temple. The women dress in traditional clothes and participate in the festivities. Everyone gathers in front of the monks to recite the ritual of going for refuge in the Buddha, Dharma, and Sangha and to receive or renew their commitment to the five moral precepts that Buddhists are enjoined to live by. Everyone recites the liturgy, repeating the lines one by one after the abbot, Bhikkhu Boupha, or after the male president of the temple society. On these days, the parishioners are particularly eager to create merit by making offerings of food, robes, and other necessities to the monks assembled on the raised platform in front of the assembly hall. Monks from other temples are invited to Wat Boupharam to participate in the ceremony to increase the "field of merit" and thus expand the attendees' opportunities to create merit. Toward the end of the service, everyone pours water into a small dish as an offering to the ancestors. The monks then perform a typical Theravada blessing ceremony in which a long string (*bhasi*) is passed to all the congregants. The congregants then cut the string into pieces, knot them, and tie them on each other's wrists. Although this ceremony may derive from Brahmanical or animist tradition, it has been thoroughly absorbed into Buddhist ritual practice. Followers wear the knotted string for at least three days after the *bhasi* ceremony as a kind of protection against misfortune. The string symbolically creates bonds of mutual protection and strengthens the community's sense of shared religious identity. After the monks have eaten, the laypeople enjoy the liberal remains of the meal that the women have prepared, and share news about their lives and activities.

Traditional patterns of gender relationships are strongly evident at Lao temples, as they are at Theravada temples in general. The nuns who are present do not sit on the raised platform, but instead sit with the laywomen. Most Lao women who become nuns do so after they have raised families, generally when they are over fifty years old.[9] Nevertheless, nuns who stay in the temple have many responsibilities and perform valuable services for the monks and the community. For example, the nuns clean the temple, organize temple activities, and cook for the monks on weekdays when the laypeople have to work. Monks in the Theravada tradition are traditionally prohibited from handling money, but because the nuns are not fully ordained and observe only eight precepts, they may be entrusted to handle monetary donations on behalf of the temple. When nuns become very old or sick, they may no longer be able to perform these tasks or to participate fully in the life of the temple. Not wanting to become a burden to the temple, they often return to their homes and stay with their children. However, when monks become old or sick, they are generally cared for by the temple community. Nuns find profound religious meaning in the services that they provide to the monks, the temple, and therefore the Dharma, but their subordinate status within the monastic hierarchy is at odds with modern-day sensibilities and expectations of gender relationships. Under the circumstances, it is rare for young women to become nuns in any Theravada Buddhist community in North America.

Except for the area of gender, where patriarchal patterns of behavior continue to persist, contemporary adaptations of Buddhist traditions are evident both in Asian and North American Buddhist communities. Buddhist monastics today are less likely to travel by foot and more likely to travel by car, bus, or air. Generally speaking, they are more likely to be provided with meals at their temples and are less likely to go for alms. Compared to previous decades, monks in general are better educated, both in Buddhist studies and

9. There is a cultural assumption that younger women are "unstable" and also an implicit aspersion that women pose a danger to the monks' celibacy or to their reputations.

the liberal arts. Monks are more likely to share responsibility for the functioning of the temple with lay devotees and to defer to lay expertise and leadership in practical matters. Although respect for the traditional *sangha*/lay distinction remains in place, in some ways the demarcation between lay and monastic is becoming somewhat less clear-cut. For example, laypeople are taking a greater interest in meditation practice, and may take the initiative to engage in intensive retreats, sometimes with even keener determination than the monks. At the same time, there is a trend for monks to take a greater interest in social service projects and income-generating activities than is customary in their home countries, where it is assumed that all monks need do is keep the precepts. Now, the age-old symbiotic relationship between the monastic and lay segments of Buddhist communities has become more crucial than ever. In accordance with tradition, the monastics are discouraged from becoming involved in secular matters and are valued for their ritual skills, ethical guidance, and counsel in matters personal and practical. But at the same time, especially as the communities struggle to construct temples in unfamiliar landscapes, where they face new economic realities, legal frameworks, and government restrictions, both monastics and laypeople are taking on new roles and becoming increasingly interdependent.

Mahayana Buddhist Communities

Mahayana Buddhist immigrant communities are more varied than Theravada schools and communities, because of their diverse philosophies, histories, and cultures. Mahayana Buddhists have migrated to North America from countries such as China, Japan, Korea, Mongolia, Nepal, Russia, Taiwan, Tibet, and Vietnam. Beginning in the 1850s, Chinese laborers, seeking respite from economic oppression and political conflict, arrived in the Kingdom of Hawai'i, Canada, and the United States.[10] The temples these early immigrants established generally blended Buddhist, Confucian, and Daoist elements, and almost all included an image of Guanyin, the Buddhist *bodhisattva* of compassion. The next wave of immigrants arrived from Japan in the 1880s. Most of these immigrants were imported to do agricultural work, and most of them were Buddhist, primarily from the Jodo Shinshu, or True Pure Land School, that emphasizes devotion to Amitabha Buddha. Missionaries from Japan and especially their wives (*bonmyo*) tackled the difficult task of running temples in a foreign, sometimes hostile environment.[11] Government restrictions eventually slowed the number of immigrants to a trickle until changes in policy begun in 1965 encouraged the next large wave of immigration. This included many from Mahayana countries such as Korea, Taiwan, Tibet, and Vietnam. Before long, there were Buddhist temples of many different descriptions in most American cities. Although interactions among Asian and Asian American Buddhists were limited, as is still the case today, Buddhism's popularity among non-Asian Americans helped ease mainstream acceptance of what had previously been perceived as an exotic, idolatrous, nihilistic, or even sinister religion. Even so, despite many adaptations to American life and sensibilities, including the increased participation of women in temple activities, patriarchy

10. A concise rendition of this early history is found in Fields, *How the Swans Came to the Lake*, 70–82.
11. For a detailed introduction to this migration, see Lori Pierce, "Origins of Buddhism in North America," in *Encyclopedia of Women and Religion in North America*, vol. 3, ed. Rosemary Skinner Keller, Rosemary Radford Ruether, and Marie Cantlon (Bloomington: University of Indiana Press, 2006, 633–58. For the lives of a Shin Buddhist minister and his wife, see Jane Michiko Imamura, *Kaikyo: Opening the Dharma, Memoirs of a Buddhist Priest's Wife in America* (Honolulu: Buddhist Study Center Press, 1998); and Tomoe Moriya, *Yemyo Imamura: Pioneer American Buddhist* (Honolulu: Buddhist Study Center Press, 2000). See also Shigeo Kikuchi, *Memoirs of a Buddhist Woman Missionary in Hawaii* (Honolulu: Buddhist Study Center, 1991); and Nobuko Fukuda, et al., eds., *Hilo Hongwanji: Recalling Our Past, A Collection of Oral Histories* (Hilo, HI: Hilo Betsuin, 1997).

persists in the hierarchical ordering of most immigrant Buddhist institutions.

Korean Buddhist temples exemplify the choices and challenges that Mahayana Buddhists encounter in the task of preserving their valued religious traditions while simultaneously adapting to American society. Korean immigrants began to arrive in the early twentieth century, first to take up agricultural work in Hawai'i, then later as picture brides and political exiles, and even later, after the Korean War, as war brides and orphans.[12] The social and psychological adjustments and tensions experienced by Korean Buddhists as they negotiate the American cultural environment are illustrated by members of Sa Chal Temple, a Korean Mahayana community in downtown Los Angeles. Not only do Buddhist immigrants face feelings of alienation as they attempt to adapt to life in the United States, but they also face criticism and coercive conversion attempts by Korean Christians. Korean Buddhists regard the Buddha's teachings as not only a source of inner transformation but also as intellectually rigorous and at the core of their culture. They regard religious affiliation as a matter of personal preference and feel uncomfortable having Christian beliefs imposed on them. To avoid public censure and disapproval from zealous Christian believers, some temple goers may not publicly identify as Buddhist; business owners may even refrain from going to the temple rather than be economically ostracized by the Korean Protestants who will not patronize businesses operated by Buddhists. Other temple goers, especially those of the older generation, appreciate the comfortable social and religious atmosphere at the temple. There is an ever-widening generation gap that exists between first-generation Korean immigrants and second- and third-generation Korean Americans. It

12. Suh, *Being Buddhist in a Christian World*, 33–4.

involves language fluency, social mores, and worldviews, and makes it difficult to attract young people to the temple.

Vietnamese temples reflect the experiences of immigrants who arrived in the United States following the Vietnam War and the passage of the Indochina Migration and Refugee Act of 1975. Many lived in refugee camps in Hong Kong, Laos, Malaysia, the Philippines, or Thailand before obtaining documents that permitted them to immigrate to the U.S. Many had served in the South Vietnamese army or were otherwise associated with the American occupying forces; others migrated to escape what they viewed as the repressive political or economic policies of the new socialist regime, including an initial suppression of Buddhism. After years in refugee camps, getting started in a new country required tremendous strength of will. Vietnamese immigrants have a strong awareness of their cultural identity, of cultural values such as compassion (derived from Buddhism) and filial piety (derived from Confucianism), and of their responsibility to represent their family and their Vietnamese heritage in a positive light. As survivors of displacement and the trauma of war, they are generally adaptable and amenable to American values such as independence and individualism. Vietnamese Buddhists turn to the Buddha for solace and to the temple as a source of cultural affirmation. Vietnamese Buddhist temples have been active in establishing Sunday programs in Vietnamese language and culture, including Buddhism, for children. For many, the Buddhist rite of going for refuge in the Three Jewels (Buddha, Dharma, and Sangha) is an antidote to fear. Serving the temple is both an affirmation of religious meaning and also a means of ensuring the prosperity of their families. As Lien Bui, a Vietnamese Buddhist who was born in Laos and lived for many destitute years in refugee camps, learned as a child: "As long as I keep the Buddha in my heart and remember to follow the Dharma teachings, no real harm can come to me. The worst that can happen is death, but that is a foregone conclusion for all sentient beings anyway."

Tibetan Buddhist immigrants exemplify patterns of migration different from other refugees, in that most migrated to India or Nepal before being able to migrate to North America. Before and after H. H. Dalai Lama fled to India in 1959, an estimated eighty thousand Tibetans made the long and difficult journey to India, where they experienced poverty and disease in addition to the trauma of leaving their country, and often their families as well. In 1990, the U.S. Congress passed a bill that enabled one thousand Tibetan refugees living in India and Nepal to obtain immigrant visas to the U.S., and several thousand more have immigrated since then. Most Tibetans take pride in their Buddhist identity and take part in religious ceremonies with highly respected religious figures such as H. H. Dalai Lama. With populations of just over nine thousand in the U.S. and four thousand in Canada, spread out over thousands of miles, Tibetans usually collaborate in organizing Buddhist events at Dharma centers established by non-Tibetans, rather than set up separate temples. Tibetans are especially likely to participate when the officiating *lama*, or teacher, is ethnically Tibetan. A large number of Tibetan centers offer teachings, meditations, retreats, and empowerments, including some with facilities for Tibetan monks and nuns, but the students are largely non-immigrant Americans. Programs for children are generally missing in these centers, raising questions about the religious identity of Tibetan Buddhists in the future.

The Precious, Tenuous Anchor of the Buddha's Teachings

Although Buddhist immigration to North America began in the mid-nineteenth century, immigrants also arrived in large numbers during the 1970s. The Buddhist teachings on impermanence, the defects of attachment, the importance of loving kindness for all beings everywhere, and the wisdom of interdependence helped make the journey of these later immigrants easier to accept and manage. However, when immigrants arrived as refugees, their Buddhist upbringing and values were not always adequate for coping with the disorientation, anxiety, economic stress, and trauma-related stress they experienced. Many refugees had lost most or all of their relatives, some had been raped, some had seen loved ones killed in front of their eyes, and most had lost all their possessions. Some suffered feelings akin to survivor's guilt, and many were deeply concerned that, due to the chaos of war, their loved ones had not received proper funeral rites. Amidst all of this turmoil, Buddhism continued to provide immigrants with comfort and meaning in their new, often incomprehensible cultural environment. Yet it is still unclear whether the Buddhism that their children inherited will be strong enough to sustain them through the stresses of intergenerational trauma, culture clash, and social dislocation.

Buddhists of all traditions have been and continue to be the objects of active conversion strategies. Well-trained and well-funded missionaries, especially of certain evangelical streams, have as their stated goal the winning over of Buddhists to the Christian point of view. Many sincerely believe that they are "doing God's work" in energetically making converts, and Buddhists are very vulnerable to their various tactics, for a number of reasons. Quite a number of immigrants from Buddhist families have converted to Christianity since arriving in North America, especially those who found themselves living in isolated locations, without family ties or a close community to affirm their Buddhist identity. Other conversions result from intermarriage, and still others are due to the failure of Buddhist education programs, which have traditionally been available only to monastics. Strong, relevant Buddhist educational programs are especially lacking among immigrant populations whose countries have been decimated by war and political oppression, such as the Cambodian, Mongolian, and Tibetan communities, where monks and nuns were frequently targeted for extermination.

Immigrants may also be inclined to convert to Christianity out of a feeling of gratitude toward the person who provided sponsorship for them to enter the country. During the 1970s, hundreds of thousands of Buddhists fleeing war-torn countries lived for several years in refugee camps, often in deplorable and seemingly hopeless circumstances. When they were finally able to immigrate to North America, many refugees felt an enormous debt of gratitude to the person who acted as their sponsor, helped them through the labyrinth of paperwork to obtain immigration papers, and then helped them obtain housing, social services, and employment when they settled in. Another reason for the success of conversion efforts is the association of Christianity with modernity and the belief that Christianity is compatible with material success. Christian churches also provide dances and enjoyable social activities for young people, whereas many Buddhist temples offer only chanting and meditation, often perceived as boring and old-fashioned by the younger generation. If the temples that Buddhist immigrants have worked so hard to establish in North America are to carry on and flourish in future generations, they will need to adopt more skillful means (*upaya*) to attract the attention and loyalty of Buddhist youth.

4

Missionaries and Immigrants, Missionaries as Immigrants

Jonathan A. Seitz

Missionaries are not a major segment of immigrants, but they have an interesting place, and often serve as intermediaries alongside other immigrants. As religious migrants, they act as instigators, translators, advocates, and aides. "Missionary" means "one who is sent," and missionaries in the past traditionally went to live in a foreign country more or less permanently (although it did not always work out this way). Mission has held an influential place in modern Western culture, often acting as the humanitarian wing for empire, but sometimes as a critic.

The country where I live, Taiwan, is an interesting case. Taiwan was held by the Qing Empire until 1895, then by Japan for fifty years

(1895–1945), and finally by the Chinese Nationalist government. Missionaries were usually separate from the foreign colonial powers and are often remembered fondly, even nostalgically. They started churches, schools, and universities that continue today. On the other hand, in China the missionary period went together with the "century of occupation" from the opium wars c. 1840 to liberation in 1949. Missionaries from Robert Morrison (arrived 1807) onward held roles in companies or government offices like the East India Company or the Imperial Maritime Customs Service, regularly served in diplomatic posts, and often went on to major academic posts. Missionary children from China alone include figures like Henry Luce, Pearl Buck, and John Leighton Stuart (the last U.S. ambassador before the communist revolution), and Buck and Stuart themselves served as missionaries. These three were some of the major interpreters of China for U.S. audiences: Luce as a publisher, Buck as a novelist, and Stuart as a diplomat. In theological scholarship, T. F. Torrance, George Lindbeck, and Ian Graeme Barbour were born in China. The missionary-as-immigrant leaves a complex legacy and many descendants.

If the U.S. early interacted with other cultures through commerce, diplomacy, or study, two of the other major cultural exchanges were immigration and mission. Before the Peace Corps or the study-abroad movement, mission was probably the main way in which Westerners intensively studied non-Western cultures. Missionaries numbered in the thousands by the late nineteenth and early twentieth century. At least one scholar has spoken of mission in the early twentieth century as deeply influencing China policy, of there being a "missionary mind" to U.S. foreign policy.[1] Today, the U.S. is still the largest sender of short-term and long-term missionaries,

---

1. James Reed, *The Missionary Mind and American East Asia Policy, 1911-1915* (Cambridge: Harvard University Press, 1983).

but has now been joined by countries like Korea, Brazil, and the Philippines. Mark Noll gives several illustrations of these changes in "from everywhere to everywhere" mission: Catholics in the U.S. now worship in more languages than ever; the highest-attendance churches in France and England tend to be black congregations made of immigrants and their children; more Presbyterians worship in Ghana than in Scotland; the largest chapter of the Jesuits is in India; and on and on.[2] By most measures, there are far more missionaries going abroad today than there were during the "high tide" of mission in the first half of the twentieth century. There may now be some 400,000 cross-cultural mission workers serving around the world, with half from the global south.[3]

Mission as religious immigration continues to have a strong influence. This essay begins with a brief overview of the rise of widespread, modern cross-cultural mission, proceeds to a discussion of how immigration and mission were part of the same process of world integration, offers a personal reflection on the missionary immigrants, and concludes with a reflection on mission and immigration.

Migration and Mission

The modern missionary movement is a bit of a historical outlier. The idea that a few nations would send out large numbers of individuals or families to live abroad for a time for mission is a modern development. Before this, communities might move because of persecution or for economic or cultural reasons. Christianity grew through conquest, through territorial creep, and sometimes through

2. Mark A. Noll, *The New Shape of World Christianity: How American Experience Reflects Global Faith* (Downers Grove, IL: IVP Academic, 2009), 20–21.
3. Center for the Study of Global Christianity, *Christianity in Its Global Context, 1970-2020: Society, Religion, and Mission* (Gordon Conwell Theological Seminary, 2013), 76. www.globalchristianity.org/globalcontext.

exilic movements. In Reformation-era Europe, cross-cultural mission was not yet a popular idea. Calvin might write a "prayer for the world" modeled after psalms that speak of the world, or Protestants might move within Europe or found new colonies in the Americas, but this was not yet the cross-cultural mission that began to accelerate c. 1800. The major Protestant confessions made no mention of mission until the twentieth century, and mission-as-theology is a very recent focus.

The missionary movement is often portrayed as an act of great intention, as if it grew from a newfound zeal *sui generis*. However, it also was the product of larger world integration, of new possibilities and opportunities, of the accumulation of wealth and improvements in technology, of the growth of empire and the rise of nations, and of new waves of immigration. The missionary intent was possible because these other things also existed. Scholars like Luis Rivera-Pagán have traced the "violent evangelism" of Latin America, which mixed together multiple modes of mission and multiple modes of forced and voluntary immigration. Mission becomes much more understandable if we see its relationship to global processes and to new patterns of migration. Such a new mission historiography must include immigrants in almost every chapter.

Missionaries and Immigrants

There is almost no research on mission and immigration, but it has often been possible to find missionaries and immigrants together, even from the mythic beginnings. For instance, the origins of the first major U.S. missionary society, the American Board of Commissioners for Foreign Missions (ABCFM), grew out of a famous New England Protestant community; key leaders were involved in the famous "Haystack Monument" incident, the Amistad, and the broader New Divinity movement that swept through places like Williams, Andover, and Yale. However, the people involved in these groups were also visibly influenced by the arrival of a Hawaiian youth, "Henry" Obookiah (1792–1818), who became a major early convert and the impetus for the Congregational Church's significant missions to Hawaii.[4] Similarly, the pioneer London Missionary Society (LMS) missionary to the Chinese, Robert Morrison, began his Chinese study with an immigrant in London, Yong Sam-Tak, several years before he went to China. In Canton, Morrison met Yong again and clearly drew upon him for help in his work.[5] Morrison went to China alone, and it is hard to see his success apart from either the initial immigrant friendship or the semi-formal sponsorship of the British East India Company that came after he married the daughter of an official. These were two of the largest missionary emphases of the time, with the Hawaiian mission representative of the ABCFM and China a major mission of the LMS. In each case, an immigrant made the mission viable.

During these early periods, Hawaiian immigrants in New England or Chinese immigrants in London were tiny in number (Obookiah may have been the only Hawaiian in the U.S. at the time, and Yong was part of a very small number of Chinese in London, perhaps in the dozens or hundreds). While mission has often been presented as an act of intention or planning, it is almost impossible to see the start of the missionary movement in these places apart from the presence and aid of immigrants. In this sense, the missionary movement was also formed around contingency, perceived opportunity, and sometimes

4. Jonathan A. Seitz, "Reorienting Early American Mission: The Conversion of Henry Obookiah" (presented at the Yale-Edinburgh Group on World Christianity, New Haven, CT, 2003). Obookiah's memoirs were published in large numbers, and the most famous mission story of the day; Edwin Dwight, ed., *Memoirs of Henry Obookiah, a Native of Owhyhee* (American Sunday School Union, 1830).

5. Jonathan A. Seitz, "Canton in London and London in Canton: Robert Morrison, Yong Sam-Tak, and Religious Translation" (presented at the Beijing University Conference on Missions and Translation, Beijing, 2004).

friendship. Immigrants were physical reminders of the broader world, language teachers and cultural guides, and models for how Christian faith might look. Obookiah was a convert who left a fascinating account, and in death he quickly became the inspiration for the sending of many, many missionaries to Hawaii.

The Missionary as Immigrant: A Personal Account

Missionaries today are probably more related to immigrant communities in the U.S. than has been recognized. I have some experience of the symbiosis of mission and immigration myself. While I lived in Beijing and Singapore as a student, my calling to Taiwan Seminary came via my next-door neighbor at seminary, Chen Shang-Jen. Through him I came to work for two years as the youth director at a local Taiwanese-American Presbyterian congregation in New Jersey. I was ordained there before coming to Taiwan, and I still visit that church whenever I am home. During summers I also occasionally see members from those churches back in Taipei, even twelve years later.

Through those at this church, I gained an introduction to the seminary in Taipei, to other Taiwanese-American churches in the U.S., and other connections in Taiwan. During our last visit home we visited Taiwanese-American congregations in Chicago, Louisville, Ann Arbor, Cincinnati, the DC area, and New Jersey. The Taiwanese-American churches are a useful foil to our work in Taiwan. Our experience is often the mirror opposite of those in these congregations. Our children attend school in Mandarin but speak English at home, we sometimes find ourselves longing for familiar food (try finding a burrito or falafel in Taipei—possible, but not easy), and we face a similar set of bureaucratic entanglements (visas, birth records, medical systems, taxes, driving licenses, etc.). In a sense, we are both privileged and alienated. The mere existence of this parallel community, which understands our needs and trials, has often been a source of encouragement. In mission history, it is also quite clear that many returned missionaries connect to immigrant communities, and have often been legal or cultural advocates. Charles McClain's *In Search of Equality* looks at the legal fight for equality where one of the major protagonists was a returned missionary.[6] One of the more famous Chinese novels of the twentieth century, Lao She's *Mr. Ma and Son*, records the lives of a father and son in England, and often mocks the overt racism of the time; a missionary figure in the novel plays an ambiguous role, providing help but also showing stereotypically English responses.[7]

Immigration is often seen as reinforcing or strengthening religious ties.[8] In the U.S., this means that the church provides one of the most visible cultural sanctuaries welcome to immigrants, often leading to conversion among those who originally followed home-country traditions. In Taiwan, we participate in an English service that is part of Taipei's largest Presbyterian congregation. The membership is the reverse of what I experience in the U.S. Attendance swells in the summer as children and grandchildren come back to Taiwan to visit older members and can fall during major holidays, when members return to their home congregations abroad or outside of the city. The worship service is often a gateway for Christian Taiwanese-Americans who wish to learn more about Taiwanese culture. They may come to study Chinese for six months, or via a missionary organization like YWAM or OMF for a year or two, but then decide to stay for a longer period of time. Only some of those who

---

6. Charles J. McClain, *In Search of Equality: The Chinese Struggle Against Discrimination in Nineteenth-Century America* (Berkeley: University of California Press, 1996).

7. She Lao, *Mr. Ma & Son: A Sojourn in London*, trans. Julie Jimmerson (Beijing: Phoenix Books, 1991); Anne Witchard, *Lao She in London* (Hong Kong: Hong Kong University Press, 2012).

8. Carolyn Chen, *Getting Saved in America: Taiwanese Immigration and Religious Experience* (Princeton: Princeton University Press, 2008).

attend are fluent English speakers, usually Taiwanese or Taiwanese-Americans, but also with English-speakers from Southeast Asia or the U.S. and Europe. For us, the congregation provides a hybrid experience. Our oldest child can go to Sunday school in Mandarin, and we have a wide range of people we can ask for help with specific challenges or worries. When we have needed help looking for an apartment, navigating schools, or understanding institutional politics, this is often the community that helps us.

It is probably also possible to speak of a broader missionary diaspora, which is organized around shared schools, institutions, and friendships. There are famous schools in India and Korea where missionaries have taught and children of missionaries have studied for generations. I am an MK (missionary kid) under only the loosest of definitions (I was born in Congo but left with my parents when I was two, and I have never returned). Nonetheless, the experience has clearly shaped me, and I was not entirely surprised to find at a gathering of Presbyterian mission workers that two other missionaries in a group of about twenty were also born in Congo; one continued to serve there, while the other has spent his adult life in Brazil. A large number of current missionaries are often themselves the children of missionaries. In Taiwan, it is not uncommon for me to encounter second-, third-, or fourth-generation missionary families. In Taiwan there were at least four or five families who returned over several generations (the Mackays and Landsboroughs are the most famous). Immigration can be long-term, and Taiwan has several missionary dynasties, where a progenitor arrived in the nineteenth century and others returned later.

Mission as a category of immigration carries with it aspects of the broader experience of relocation or dislocation. One of these is simply the lived experience of visible difference. Part of the challenging experience of immigration is the profound and continuous experience of difference. Our children are often noticed in public, and usually for physical traits (their hair, their eye color, their skin), and sometimes people comment on them using the expression *yang wawa*, "foreign baby" (the mirror image, perhaps, of "china doll"?). For good and bad, they are immediately visible as different, just as immigrants are almost anywhere else. Stigmas, positive and negative, attach to them, which is always a challenge for the parent. Similarly, their behavior, better or worse, is sometimes described back to them as characteristic of being "American" (whatever that means). Although, cognitively, I knew that immigrants suffered from being singled out or taken as representative for an entire group, experiencing it firsthand is stressful in a different way.

There is a type of cognitive dissonance that comes from living between cultures, and the temptation to resolve this tension is dangerous. Missionaries have reacted, sometimes in alarming ways, to being called "barbarians," "foreigners," or more pejorative terms. Even when the terms were not intended with any offense, they could infer offense. For instance, Lydia Liu has written about how Robert Morrison initially took no offense at a common Chinese term for "foreigner," but later advocated the term's elimination. The term was eventually outlawed under opium war conventions.[9] Missionaries resented being described as permanently other and sometimes took steps via the colonial enterprise to suppress ways of speaking. As a historian of religion and a missionary, I am ambivalent about how to respond to such markers of foreignness. Taipei is cosmopolitan such that it is easy to blend in, but when we travel we frequently have people comment on our existence ("foreigners!"), throw out an

---

9. Jonathan A. Seitz, "Canton in London and London in Canton: Robert Morrison, Yong Sam-Tak, and Religious Translation" (presented at the Beijing University Conference on Missions and Translation, Beijing, 2004). Lydia He Liu, *The Clash of Empires: The Invention of China in Modern World Making* (Cambridge, MA: Harvard University Press, 2004).

English greeting (*Halou*, the Chinese pronunciation of "hello"), or just snap some pictures. For a tourist these experiences are tolerable, perhaps even flattering, but for a long-term resident they wear thin quickly. U.S. immigrants have termed such behaviors "micro aggressions," and, again, they mimic the ways in which nationals may single out immigrants as foreign.

A separate distinctive challenge for missionaries is that they may elect to live locally ("gone native") or in a foreigner bubble. Just as other immigrants may live in their adopted land and never learn the local language, the same is true for missionaries. It is common to choose housing, schools, or churches that are more or less foreign to the local culture. Sang Hyun-Lee describes the immigrant church as a "refuge and liminal space."[10] For many immigrants, the church is the primary harbor of one's original culture. Language, food, and customs mimic the home culture and provide respite from the host culture. Chinese language is particularly challenging, and even a number of our Taiwanese colleagues have found it difficult to maintain schooling in the local language.

Conclusion

Missionaries and immigrants hold some unique attachments. There is so little formal research on this topic that it is hard to make the case for an exact relationship. From the above, it is clear that the missionary movement was always rooted in global processes of migration, and that missionaries relied on and were inspired by immigrants in their own work. A personal reflection showed how mission movements continue to draw on the immigrant experience and how cross-cultural mission today draws on complex genealogies of migration. There is still a heroic imagination about mission that

10. Sang Hyun Lee, *From a Liminal Place: An Asian American Theology* (Minneapolis: Fortress Press, 2010), 127.

depicts solitary missionaries converting foreign peoples, but the truth is that mission has usually been a dialogical process that requires mutuality and relationship for any modicum of success or sustainability.

Missionaries and immigrants travel the same routes, albeit in opposite directions. They share interests, friendships, and affinities. Today there are probably as many missionaries serving abroad as at any point in history, although the composition and the nature of the work have shifted. At the same time, the long-term movement has been joined by massive and growing waves of short-term mission, sometimes essentially "religious tourism."

Sang Hyun Lee has developed the image of Korean immigrants as a "pilgrim people." This is also an appropriate model for mission. Just as many immigrants plan to return to their first homes, missionaries also see even long-term service as eventually leading to a return "home" someday. The pilgrim, however, is perhaps different from the exile: they go to better live the life of faith and to share it with others. Luis Rivera-Pagán has spoken of "xenophilia" as a love of the foreigner or the other.[11] "Xenophobia" is far and away the better-known word. At its core, love of the other is the stated ideal of Christian mission, an effort to love those who are different. It brings its own challenges. Samuel Escobar speaks of three challenges related to migration and mission: "the challenge to Christian compassion and sensitivity," "the need for the churches to take a prophetic stance in the face of society's unjust treatment of immigrants," and "the fact that migration is an avenue for the evangelistic dimension of mission."[12] It may be that the flip side to mission as love-for-the-foreigner is mission as love-of-the-foreigner. The church grows its capacity for compassion, for

11. Luis Rivera Pagán, *Essays from the Diaspora* (Mexico City: Publicaciones El Faro, 2002).
12. Samuel Escobar, "Migration: Avenue and Challenge to Mission," *Missiology* 31, no. 17 (2003): 17–28.

prophetic justice, and for evangelism through its going as well as through its receiving. Being immigrants, we have more compassion for the immigrants we meet.

While Christianity has often been a territorial faith (i.e., "Christendom"), it has also been a missionary faith; and this missionary faith is reflected through the modern tradition of the missionary movement. This movement grew out of a broader globalization, and missionaries and immigrants sometimes partnered for their mutual benefit. Missionaries themselves became immigrants. These discrete immigrations (from, for instance, New Jersey to Taipei) are part of a larger set of immigrations in many directions. While missionary immigrants have been a small part of the larger flow of immigrants, they raise enduring questions and demonstrate in striking ways the possibilities for cross-cultural exchange. Often imperfect witnesses, they nonetheless attempted to translate and share their faith across languages and cultures.

PART II

Abrahamic Tradition

5

———

Singing the Songs of the Lord in a Strange Land

Forced Exile versus Chosen Exile in Early Jewish History

Daniel Maoz

Introduction

Throughout Jewish history, exile and immigration largely have been perceived and explained by terms established within narratives of exile and return in the Hebrew Bible. This understanding presupposes that the land of Canaan was gifted to the Hebrew people and when removed from this Land of Promise, they became exiles. Yet, claims to Israel's possession of the Promised Land are set in balance by declarations that *Eretz* Israel is and remains, in fact, God's possession. Narratives identifying the Hebrew people as foreigners and strangers, even when living in the Land of Promise, appear throughout the Hebrew Bible.[1] This chapter addresses the concept of exile by considering viewpoints I have classified as "forced" or "chosen." In so doing, I also offer an alternate approach to Lemche's recent questioning of the historicity of the Babylonian exile as recorded in the Hebrew Bible.[2]

Theory

Problematic is the matter of theodicy—exculpation of any expression of divine justice that condones and initiates suffering, evil, punishment, or even death in order to bring about a state of goodness, kindness, or love to Israel. Bakon summarizes the standard explanations of theodicy from three distinct Jewish perspectives.[3] Each provides a competing theoretical basis for this study.

The first approach considers God's actions as an exercise of divine retribution against human transgression as a means to establishment and exercise of divine justice, with a caveat that repentance can stay the hand of judgment. The second examines the life of Job and explains that no transgression was committed, therefore no need for or exercise of retribution was involved—God unilaterally makes a deal with Satan, Job thus becoming the subject of an exhibition of how righteousness (Job's life) prevails against unmerited suffering (Satan's test). The third contains two phases, but involves voluntary acceptance of suffering as a servant's prerogative to participate in the redemption of the world: the prophet first and then Israel as a people make the self-offering in order to bring about *Tikkun Olam* ("repair

---

1. While it is tempting to say "believing Israel," I aver that all Jews—those who express faith in God, those who doubt the existence of God, and those who categorically reject any idea associated with God—are under covenant according to the terms of Sinai.
2. Niels Peter Lemche, *The Old Testament* (*sic*) *between Theology and History: A Critical Survey* (Louisville: Westminster John Knox, 2008), 330.
3. Shimon Bakon, "Suffering: Three Biblical Views," *The Jewish Bible Quarterly* 30, no. 3 (2002): 183–90.

of the world"). Bakon presents these models as three competing theories, not as a complex system of unified thought.[4]

Methodology

The discussion of exile becomes problematized when the range of perspectives present in the biblical text is brought to light. Five vantage points dealing with exile in the Hebrew Bible are considered in this study: first, through the eyes of an exiled people (a strictly human perspective); second, from the language of Scripture representing divine action leading directly to exile of Israel; third, from exiled Israel coming to terms with God initiating and choreographing all aspects of their exile; fourth, from exiled Israel viewing their plight as a result of human force alone; and fifth, from the perspective of self-exile, a willingness to enter or remain in a state of exile rather than act according to the stated will of God. This study applies the terms "forced exile" and "chosen exile" polyvocalically in analyzing certain of these vantage points.[5]

Forced Exile versus Chosen Exile:
Case Studies from Jewish Biblical History

Biblical lament reinforces several traditional themes relating to the Promised Land, with inheritance, home, and freedom at the top of the list. When Israel was thrust into exile, loss of inheritance to strangers, forfeiture of homes to foreigners, and enslavement to foreign power become primary reasons for lament:

4. "There are three biblical views on suffering, existentially a corollary of evil" (Bakon, "Suffering," 183).

5. Polyvocality expresses similar concepts in different words; polyperspectivity expresses different concepts employing similar language. See Daniel Maoz, "Chimes of Freedom Clashing," *The Journal for the Society of Textual Reasoning* 7, no. 1 (March 2012), for early application of this terminology. The five categories discussed herein are my own, created with the intention of emphasizing the polyperspectivity of interpretive vantages, thereby highlighting important component parts of this complexity commonly overlooked when viewed as a unified system.

Our inheritance was turned over to strangers (זָרִים), our homes to unknown people (נָכְרִים). We became orphans without a father; our mothers became like widows. The water we drink *we pay for* with silver; our wood comes at a price. We are pursued to our *very* necks; we are weary and rest is not given to us. We submitted to the hand of Egypt and Assyria *in order to* have enough bread to be satisfied. Our fathers transgressed and are no more, and we bear their punishments. Slaves rule over us, and there is no one to free us from their hands. (Lam. 5:2-7)[6]

Two particular exiles are emphasized in the Hebrew Bible in detail, the Assyrian exile (722 B.C.E.) and the Babylonian exile (586 B.C.E.). The two exiles were significantly different in nature, though from a perspective of one dwelling in a land being conquered, similar effects would be felt. These accounts developed an exile language—"a kind of scarlet thread that runs through biblical historiography from one end to the other"—that would inform subsequent Jewish exiles to present times.[7] Inhabitants of Israel (the Northern Kingdom) experienced their land annexed by an Assyrian Empire that had conquered the lands to their north in the prior century (850–722 B.C.E.). Consequentially, the people of Israel were involuntarily placed under foreign and initially hostile authority. According to Sargon II's extant cuneiform records, Assyria captured Samaria, the capital of the Northern Kingdom, in the first year of his reign:

Samaria I besieged and conquered . . . 27,290 people I took into captivity, 50 chariots for my military use I removed . . . I renewed, made it higher than before; people out of all lands, my captives of war. I settled there; my officer I made governor over them. Tribute and taxes like the Assyrians I laid upon them.[8]

---

6. All Hebrew Bible references are my own translations. When comparing to standard English translation, I use JPS (*Tanakh – The Holy Scriptures* [Philadelphia: Jewish Publication Society, 1999]).

7. Lemche, *The Old Testament* (sic) *between Theology and History*, 154.

8. Schraeder, *Keilinschriftliche Bibliothek*, ii; as cited in James A. Montgomery, *The Samaritans, the Earliest Jewish Sect: Their History, Theology, and Literature* (Eugene, OR: Wipf & Stock, 2006), 50.

No relief was gained when Sargon II died, as his successor, Sennacherib, closed in on the Southern Kingdom, constraining its inhabitants to become prisoners in their own land:

> Hezekiah of Judah did not submit to my yoke, and I laid siege on 46 of his strong cities surrounded by walls, and the many villages surrounding them. I captured all of them. . . . 200,150 people were forced out. . . . I made Hezekiah a prisoner in Jerusalem, his royal residence, like a bird in a cage.[9]

The Hebrew Bible attests to a Neo-Babylonian incursion that forced thousands of Jerusalemites to move to Babylon.[10] The Babylonians besieged the Southern Kingdom (Judah), pillaging and burning Judah's capital city, Jerusalem, and destroying the Temple (587–586 B.C.E.). The line of Davidic rule came to an end with the deportation of a majority of the surviving inhabitants from the Southern Kingdom. Few managed to escape to another land (e.g., Jeremiah to Egypt). Famously, the Psalms and Amos recall this exile in melancholic phrase:

> By the rivers of Babylon, there we sat down, and we wept when we remembered Zion. (Ps. 137:1)

> Maiden Israel is fallen *so that* she shall not rise again. She is abandoned on her land. No one will lift her up. (Amos 5:2)

The gift of land came with responsibility: rid inhabitants, destroy graven images, remove high places, and distribute land among yourselves according to lot. Negative repercussions would follow if these conditions were not fully met, God declared, "and then that which I plan to do to them I will do to you."[11] Punishment came

---

9. Extract from the hexagonal black obelisk known as the Prism of Sennacherib, discovered in the ruins of Nineveh. See Lemche, *The Old Testament* (*sic*) *between Theology and History*, 117.

10. 2 Kgs. 24:14-16. See Lemche, *The Old Testament* (*sic*) *between Theology and History*, 154–56, 219–32, for discussion about its historicity.

to Israel in the form of chosen exile. Israel chose not to satisfy stated conditions and therefore brought exile upon herself. While the hand of judgment appeared in human form—"an enduring nation, an ancient nation, a nation whose language you do not know, neither do you understand what they say"—Israel was to understand that this was actually an extension of divine enactment—"I will bring a nation upon you from far." Thus a foreign nation impoverished the gifted land by consuming its harvest, its bread, its vines, and its figs.[12] Israel experienced an exile that was mutually chosen by God and Israel as a result of Israel walking "after the imagination of (their) evil heart," and was cast out of the gifted land and thrust into an unknown land.[13] Any hope of reversing this judgment thereafter lay in living peaceably among their captors and praying for their well-being.[14]

From the chronicler's perspective, the psalmist distinguished between perception and reality when praising God about a forthcoming Temple. While from a human perspective, material possessions, land, and all that it contains may appear to belong to human owners, but in reality, everything belongs to God, including the Temple about to be constructed, as all came from God's hand.[15]

How then can one speak of being exiled from a place that never belonged to anyone else except God? The Book of Job explores what can be described as an inner, spiritual exile. If, according to longstanding theory, the Book of Job was authored during the time of exile in a non-Israelite setting,[16] Bakon's second category for

---

11. Num. 33:52-56.
12. Jer. 5:15; 6:17-18.
13. Jer. 16:12-13.
14. Jer. 29:9.
15. 1 Chron. 29:10-16.
16. See Robert Watson, *Expositor's Bible: The Book of Job* (New York: Funk & Wagnalls, 1900), 343. More recently, Larrimore devotes a chapter to understanding Job's personal exile as a model for people in exile: see Mark Larrimore, *The Book of Job: A Biography* (Princeton: Princeton University Press, 2013), chapter 5, "Job in Exile." Cf. Job 12:13-23: "To God belong wisdom and power; counsel and understanding are his. What he tears down cannot be rebuilt;

understanding theodicy that involves Job's story line offers insight into the mind of those in exile as well as establishes an exilic pattern (לְיִשְׂרָאֵל מָשָׁל),[17] a consolation for those who would otherwise correlate national sin with personal suffering. From this perspective, Job experienced unwarranted exile in Sheol,[18] hoping that through faith his exile would end redemptively:

> Water disappears from the sea and the riverbed becomes parched and dry; so a person lies down and does not rise; until the heavens no longer exist, people will not awake or be roused from their sleep. Who will grant that you would hide me in the grave and that you would conceal me until your anger has passed? *Who* will set a fixed time for me after which you will remember me? If a person dies, will he live again? All the days of my service I will wait until my replacement comes. You will call and I will answer you; because you will long for the creature your hands have made. Surely then you will count my steps but not keep track of my sin. My offenses will be sealed up in a pouch; you will cover over my sin. (Job 14:11-17)

The concept of exile, removed from its literal domain, is extended metaphorically in early Rabbinic Judaism:

> Rabbi Nehorai said: "Exile yourself to a place of Torah—and do not assume that it will come to you—for it is your colleagues who will cause it to remain with you; and do not rely on your own understanding."[19]

It is clear that language has an innovative flexibility that linguists identify as linguistic domain and range. So it is in the case of the

---

the man he imprisons cannot be released. If he holds back the waters, there is drought; if he lets them loose, they devastate the land. To him belong strength and victory; both deceived and deceiver are his. He leads counselors away stripped and makes fools of judges. He takes off the shackles put on by kings and ties a loincloth around their waist. He leads priests away stripped and overthrows men long established. He silences the lips of trusted advisers and takes away the discernment of elders. He pours contempt on nobles and disarms the mighty. He reveals the deep things of darkness and brings deep shadows into the light. He makes nations great, and destroys them; he enlarges nations, and disperses them."

17. Franz Delitzsch, *Biblical Commentary on the Book of Job* (Edinburgh: T. & T. Clark, 1869), 1.20.

18. Norman C. Habel, *The Book of Job: A Commentary* (Philadelphia: Westminster, 1985), 243.

19. Bavli, *Pirke Avot* 4.18.

term "exile." Depending on the context of usage, the term may range from unwanted literal enslavement or displacement (biblical *galut*) to willful isolation or focus for the sake of learning (Talmudic *goleh*). A repeated theme throughout Jewish biblical history is the concept of "strangers and settlers" (וְתוֹשָׁב גֵּר) on earth. It was on this understanding that Abraham based his request to the Hittites for a burial plot for his departed wife, Sarah:

> I am a foreigner and settler (וְתוֹשָׁב גֵּר) among you. Sell me some burial property that is in your possession so I may bury my dead while I remain here. (Gen. 23:4)

When declaring "the land which I am about to give to you," God indicated that the Israelites would not be residents in this Land of Promise but foreigners and strangers in the Lord's land. In addressing land responsibilities during a Jubilee year, God instructed:

> The land must not be sold permanently, because the land is mine and you are *residing in my land* as strangers and settlers (גֵּרִים וְתוֹשָׁבִים). Throughout the land that you hold as a possession (of mine), you must provide for the redemption of the land. (Lev. 25:23–24)

The language in this passage appears to contradict itself, especially as the narrative develops. Those who are identified as foreigners and strangers are then admonished to treat their indebted fellow Israelites as hired workers and temporary residents until their debt is paid in full or until they are fully forgiven during the year of Jubilee. Again, however, the initial language is revisited toward those to whom the debt is owed (i.e., servants of God as "tenants" on God's land):

> If any of your fellow Israelites become poor *while living* among you and should sell themselves to you, do not give them work as slaves. They are to be treated as hired workers (כְּשָׂכִיר) or as settlers/temporary residents (כְּתוֹשָׁב) among you; they are to work for you until the Year of Jubilee. Then they and their children are to be released, and they will go back

to their own families and to the property of their ancestors, because they are my servants whom I brought out of the land of Egypt. They must not be sold as slaves. Do not rule over them ruthlessly, but fear your God. (Lev. 25:39-43)

Elsewhere, the psalmist recognized that not only was the Land of Promise not his "home" residence; he knew that this perspective had been held throughout his ancestors' history as well:

Hear my prayer, Lord, and my cry for help. Listen to my weeping; do not be deaf. I am a stranger (גֵר) with you—a settler (תּוֹשָׁב)—as all my ancestors were. (Ps. 39:13)

Understanding the significance of getting it right, the psalmist appealed to God to remind him that he does not possess an earthly kingdom (quite striking when one considers the psalmist to be King David, chosen ruler of the Promised Land); David is but a "stranger" on earth:

Open my eyes, that I may see wonderful things from your Torah. I am a stranger (גֵּר) on earth; do not hide your *mitzvot* from me. (Ps. 119:18)[20]

The chronicler repeated this language later in Israelite history, spiritualizing the matter in a manner that implies that no place on earth is "home" to the Hebrew people. Everywhere they reside, anywhere on earth—including the Land of Promise—they are foreigners and strangers:

We are strangers and settlers (גֵרִים וְתוֹשָׁבִים) before you, as all our ancestors were. Our days on earth are like a shadow, and there is no hope. (1 Chron. 29:15)

---

20. Elsewhere, Isaiah employs גֵרִים to describe strangers who benefit from Israel's exile (5:17), while Jeremiah lays out a condition for living in the gifted land: do not oppress the alien ((גֵּר 7:6)); these are based on a Torah command for the people of Israel to treat justly the stranger (גֵּר) among them, neither wronging nor oppressing, because they too were strangers (גֵרִים) in the land of Egypt (Exod. 22:21).

Spiritualization of homeland was carried over, adapted, and reapplied in a New Testament context for Christian appropriation of the biblical theme of exile:

> Dear loved ones, I urge you, as foreigners and resident aliens (παροίκους καὶ παρεπιδήμους), to abstain from carnal desires, which are waging war against your soul. (1 Pet. 2:11)
>
> All these people died with faith, not having received the promises, but having seen them far off, they welcomed them, confessing that they were foreigners and resident aliens (ξένοι καὶ παρεπίδημοί) on earth. (Heb. 11:13)[21]

While Christian applications diverge from scriptural usage, as indicated above, it is clear that the notion of exile relating to the hereafter was constant throughout the periods of the Hebrew Bible and well into the New Testament period.[22]

Biblical exile became a metanarrative for subsequent descriptions throughout Jewish history as related to forced and voluntary living in Diaspora, persecution, pogrom, and expulsion. Combined with the image of the wandering Jew, negative stereotypes reinforced misuse of language and validation of the now Christianized concept of spiritual exile that awaited a home in the heavens.[23]

---

21. Too much can be made of differences between παροίκοι and ξένοι, as they may merely act as synonyms in these two texts. However, Eph. 2:19 employs both terms, where translators seem to make παροίκοι synonymous with παρεπιδήμοι.

22. To say the Land of Promise belonged to Israel instead of God is parallel to saying that any land belongs to any nation, whereas the biblical understanding is that "the earth is the Lord's" (i.e., belongs to the Lord) and no nation owns any part of it except for temporary stewardship on behalf of a divine landlord; the prophets of Israel and thereafter the people of Israel identified themselves as strangers and foreigners on earth, even when living in the Land of Promise.

23. Throughout Christian history into the present age, much has been made of the myth of the wandering Jew wherein Ahasverus, a typecast Jew, was eternally cursed for denying a Golgotha-bound Christ a resting place. See Stefan Heym, *The Wandering Jew* (Evanston, IL: Northwestern University Press, 1981) for a modern retelling of the myth.

Conclusion

Traditional views of Israel, God, and exile are herein challenged. First, God gave a land to Israel as a possession, but identified them as stewards of the land God called "my possession." The Hebrew people remain strangers and foreigners on earth, even when dwelling in the Land of Promise.[24] Second, their stated "homeland" was in the afterlife, in the company of the God of creation, including the earth and all that is in it. And third, the language of accommodation depicts the Hebrew people as exiles in foreign lands, that is, in lands in which they were forced to live as a result of being removed (exiled) from their Land of Promise.[25]

The nuanced discussion of exile, chosen and forced, has never had a more relevant and challenging opportunity to be addressed. And never has more been at stake for Jews as well as non-Jews in the process. From this perspective, Israel has a commitment to God with respect to gifted land and an equally solemn responsibility to her neighbors as concerns proper stewardship while awaiting a land hereafter. From a biblical perspective according to Jewish tradition, God has been moving Israel about from place to place and from pasture to pasture to make her name great. God declared long ago: "I will establish a place for my people Israel. I will plant them so that they can have a home of their own, so that they will no longer be disturbed" (1 Sam. 7:1-17).

---

24. Biblical texts cited throughout this study highlight the proviso that God claimed the Land of Israel as "my possession" while gifting it to the Hebrew people. For Israelites to say it is "our possession" acknowledges human "ownership" framed within covenantal terms, both established and maintained by the Creator of the land who gifted it to Israel.

25. From biblical to present times, a common understanding of Jewish exile includes living anywhere outside the gifted land of Israel. The Declaration of the State of Israel (1948) declared: "The State of Israel will be open for Jewish Immigration and for the Ingathering of the Exiles." Distinguished from spiritual exile, physical exile of this nature has been traced recently in James M. Scott, ed., *Exile: Old Testament (sic), Jewish, and Christian Conceptions* (Leiden: Brill, 1997).

While living as strangers and foreigners in gifted land that belongs to God, amidst a world of nations who live in lands that also belong to God, promised rest from all Israel's enemies will undoubtedly have to wait a little while longer.

6

Immigration Theology in Islam

Muhammad Shafiq

Immigration Theology in Islam

The word *hijrah* is most commonly used in Arabic for immigration. The male immigrant is called *muhajir* (pl. *muhajirun*) and *muhajirah* (pl. *muhajiraat*) refers to the female immigrant. The root word *hajarah* literally means to leave something behind. This "something" could be home, drug addiction, one's belongings, or even one's family members. The word *yuhajir* refers to an intshowentional immigrant. *Hijrah* and its derivatives are mostly used in the Qur'an for the immigration of the Prophet and his companions from Makkah to Madinah. Migration in the Shari'ah (Islamic Law) was necessary from non–Muslim lands where Muslims had no freedom of religion and were persecuted, to a Muslim land where their human rights were guaranteed. The main example in the Qur'an of a place to emigrate from is Makkah, where the early Muslims, including the Prophet, were persecuted, while in Madinah their human rights were secured and they were promised freedom of worship.[1] The word *kharaja* (pl. *khuruj*) also means to immigrate (Qur'an 2:243). The biblical word translated into Greek as Exodus is translated into Arabic as *khuruj*. It can also refer to the day of resurrection (*yaum al kharuj*, 50:42) or even ritual purification (leaving a state of impurity for one of purity [40:11]).

Muslims are asked in the Qur'an to emigrate to save themselves from immediate danger or from oppression. The word *zulm* (injustice, usurpation of fundamental rights) and its derivatives are used in the Qur'an (16:41) to justify emigration from a land of persecution. *Fitnah* (trial, obstruction, and even persecution, as in Qur'an 16:110) is also used to rationalize the desire to emigrate. Those who face the worst life conditions, for whom the Qur'an uses the word *mustad'afin* (weak, suppressed, underprivileged, and deprived), are commanded to search for a better land. The Qur'an says: "When angels take the souls of those who die in sin against their souls, they say: 'In what [plight] were ye?' They reply: 'Weak and oppressed were we on the earth.' They say: 'Was not the earth of Allah spacious enough for you to move yourselves away [from evil]?' Such men will find their abode in Hell,—What an evil refuge" (4:97). Such verses encourage believers not to live under oppression, but rather to seek opportunities for a better life elsewhere in the world. To live under *zulm* (oppression) in Islam is, according to this and similar verses, to commit a sin. That is why the full meaning of the word *mustad'afin* in the Qur'an includes not only the fact of

---

1. For detail on the meaning of *Hijrah* in Arabic, see *Lisan al `Arab* or *Qamus*: www.baheth.info/all.jsp?term=.

oppression but also the steps taken to achieve religious freedom and to advocate human rights for all people. Negatively, the above verse refers to oppressed Muslims who did *not* emigrate from Makkah to Madinah with the Prophet.

To those who do emigrate for freedom of their faith, for human rights, and for release from persecution, God promises huge rewards in this life and in the hereafter. The Qur'an says: "He who forsakes his home in the cause of Allah, finds in the earth many a refuge, wide and spacious: Should he die as a refugee from home for Allah and His Messenger, his reward becomes due and sure with Allah. And Allah is Oft-forgiving, Most Merciful" (4:100). Those in the new lands who welcome the immigrants, receiving them with hospitality and giving them support, are called the *Ansar* (the helpers, the supporters, referring to the people of Madinah who received the Muslim emigrants from Makkah). God honors them in the Qur'an with blessings in this life and in the hereafter. Praising the *Ansar* of Madinah, the Qur'an says: "But those who before them had homes [in Medina] and had adopted the Faith, show their affection to such as came to them for refuge, and entertain no desire in their hearts for things given to the [refugees], but give them preference over themselves, even though poverty was their [own lot]. And those saved from the covetousness of their own souls, they are the ones that achieve prosperity" (59:9).

The Qur'an narrates stories of prophets who were persecuted in their lands and became successful in spreading the message of God after they emigrated. For example, in several places the Qur'an speaks of Abraham, who was persecuted in his homeland of Ur, an important Sumerian city in ancient Mesopotamia (now Iraq). His people, rejecting his monotheistic faith, turned against him. They decided to burn him alive.[2] But God asked him to emigrate to the land of Palestine and Israel. God blessed him with children and followers, and today Abraham is the chief patriarch of three great communities: of Jews, of Christians, and of Muslims.[3] Another important story involving emigration is told of the Prophet Moses. Growing up in the house of Pharaoh, he was afraid of persecution. So he left for Midian and married there. Upon his return to Egypt, he asked Pharaoh to accept his message about God and to free the Israelites. Pharaoh frowned upon him and refused. When the Israelites, persuaded by Moses, left the land of Egypt for the sake of freedom, arrogant Pharaoh and his army pursued them. Moses and his followers peacefully crossed the Red Sea in which Pharaoh and many of his army were drowned.[4] Afterwards, the Israelites were blessed with many opportunities thanks to their emigration from Egypt into Sinai.

First *Hijrah* in Muslim History

When Muslims' lives at Makkah became unbearable because of torture and murder at the hands of the Quraysh (Makkah's dominant tribe), Prophet Muhammad saw no other alternative but to urge those who were especially vulnerable in the new community to emigrate to a secure land. Looking for a Christian land as a safe haven, he chose Abyssinia, and urged the believers to go there, for king Negus, known as Al Nijashi in Arabic, was a just man. Some fifteen people, eleven men and four women, took part in the first emigration in 613, some four years after the prophecy of Muhammad. The group returned to Makkah after about three months once they heard rumors that Makkah had embraced Islam. Soon afterwards, in 615, a second

2. Qur'an 21:51-70.
3. The story of Abraham is narrated throughout the Qur'an, and chapter 14 of the Qur'an is named after him. For more reading about Abraham, see Qur'an 2:124-40; 3:65-97; 11:69, 76; 19:41-56; 21:51-69; 37:83-109.
4. The story of Moses is narrated in detail in the Qur'an. See 2:51-136; 5:20-25; 7:103-70; 18:62-76; 20:11-96; 26:24-65; 28:7-76 and many others.

group of close to a hundred people, led by Ja`far ibn Abi Talib, immigrated to Abyssinia.

The Quraysh leadership was frightened to see Muslims finding shelter in a protected land. They sent two ambassadors loaded with gifts to Abyssinia to petition the king to return the Muslims to Makkah. But the king, after hearing Ja`far ibn Abi Talib's side of the matter, rejected the Quraysh request and permitted the Muslims to stay in Abyssinia as long as they wanted. It is said that they stayed there for many years and that later some immigrated to Madinah in 630 ce, in the seventh year of the *Hijrah* (Prophet Muhammad's emigration from Makkah to Madinah).[5]

Prophet Muhammad's *Hijrah* to Madinah

After Muhammad's wife Khadijah and his uncle Abu Talib died, both of whom had given him support and comfort, the Quraysh increased their persecution of Muslims. They even plotted to assassinate Muhammad himself. Muhammad went to Ta'if, a town near Makkah, to persuade its people to adopt Islam or, failing that, at least to give refuge to him and his companions. But in return, the people of Ta'if ordered their children to throw stones at Muhammad and wound him. Then Muhammad experienced a change of fortune. During the height of his despair at the Makkans' and others' resistance to the call of Islam, he met twelve men from Yathrib (the old name of Madinah) who had come to Makkah during the pilgrim season in the year 621. Muhammad presented the message of Islam to them and they all accepted the faith. Pledging him their full support, they invited Muhammad and his followers to immigrate to Yathrib. Instead of immigrating himself, however, Muhammad sent Mas`ab ibn `Umayr with the twelve to teach them and others at Yathrib the Qur'an

---

5. Muhammad H. Haykal, *The Life of Muhammad*, trans. Isma`il R. Al Faruqi (North American Trust Publications, 1976), 97–104.

and to spread the message of Islam. Mas`ab's success is measured by the fact that some seventy-five other residents of Yathrib came to Makkah to meet Muhammad in the following year of 622. They all not only embraced Islam, but they also entered into a covenant with Muhammad known in Muslim history as the Second Covenant of `Aqabah. This Covenant cleared the path of emigration for all Muslims to leave Makkah for Yathrib.[6]

While Muhammad allowed the Makkan believers to emigrate to their new home, he himself stayed behind waiting for Allah's permission to depart. Meanwhile, the Quraysh leadership, highly disturbed when they heard of this new Covenant, increased their persecution of the Muslims. They took measures to prevent their emigration and persecuted those who were caught fleeing from Makkah. However, the Muslims eluded them, fleeing secretly one by one and all making their way to Yathrib.

Then came Muhammad's turn to emigrate. One night while Makkan mobs intent on murdering Muhammad surrounded his house, the Angel Gabriel delivered God's permission to Muhammad to emigrate. The prophet asked `Ali, his nephew, first to lie in his bed as a decoy, then to return the deposits of some Makkans who had placed them with him as a trust, and finally to join him in Yathrib. Muhammad left his home unobserved by those waiting to kill him. He went to Abu Bakr's house, and the two left on their journey to Yathrib.[7] With his immigration, Yathrib became Madinatun Nabi (the city of the Prophet), or in its shorter form Madinah, which is how it has been known throughout Muslim history and today.

Most of the Qur'anic references to the *Hijrah* are about this immigration of Muhammad and his companions to Madinah. The significance of this day in Muslim history can be seen from the fact

6. See Haykal, *The Life of Muhammad*, 148–60.
7. See the whole story in detail in ibid., 148–99.

that the Muslim calendar does not begin with the birth or death day of Muhammad or with the day Muhammad was appointed as a messenger or with the day he was taken into heaven, but rather with this *Hijrah*. The *Hijrah* stands for freedom from oppression, and the right to become part of a commonwealth where everyone, irrespective of belief or caste or ethnic affiliation, can enjoy full human rights. *Hijrah* in its broadest meaning refers to spiritual, religious, political, and economic freedom and opportunity based on social justice for all humanity.

The Muslim Golden Age began with this *Hijrah* and lasted for hundreds of years. After the prophet instructed his companions at his farewell pilgrimage in 631, in the ninth year of *Hijrah*, to take the message of *Hijrah* across to the world, many of them made their way to Africa and parts of Asia and Europe to deliver the message. Many did not return and were buried where they died. Others went on business trips, especially in the medieval period of Islam, to different parts of the world and carried the message of Islam with them. Some married in far places and remained; others returned. Parts of Africa and Asia became Muslim through these business trips.[8]

The Muslim theology of immigration was developed during this golden era. It was based on the idea that Muslim power and the vigor of its social-justice teachings would endure forever. Perhaps those who developed this theology never thought of the downfall of that power and vigor. On visiting the Alhambra (in Spain) in 2008, I found a written Arabic script on its walls claiming that with God's favor Muslims would stay in power forever. It is true that during the West's Dark Ages, the Muslim world offered a comparatively better place to live. Baghdad, Spain, and later Delhi were showcases of Muslim civilization, where dialogue was encouraged and freedom

8. Caesar A. Farah, *Islam*, 6th ed. (Barron's Educational Series, 2000), esp. chs. 12 and 13.

of religious worship was guaranteed. Perhaps Muslim scholars never thought that one day Muslim lands would become despotic and that the West would carry the torch of human dignity and freedom to them. It is for this reason, as we will discuss below, that in Muslim medieval literature there was never any thought of immigrating to a non-Muslim land for freedom—in order to escape oppression in Muslim lands.[9]

The collapse of Muslim rule during the colonial period and after led to many theological issues within Islam. The first issue was raised by the slave trade. Many of those who were brought as slaves from Africa to Europe were Muslims. They not only lost their fundamental human rights; they were also forcibly converted to Christianity. Later, as a result of their subjugation during the colonial period from the early nineteenth century to the middle of the twentieth century and then afterwards as a result of their independence during the postcolonial period, Muslims encountered challenges never faced before. Colonization faced them with non-Muslim rule, and when they got their independence from their colonial masters, they found their own Muslim rulers tyrannical and cruel. A peaceful life became difficult to attain in many Muslim lands. And further: ethnic rivalries, sectarian differences, border disputes, and Western interference in Muslim countries forced many Muslims to leave their homelands in search not only of freedom but also of survival itself. Today millions of Muslims are living in non-Muslim lands all over the world, including in Europe and America. Some of these Muslims are indigenous. Others are refugees who immigrated to obtain a better life or to escape tyranny.

9. Muslims in their medieval period promoted interfaith dialogue. See Akbar S. Ahmad, *Islam Today: A Short Introduction to the Muslim World* (London: I. B. Tauris), 62–64. Also see Muhammad Shafiq and Mohammed Abu Nimer, *Interfaith Dialogue: A Guide for Muslims*, 2nd ed. (London: International Institute of Islamic Thought, 2011), 93–100.

The phenomenon of Muslims living in non-Muslim countries whether as indigenous inhabitants or as refugees has raised a new issue: whether it is permissible under Shari'ah law for any Muslim to live permanently in a non-Muslim country. There are, however, precedents. The first *Hijrah* to Abyssinia was motivated by a search for freedom from persecution, and the *Hijrah* of Prophet Muhammad to Madinah was supported by many Qur'anic verses. Madinah became a safe haven for Muslims who were under attack by idolatrous Makkans. Muslims were asked to immigrate to their new home not only in self-defense but also in order to enjoy a life of religious and social freedom there. But does Shari'ah law countenance a permanent state of residence in non-Muslim lands?

When the number of Muslims in America increased in the 1990s, I heard three types of opinion. One was that America was an abode of peace (*Dar al Amman*),[10] allowing Muslims to worship freely and receive social justice. Most of the modern educated Muslim professionals I knew were of this opinion. These professionals based their opinion on the precedent of the Muslim immigration to Abyssinia. A second opinion was held by some Muslim scholars and Imams. They justified Muslims living as a minority in non-Muslim countries as a missionary opportunity. Muslims would see themselves as making Da`wah (delivering the message of Islam): not only practicing Islam themselves but also sharing it with others. The third opinion was that the host countries were no more than places of temporary refuge. Muslims were to stay in these countries only until it became possible to return to their homes. Some Muslim leaders holding this opinion advised their co-religionists not to take American and European citizenship. Others went further,

10. For the word *Dar al Amman* and other related terms and about Muslims living in non-Muslim countries, see http://worldmuslimcongress.blogspot.com/2008/01/dar-al-islam-dar-al-harb.htmlnd.

condemning the taking of American citizenship itself as *Shirk* (associating others with God).

The extremity of that latter opinion came home to me one evening in the early years of the 1990s after I had given a speech in Atlanta at a Muslim conference. The speaker following me raised the issue of *Hijrah*, asking the audience to refuse to adopt American citizenship (arguing that taking the citizenship oath was to pledge allegiance to something other than God and therefore dangerously close to committing *Shirk*). The audience, mostly African American, rose in protest. I had to stand up to appease the listeners. A similar experience happened to me at another conference where a speaker asked people to be ready to pick up and leave. Again, the audience of African Americans was offended by the speaker's comments. I expressed my disagreement with the speaker's approach and tried to reassure the audience that our living in America was very much according to the tenets of our religion as long as we practiced it faithfully ourselves and were ready to convey the message to others. With the gradual worsening of conditions in the Muslim world through the 1990s and their more precipitous decline especially after 9/11, I no longer heard speakers make this argument.

Those who oppose Muslim citizenship in or immigration to non-Muslim lands derive their arguments from certain verses of the Qur'an and certain Hadith (stories or sayings from the Prophetic traditions) and from some medieval Muslim literature. Most of the discussion is based on the Qur'anic verses 4:88 and 4:97. These verses refer to those Muslims at Makkah who did not immigrate to Madinah though they had the means to do so. The verses warned such people with hell fire as their final destiny. Supporting these verses are a few Hadith from the Prophet saying that he will have nothing to do with those Muslims who stay and live with *Mushrikun* (idolaters).[11] But with the conquest of Makkah, Islam became triumphant, and it is said that the Prophet proclaimed the *Hijrah* to have ceased as of that day.[12] `A'isha, the wife of the prophet, is reported to have said:

> Today there is no (*Hijrah*) emigration. A believer used to run away with his religion to Allah and His Apostle lest he should be put to trial because of his religion. Today Allah has made Islam triumphant, and today a believer can worship his Lord wherever he likes. But the deeds that are still rewardable [in place of emigration] are Jihad and good intentions.[13]

The ruling of verses 4:88 and 4:97 applied, therefore, to those Muslims living at Makkah, who, having the means to immigrate to Madinah, did not do so. `A'isha's statement that the *Hijrah* had ended applied to those Muslims who were still living in Makkah when Makkah came under Islam; they were told not to emigrate, since Islam had triumphed.

Muslim scholars who translated and wrote commentaries on the Qur'an in the late twentieth century broadened the interpretation of verses 4:88 and 4:97. Referring to verse 4:88 and then 4:97, a renowned Muslim scholar, Mawlana Abu al A`la Mawdudi (1903–79), explained that the word "hypocrite" could be applied to any Muslim who, living under oppression and having the means to emigrate, refused to do so. If, according to Mawdudi, there were a Muslim country where social justice was established and would welcome other Muslims to come and enjoy freedom of life there,

11. For this Hadith and the discussion on prohibition of living in non-Muslim lands, see http://hijrafeesabilillah.blogspot.com/2007/05/condition-of-muslim-that-doesnt-intend.html and available on http://www.islampolicy.com/2011/02/importance-of-making-hijrah-from-lands.html.
12. The *Hadith* is narrated in Sahih Bukhari by Abdullah Ibn `Abbas, http://ahadith.co.uk/hadithsearchfilter.php?id=1&q=hijra.
13. Shahih Bukhari; for reference see http://www.quranexplorer.com/Hadith/English/Hadith/bukhari/005.058.240.html. For more details to understand the issue of *Hijrah*, please see the following websites: http://www.islamweb.net/emainpage/index.php?page=showfatwa&Option=FatwaId&Id=83200, http://www.sunniforum.com/forum/archive/index.php/t-38081.html, http://www.al-islam.org/a-code-of-practice-for-muslims-in-the-west-ayatullah-sistani/migration-non-muslim-countries.

then it would be necessary for those Muslims who lived under oppression anywhere to immigrate to that country so that they could live peacefully and practice their religion. However, Muslims living in a Muslim or even a non-Muslim state where there was social justice and freedom of worship would not need to emigrate.[14] Mawlana Amin Ahsan Islahi (1904–97), another Muslim scholar, in his commentary on verse 4:97 explains that *Hijrah* in modern times applies only to those Muslims who, living under oppression, have no freedom to practice their religion. It would be better for them to immigrate to any land where they could live freely and practice their religion. However, it would be even better to immigrate if that land were an abode of peace inhabited and ruled by other Muslims. But he stressed the general rule that Muslims who live under oppression must seek to emigrate to a land, whether ruled by Muslims or not, where there is freedom of worship and peace.[15]

The distinction between lands where peace and justice rule and those where they do not is similar to the distinction between *Dar al Islam* or *Dar al Salam* ("Abode of Peace") and *Dar al Harb* ("Abode of War") in the Muslim medieval period. During that period, the term *Dar al Islam* clearly referred to the political domination of Islam and the assumption that such domination brings peace and justice. Though the term *Dar al Harb* is not used in the Qur'an, the term *Dar al Salam* is: "Theirs shall be an abode of peace (*Dar al Salam*) with their Sustainer; and He shall be near unto them in result of what they have been doing" (6:127). In another place the Qur'an says: "And [know that] God invites [man] unto the abode of peace, and guides him that wills [to be guided] onto a straight way" (10:25). But these

---

14. Mawlana Mawdudi, *Tafheem al Qur'an* (Lahore: Idara Turjaman al Qur'an, 1998), esp. 4:88 and 4:97.
15. Amin Ahsan Islahi, *Tadabur al Qur'an* [Urdu], vol. 2 (Lahore: Faraan Foundation, 1991), 4:97.

verses refer, according to the commentators, not to life in this world, but to life in the hereafter.

There are, however, some other references in the Qur'an, in Hadith, and in Islamic historical literature that support the political use of the terms *Dar al Islam* and *Dar al Harb*. Those early jurists who had voiced a different opinion were ignored. The British rule of India provides a significant case study. After Muslims lost power to the British, their first reaction was emotional, both politically and religiously. Struggling against the British occupation of India, Shah `Abd al `Aziz Dehlavi (1745–1823), a very respected Muslim scholar and religious leader, declared India to be *Dar al Harb* in 1803. Sayyid Ahmad Barelvi (1786–1831), a Muslim scholar and political activist who was influenced by the Shah `Abd al `Aziz Dehlavi's teachings, started a Jihad movement from the Northwest Frontier Province, calling upon the Pushtun tribes to liberate India. When a country is considered to be *Dar al Harb*, Muslims are obligated to immigrate to *Dar al Islam* and then wage Jihad against *Dar al Harb*. A few did emigrate from India but the rest stayed, including Shah Abd al `Aziz. Later on, accepting the reality of the situation, Muslim jurists of India debated whether India under the British should be considered *Dar al Harb* or *Dar al Islam*. Looking back at the Hanafi Fiqh (jurisprudence), many came to the conclusion, including some in the Deoband Seminary, that as long as a country provides religious freedom for Muslims, that country could be considered *Dar al Islam*.[16]

To understand this issue in its contemporary application, "Muslims' Place in the American Public Square" is an important source. In chapter 1 of his book *Toward a Fiqh for Minorities: Reflections*, Taha Jabir al Alwani comes to the conclusion that *Dar al Islam* is any place

16. For detail on this subject, see Peter Hardy, *The Muslims of British India* (Cambridge: Cambridge University Press, 1972). Also for more discussion on *Dar al Islam*, see Muhammad Shafiq and Mohammed Abu Nimer, *Interfaith Dialogue: A Guide for Muslims*, 73–75.

where a Muslim can live in peace and security even if he/she lives in a non-Muslim majority country. *Dar al Harb* or *Dar al Kufr* is any country where a Muslim lives under threat even if the majority there adheres to Islam and Islamic culture. In that case, he/she is obligated to emigrate to a land of freedom. Taha Jabir al Alwani quotes Al Mawardi's saying that if a Muslim is able to practice his religion openly in a non-Muslim land, then that land becomes *Dar al Islam* by virtue of his settling there. Settling in such a country is preferable since other people, coming under the Muslim settler's influence and example, would be likely to convert to Islam. Al Alwani also quotes the Muslim theologian Imam Fakhr al Din al Razi's (1149–1209) citing of Al Shashi's opinion that it would be better to rename *Dar al Harb* or *Dar al Kufr* as *Dar al Da`wah* ("a House delivering the Message of Islam or even abode of Dialogue"), and rename *Dar al Islam* as *Dar al Ijabah* ("an Abode of Acceptance"). He names non-Muslims in a country granting freedom to Muslims as the *Ummah al Da`wah* and Muslims living there the *Umma al Ijabah*.[17] Most recently, the *Dar al `Ulum*, a Muslim Seminary at Deoband, India, named India under Hindu rule *Dar al Amman* ("Abode of Peace," a place of protection and peace). The Vice Rector of the Seminary, Mawlana Abdul Khaleque, was quoted in the *Hindustan Times* of 22 February 2009, as saying that Muslims in India are free to practice their religion and that therefore India is *Dar al Amman* for all Muslims.

Conclusion

The main thrust of the Qur'anic teaching on *Hijrah* or immigration is to promote the protection of life and security for the immigrant, under the condition that the receiving country foster coexistence by

17. Taha Jabir al Alwani, "Toward the Fiqh of Minority: Reflections," in *Muslims' Place in the American Public Square*, ed. Zahid H. Bukhari et al. (Lanham, MD: AltaMira, 2009), 28.

providing social justice for all irrespective of caste, creed, color, or ethnic affiliation. This teaching emerges from historical experience. Muslims living in pre-Islamic Arabia were persecuted and oppressed. Their lives were in danger, and they had no freedom. In order to save Muslims' lives and to protect their human rights, Prophet Muhammad looked for refuges. He allowed Muslims to immigrate to Abyssinia to escape persecution. Later, he and the rest of his followers immigrated to Madinah. Then, after Madinah, having become a protected home both for Muslims and non-Muslims, was threatened with war by the Makkans, the Qur'an asked all Muslims to immigrate to Madinah not only to save themselves from persecution but also to defend their new home from its enemies. The command to immigrate ended with the conquest of Makkah.

Following the Qur'anic command, Muslims were able to establish social justice and security and to offer peaceful coexistence to all citizens during most of its caliphate period. Thomas Arnold, a British missionary, rightly observed in his *Preaching of Islam* that Christians living with their Muslim neighbors in the Holy Land were pleased by the defeat of the Crusaders and welcomed the return of the Muslims to Jerusalem.[18] Speaking comparatively, we can say that people had more freedom, peace, and security living under the Caliphate than elsewhere. Welcoming immigrants to its lands, Cordoba and Baghdad became great centers of interfaith dialogue and freedom of thought.

Muslims never thought that they would experience a downfall. Muslim scholars in all fields—theologians, jurists, economists, and political theorists—wrote their treatises at the height of Muslim power, culture, and civilization, during the era Muslims could have described as "modern." The word "modern" as used in Western

---

18. Thomas Arnold, *The Preaching of Islam* (New York: AWS Press, reprint of 1913 edition).

history refers to the period of the Renaissance and Reformation, marking the end of Europe's Dark Ages and its entry into an age of light. But Europe's enlightenment marked the beginning of a dark age for Muslims.

Living in their own "modern" age, the West adopted human rights, established security, and promoted peaceful coexistence as marks of their new age—the values the Muslim world had adopted during its own "modern" era. As Muslims had done before them, the West opened its doors to immigrants, promising them protection, freedom from persecution, and the opportunity to seek a better life. Meanwhile, Muslims had become divided into small nation states, many of whose political leaders oppressed their own people. The natural resources in many of these countries were controlled by their authoritarian rulers while the masses lived a life of poverty. Life in many of these new Muslim states became terrible for its Muslim and non-Muslim citizens alike. Political chaos, tyranny, poverty, and insecurity forced all citizens to look for refuge. The West opened its arms and welcomed both educated elites and poor refugees to their own lands.

We are living today in a global society where citizens seek to live in societies that promise freedom of thought and religion and guarantee the protection of human rights. These drastic changes in the political, economic, and social demographics of today's world should inspire Muslim scholars to reconsider Islam's theology of immigration in the light of the often-negative conditions Muslims are living in today.

Freedom, proper nourishment, and safety are the most highly valued political goods in Islam. All other goods come after them. Certainly every Muslim would wish to live and raise his or her family in a Muslim state that actively promotes social justice and human flourishing, but when a Muslim state becomes oppressive and threatens its own citizens, then living in America and the West becomes the best path to a life that offers security and religious freedom.

7

The Islamic Doctrine of *Hijra* (Migration)

Theological Implications

Hussam S. Timani

Introduction

Immigration issues have been hotly debated in the United States and Europe, and many laws (sometimes very harsh) have been made to restrict, punish, or manipulate immigrants, whether they are in the adoptive country legally or otherwise. According to *The Washington Post*, many people ask, "Does affluent America have a larger moral or spiritual obligation to help illegal immigrants who are trying to better their lives? What about religious obligations to welcome the stranger? Are we our brother's keeper?"[1] The same questions apply to Muslims (especially in the Persian Gulf region) who employ

---

1. On Faith Panel, "Stopping Illegal Immigrants with Immoral Laws?" *The Washington Post*, 29 May 2010.

a significant number of legal migrant workers from south and Southeast Asia but treat them as strangers and, in many cases, as slaves. Migrant workers in Muslim societies have no rights and live on the margins of society, often in utter oppression and suffering. Suicide is on the rise among migrant workers in Lebanon, Saudi Arabia, Kuwait, and other Muslim countries due to harsh conditions and sufferings, and little to no attention has been given to their plight and living conditions.

In the U.S., the debate includes those who advocate policies that would deport immigrants and those who support laws that would construct walls at the borders to keep migrants out. Many immigrants who would be affected arrived with their parents as infants, speak only English, and feel America is the sole country to which they feel they belong. Some European countries, like France and Switzerland, have introduced laws that are unwelcoming to Muslim immigrants, such as banning the Islamic veil or putting restrictions on Muslim places of worship. Religious scholars and leaders ask a central question: What does theology offer to the field of migration studies, and how may it alter the ongoing debate on illegal immigration (and immigration in general) in America, to make Europe more welcoming to outsiders, and to improve the status of immigrants in Muslim societies? In this chapter, I reflect on the doctrine of *hijra* in the Qur'an as a way to suggest that a theology of migration, whether Islamic or interreligious, is needed today to counter the challenges that migrants face in the age of globalization.

In this chapter, I first demonstrate how migration is an experience that encompasses different cultures and religious traditions, then proceed to discuss the doctrine of *hijra* in Islam and how migration is a spiritual journey that establishes a point of communication between humans and the divine, and then conclude with a brief discussion of the Islamic doctrine of *tawhid* ("oneness of God," or "Unity of Being") to demonstrate that the separation of the self from the other runs counter to basic Islamic beliefs. I attempt in this chapter to construct an Islamic theology of migration that transforms the self to become the other so strangers may become at the center of the communities they live in rather than being at the peripheries.

Globalization and the Role of Religion

The rise of globalization is a threat to religious values as a means to protect the dignity of persons as historical agents. The loss of these values, according to William Schweiker, threatens to reduce our world to "one system of measurement (say, money) and feed human vice, especially greed."[2] Therefore theologians who have expressed their concerns about the loss of religious values due to globalization believe that theological principles may be a key to preserve these values and human dignity. Theodor Damian writes: "When globalization becomes militant and economically hegemonic, and runs the risk of de-humanizing the individual, the Christian Church has a well-acknowledged, powerful tool in defense of human dignity: traditional religious values."[3]

Abdulaziz Sachedina argues in more general terms. He writes: "Globalization of any form of militancy, whether religious or secular, is in need of ethical, universal criteria to prevent it from becoming a source of further destruction to the sanctity of human life and dignity."[4] The above-mentioned statements by scholars of religion speak to the fact that religious traditions in general and theological

---

2. William Schweiker, "Responsibility in the World of Mammon: Theology, Justice, and Transnational Corporations," in *God and Globalization*, ed. Max L. Stackhouse and Peter J. Paris (New York: T. & T. Clark, 2000), 108.

3. Theodor Damian, "Christianity as Ideal Paradigm of Globalization," *Journal of Interdisciplinary Studies* 20 (2008): 163.

4. Ibid.

principles in particular play a key role in preserving human dignity against the rise of globalization.

In an era of globalization, more people are on the move than ever before. For example, in the world today, approximately thirty to forty million people are undocumented immigrants, twenty-four million people are internally displaced, and almost ten million people are refugees.[5] The twenty-first century has been referred to by some scholars as the "the age of migration."[6] According to Daniel G. Groody, "migration studies and migration theory had encompassed almost every discipline and field from economics and history to politics, sociology, law, and psychology, but theology has never been mentioned in major works on migration studies."[7]

Terms like "alien," "illegal immigrant," "refugee," "asylum seeker," "migrant worker," or simply "immigrant" identify the political status of immigrants rather than their human identity, according to Groody. Thus the role of a theology of migration, Groody adds, "is to bridge the gap created by these labels, challenge the dehumanizing stereotypes created by these labels," and build up, in the words of Paul VI and John Paul II, "a civilization of love" and "a culture of life."[8] In the words of Gioacchino Campese, "The goal of theology is not simply to understand, but to understand in order to transform the reality of oppression, violence, and sin in which people live as they journey toward the realization of the reign of God."[9] Some theologians have argued that an approach rooted in Catholic social thought must, in the words of Mary DeLorey, "include both the

5. Daniel G. Groody, "Crossing the Divide: Foundations of a Theology of Migration and Refugees," *Theological Studies* 70 (2009): 639.
6. Ibid., 640.
7. Ibid.
8. Ibid., 644.
9. Gioacchino Campese, "The Irruption of Migrants: Theology of Migration in the 21st Century," *Theological Studies* 73 (2012): 6.

reduction of the need to migrate and the protection of those who have little choice but to do so."[10]

Today the major world religious traditions may provide humanity with some form of immigration theology, for the migration experience is a shared and central theme in their traditions. In Christianity God migrated to this world in the form of the human Jesus; the Hindu god Krishna descended to earth to become a charioteer, a human being (*Bhagavad Gita* 1:20-47);[11] and the Buddha "becomes Awakened"[12] only when he became a wanderer and a stranger. The migration experience is not only metaphorical but also real for Abraham, who was commanded by the Lord to leave his country, his people, and his father's household (Genesis 12:1);[13] for Muhammad who was chased out of his city; and for the Jews who were forced "into exile" (2 Kings 25:11) to live as strangers for centuries. Thus I would argue that in the age of postmodernity, relativism, and pluralism, religious traditions are in an excellent position to provide us with the necessary theology that can help us formulate policies that are compassionate to the strangers. In the following pages, I demonstrate how Islam can provide such a theology.

The Doctrine of *Hijra* (Migration) in Islam

The term for migration in Islam is *hijra*. The person who makes the *hijra* is *muhajir*. Both terms have a connotation of being strange, a refugee in a specific place. *Hijra* involves permanent relocation. A very famous Arabic statement, "the stranger is blind even if he has

---

10. Cited in Kristin E. Heyer, "Reframing Displacement and Membership: Ethics of Migration," *Theological Studies* 73 (2012): 199.

11. *The Bhagavad Gita*, trans. Juan Mascaro (Baltimore, MD: Penguin Books, 1962).

12. *Life of the Buddha*, trans. Patrick Olivelle (New York: New York University Press, 2009), 417.

13. Biblical passages taken from *The Thompson Chain-Reference Bible* (Indianapolis: B.B. Kirkbride Bible Co., Inc., 1983).

eyes," speaks to the vulnerability and weakness of the immigrant. In the religious, and Islamic context especially, *hijra* has an additional aspect, one of purification, piety, and redemption. The Qur'an speaks of the migration experiences of many prophets prior to Islam, such as Adam, Abraham, Lot, Jonah, Jacob, and Moses. Also, important figures in Islam such as Muhammad, Hagar and her son Ishmael, and Mary and Jesus were migrants and strangers. In Islam, all human beings are migrants because Adam, the father of humanity, migrated from heaven to earth. Therefore, in the words of Zeki Saritoprak, "the primordial fatherland of humanity is heaven, while the earth is a place for relocation."[14]

The Qur'an speaks of oppressed, weak people on earth and suggests they could migrate from their oppressed positions to another land of God. In 4:97 the Qur'an says: "But was God's earth not spacious enough for you to migrate to some other place?"[15] The verse suggests that those who have authority should take care of refugees, for it speaks of God as the owner of the land. Moreover, verses 4:98-100 say: ". . . the truly helpless men, women, and children who have no means in their power nor any way to leave—God may well pardon these. . . . Anyone who migrates for God's cause will find many a refuge and great plenty in the earth." This verse suggests that God will not pardon those who have the means to migrate but fail to do so. This verse may be interpreted to say that migration is a religious duty for the believer.

Migration becomes an expression of piety because it is required. Only those who cannot migrate are exempted from God's wrath and therefore earn his grace. Therefore, *hijra*, one may argue, is an

14. Zeki Saritoprak, "The Qur'anic Perspective on Immigrants: Prophet Muhammad's Migration and Its Implications in Our Modern Society," *The Journal of Scriptural Reasoning* 10, no. 1 (August 2011): 1.

15. Passages taken from *The Qur'an*, trans. M. A. S. Abdel Haleem (Oxford: Oxford University Press, 2005).

important pillar in Islam. Verse 16:110 says: "But your Lord will be most forgiving and most merciful to those who leave their homes after persecution, then strive and remain steadfast." Thus *hijra* is placed in the category of pious acts like jihad and patience.

In Islam, the *hijras* of Adam, Abraham, Hagar and her son Ishmael, Mary and Jesus, and Muhammad were for purification and redemption, and *hijra* was a prerequisite for prophecy. Adam migrated from his own disobedience (purification). Abraham migrated from the land of his father to Canaan; in the Qur'an, Abraham migrates to Mecca. Thus, being on the move and constant mobility meant further purification and piety. Hagar migrated from the house of Sarah to receive a word from God, Mary "withdrew from her family to a place to the East and secluded herself away" (Q. 19:16-17), and Jesus was conceived and born in a "distant place" (Q. 19:22). Muhammad was a migrant before receiving God's revelation, when he led caravans to Syria, and then making the *hijra* as a prophet from his own town and tribe. Thus, according to Kip Redick, migration is an experience "that does not fit into any particular religious tradition, but involves a spiritual journey . . . that produces a certain mood or feeling in the person"[16] and establishes a point of contact with the divine. Thus the spiritual journey that Redick highlights is the Islamic *hajj* or pilgrimage, and to make the *hajj* is to live the experience of being a stranger and an immigrant at least once in a lifetime.

Pilgrimage (*hajj*) is a form of *hijra*, albeit a temporary one, that every Muslim should perform provided he or she can afford it. The purpose of *hajj* is to submit the soul to the process of migration, to the experience of being a stranger as a way of purification. The state

---

16. Kip Redick, "Wilderness as *Axis Mundi*: Spiritual Journeys on the Appalachian Trail," in *Symbolic Landscapes*, ed. Gary Backhaus and John Murungi (Dordrecht: Springer, 2009), 1.

of being a pilgrim establishes, renews, or revives submission, i.e., the trust in God, in the individual. According to Groody, migration is deliverance "not only from a specific national territory but also from a narrow way of thinking."[17] Groody adds:

> [The] liberation [of Israel] at Sinai means more than simply taking off the shackles. It involves a cognitive migration, taking on a new mindset, adopting a new way of looking at the world, living out a different vision, and ultimately learning to love as God loves.[18]

Campese argues that "the true Christian is the person who acknowledges in every moment the fact of being on a journey, of being a pilgrim for the reign of God, for this is the final goal of those who believe in the God revealed by Jesus Christ."[19] Thus the goal of the pilgrimage, whether in Islam or in any other religious tradition, is not *the* sacred place but the journey *to* the sacred place. It is the journey, that is, the experience of being a stranger, an immigrant, and a wanderer that enriches the soul of the believer, rather than the sacred place.

Abraham submits in the midst of his experience as a pilgrim. Abraham, *pater familias* of Israel, is first placed in Ur of the Chaldeans. From the heart of the civilization of Sumer, Abraham's family moves to Haran in northern Mesopotamia. It is while dwelling in Haran that Abraham hears the instructions from God to leave family and home and go "to the land I will show you" (Genesis 12:1). He journeys to Canaan and establishes a point of communication with the Divine. There he builds an altar to the Lord, who appears to him. In the unknown territories, God speaks to Hagar when she is a migrant and a stranger (Genesis 16). Hagar is forced into the wilderness and becomes a stranger. Out of her experience as an immigrant and a

17. Groody, "Crossing the Divide," 662.
18. Ibid.
19. Campese, "The Irruption," 22.

stranger, and while in the middle of her journey, God entrusts her with a special mission: "I will so increase your descendants that they will be too numerous to count" (Genesis 16:10).

In the middle of her journey as a pilgrim, Hagar receives a word from God. Hagar is an outcast in the land of Sarah, but when she goes on the journey and becomes a stranger, God rewards her. In the words of Steven Kepnes: "Since Hagar flees [migrates from] Sarah's home in Canaan . . . her journey reminds us of Abraham's journeys. Like Abraham, Hagar is a wanderer who comes to hear the word of call and fulfill a divine mission."[20] Kepnes adds that Hagar is a counterpart to Abraham as another Prophet of the One God. Hagar begins her mission by going out to the wilderness, by being an immigrant and a stranger. Like Hagar, Mary withdraws from her own family and town, and as a refugee and stranger, she receives word from God (Q. 19:24-26). Thus this unknown, strange place becomes the point of communication between the stranger and God, just as Medina became the point of communication between Muhammad and God.

Muhammad the Immigrant

Upon Muhammad's arrival in Medina as an immigrant, God addresses him more personally (Q. 65). Medinan verses are more personally directed toward Muhammad than are the Meccan ones, which seem directed at unbelievers and society in general. Thus Medina becomes the point of communication between Muhammad—the immigrant—and his God. Muhammad's *hijra* to Medina was the driving force behind the creation of a community of brotherhood. The immigrants (*al-muhajirun*) who sought refuge in

20. Steven Kepnes, "Islam as Our Other, Islam as Ourselves," in *Scripture, Reason, and the Contemporary Islam-West Encounter: Studying the "Other," Understanding the "Self,"* ed. Steven Kepnes and Basit Bilal Koshul (New York: Palgrave Macmillan, 2008), 110.

Medina left all their belongings behind. Their problems of poverty and weakness were to be solved through the wisdom of the Prophet. Muhammad had to integrate the immigrants with the local people, and in order to do so, he declared a state of brotherhood between the immigrants and the locals. This historical brotherhood in Medina is called *mu'akhat*. The Qur'an praises this *mu'akhat* between the immigrants and the local people:

> Those who were already firmly established in their homes [in Medina], and firmly rooted in faith, show love for those who migrated to them for refuge and harbour no desire in their hearts for what has been given to them. They give them preference over themselves, even if they too are poor: those who are saved from their own souls' greed are truly successful. (Q. 59:9)

The brotherhood the Prophet declared brought prosperity, solidarity, tolerance, and peace to the community. According to Saritoprak, "It was not only a material cooperation, but a spiritual one as well."[21] The Qur'an says of this cooperation: "Remember God's favour to you: you were enemies and then He brought your hearts together and you became brothers by His grace" (3:103). Thus this brotherhood the Prophet declared and the Qur'an praises occurred between the immigrant Muslims and the people of the city. The Prophet's brotherhood helped to create a welcoming environment for immigrants, one that strengthened society.

The Prophet achieved a full inclusion of immigrants through the Medina covenant or constitution, or what is known in Arabic as *Mithaq al-Madina*. It begins:

> In the name of God, the Merciful, the Compassionate! This is the writing of Muhammad the prophet between the believers and Muslims of Quraysh and Yathrib [Medina] and those who follow them and are

21. Saritoprak, "The Qur'anic," 3.

attached to them and who crusade along with them. They are a single community distinct from other people.[22]

Some scholars have read the constitution to mean building bridges between Muslim and non-Muslims or between different religious communities. For instance, Sean William White writes that

[t]he society was pluralistic, and it was not repressive. The Prophet never imposed Islam upon the people of Medina, which meant that they could still practice without disruption their religions and customs, aspects of life that were important to them.[23]

In fact, the *Medina Constitution* was not a covenant between Muslims and non-Muslims; rather, it was a covenant to establish a place for the marginalized in the new community and to close the gap between *al-Muhajirun* ("the immigrants") and *al-Ansar* ("the supporters"). So, through the Constitution, Muhammad offered a place for the immigrants in a new community.

The Muslim community in Medina resembles Jesus' new communities in God's kingdom "so that you may eat and drink at my table in my kingdom" (Luke 22:30). Through table fellowship, in Groody's words, "Jesus fulfills the message of the prophets, invites all people to salvation, and promises his disciples a place at table in God's kingdom."[24] Jesus invited to the table those who were marginalized and those who were deemed insignificant or rejected by society. Like Jesus' table fellowship, Muhammad's constitution established a place for the newcomers—those who were rejected and deemed insignificant. According to Groody, "Jesus' practice of table

22. Ashgar Ali Engineer, "Islam and Pluralism," in *The Myth of Religious Superiority: A Multifaith Exploration*, ed. Paul F. Knitter (Maryknoll, NY: Orbis, 2005), 216.
23. Sean William White, "Medina Charter and Pluralism," accessed 24 Feb. 2012, http://www.islamicity.com/Articles.
24. Groody, "Crossing," 657.

fellowship situates him against the backdrop of covenant theology, which is internally related to the notion of migration."[25]

Abraham and Moses made a covenant with God that was related to migration. A covenant was a binding agreement between two parties, which resulted in a new relationship and served as a bridge between communities. It helped overcome division and fostered justice and peace. *The Constitution of Medina* guaranteed "dignified existence and rights" to those who were marginalized.[26] It unified diverse groups, cultures, religions, and languages. As White notes, "The Prophet came to Medina with tolerance—an aspect of Islam which is fundamental to the manner in which the religion operates in foreign lands."[27] Thus what we should learn from Jesus' table fellowship and Muhammad's Constitution is that the absence of an international covenant to frame just and sustainable immigration and integration policies could result, in the words of Dhananjayan Sriskandarajah, in "permanent social exclusion for some groups of migrants, strains on social cohesion, and increasing global inequality."[28] Fifteen centuries ago, the Qur'an spoke against the exclusion of the stranger (and the other) and provided a framework that can be used today to construct an Islamic theology of migration that would help the weak and the vulnerable in an age of globalization.

The Stranger in the Qur'an

In the Qur'an, the immigrant or the stranger is entitled to the distribution of wealth. Verse 8:41 says: "Know that one-fifth of your battle gains belongs to God and the Messenger, to close relatives and

25. Ibid., 658.
26. Engineer, "Islam and Pluralism," 216.
27. White, "Medina."
28. Dhananjayan Sriskandarajah, "Migration Madness: Five Policy Dilemmas," *Studies in Christian Ethics* 19 (2006): 37.

orphans, to the needy and travellers [*ibn al sabil*]."[29] Giving to the stranger is rewarding: "So give their due to the near relative, the needy, and the wayfarer [*ibn al-sabil*]—that is best for those whose goal is God's approval: these are the ones who will prosper" (30:38). Verse 9:60 identifies *ibn al sabil* among the recipients of alms: "Alms are meant only for the poor, the needy, those who administer them, those whose hearts need winning over, to free slaves and help those in debt, for God's cause, and for travellers [*ibn al-sabil*] in need." This verse leaves out God and the Messenger and has two categories in common with the previous two verses, the poor and travelers.

The stranger also occupies an important place in Qur'anic verses concerned with piety and virtue. For example, the Qur'an demands believers to be good to their "parents, to relatives, to orphans, to the needy, to neighbours near and far, to travellers in need, and to your slaves" (4:36). Moreover, "The truly good are those who believe in God and the Last Day . . . who give away some of their wealth . . . to their relatives, to orphans, the needy, travellers and beggars" (2:177), and whatever the believers "give should be for parents, close relatives, orphans, the needy, and travellers . . ." (2:215), and those "who have been graced with bounty and plenty should not swear that they will [no longer] give to kinsmen, the poor, those who emigrated in God's way: let them pardon and forgive" (24:22). Michael Bonner notes that "[s]ome of the recipients appear only once, and others . . . reappear constantly. Most common is the triad of kinsfolk, poor, and travelers . . ."[30]

"The exegetical literature," according to Bonner, defines *ibn al-sabil*, literally "son of the road," as someone encountered by chance

29. The literal translation of the Arabic term *Ibn al sabil* is "the son of the road," meaning someone who is in constant travel. This term is discussed further below.

30. Michael Bonner, "Poverty and Economics in the Qur'an," *Journal of Interdisciplinary History* 25, no. 3 (Winter 2005): 401.

who is in need. Some exegetes define him as the guest, entitled to three days' hospitality—after which his entertainment becomes *sadaqa*, voluntary alms. One way or another, he is someone unknown, as opposed to kinsman.[31]

Those who are in need and entitled to distributions are defined in the Qur'an as the "poor emigrants [*al-fuqara' al-muhajirin*] who were driven from their homes and possessions" (59:8). Bonner writes that "this passage of Qur'an reveals that this group is central to the community, if not identical to it."[32]

The emphasis on *hijra* in the Qur'an was so great that it became the criterion of *iman* ("belief") and *kufr* ("unbelief"). God categorically declares in verse 8:72: "As for those who believed but did not emigrate, you are not responsible for their protection until they have done so." Thus *hijra*, as an act of *iman* against *kufr*, is reflected in the behavior of some early and modern Islamist groups. This theological notion of declaring Muslim infidels then migrating to another territory was applied in early Islam by the Kharijites, who declared other Muslims *kuffar* (infidel) and then withdrew from society. Similarly, modern-day *Takfir* and *Hijra* groups of Egypt made the *hijra* out of Cairo, believing that a true Muslim must migrate away from the infidels.[33] This separation of the self from the other and the erecting of barriers to enforce this separation run counter to the Islamic doctrine of *tawhid* ("the oneness of God" or "the Unity of Being"), which I discuss briefly below.

31. Ibid.
32. Ibid., 401–2.
33. See, for example, Hussam S. Timani, *Modern Intellectual Readings of the Kharijites* (New York: Peter Lang, 2008).

The Islamic *Tawhid* and the Other

The Islamic *tawhid* rejects arrogance and boastfulness because they are traits that lead not only to tyranny, injustice, and oppression but also to the destruction of the self as well as the other. Therefore, the integration of man with other men, of man with the whole universe, of man with God, of the other with the self leads to absolute nothingness, a state in which arrogance, boastfulness, and egotism are destroyed. Mystical *tawhid* eliminates all forms of injustice because mysticism, as Walter T. Stace points out, is "the apprehension of *an ultimate nonsensuous unity in all things*, a oneness or a One to which neither the senses nor the reason can penetrate."[34] The nonsensuous unity of all things where neither the senses nor reason can penetrate is the *fana'* ("annihilation") of the empirical selfhood, "when the ego-consciousness is completely dissolved into the consciousness of Reality, or rather, consciousness which *is* Reality."[35] In a world where egotism drives our appetites and desires and prevents us from caring for the other, where our selfhood demands from us to care less about our neighbor, to shun the immigrant and the stranger, and to look down at those who look different, the *fana'* of our ego into the consciousness of Reality is the best recipe.

The *fana'* of our ego is not only at the core of the Qur'anic message, but also it was mandated and practiced by Muhammad and early Muslims. According to a *hadith*,

> The best person in the eyes of [the Prophet Muhammad] was the one who wished everybody well. The one with the highest status in the eyes of [Muhammad] was that person who considered, comforted, and helped the creation the most. . . . The whole creation was equal before him as far as rights were concerned. . . . All were regarded as equals

34. Walter T. Stace, *The Teachings of the Mystics* (New York: New American Library, 1960), 14–15.
35. Toshihiko Izutsu, *Creation and the Timeless Order of Things: Essays in Islamic Mystical Philosophy* (Ashland, OR: White Cloud, 1994), 11.

among themselves. (A person was not regarded according to his lineage or genealogy). The [virtue] of one over the other was according to the *taqwa* (piety) possessed. The small ones were loved. The needy were given preference. Strangers and travellers were cared for.[36]

The second Caliph, Umar b. al-Khattab (d. 644), once said: "If I were to live again the past which I have already lived, I would take the surplus from the rich and distribute it among the poor immigrants (*muhajirun*)."[37] These anecdotes about the Prophet and his Companions demonstrate how early Muslims not only destroyed the barriers of the old *jahili* (pre-Islamic system) but also learned how to experience *fana'* by applying Islamic *tawhid* as a means to destroy the egotistic attitude that prevailed at that time, an experience that Islam requires us to go through in the twenty-first century to elevate and improve the living conditions of the strangers who live among us.

Fana' is "man's experiencing the total annihilation of his own ego and consequently of all things that have been related to the ego in the capacity of its objects of cognition and volition."[38] *Fana'* is "the ontological stage of 'unification,'" or gathering, when the "essential demarcations separating one thing from another, are no longer here," and when "multiplicity is no longer observable."[39] *Fana'* thus can be achieved, as Toshihiko Isutzu points out, when "there is no ego-consciousness left."[40] Globalization can be transformed into a positive force if egotism disappears in the experience of *fana'*.

Globalization is supposed to bring all humanity together, to unite the world, to elevate those who are at the bottom of the society, to open borders and destroy boundaries between nations and social

---

36. *Shama-il Tirmidhi*, ch. 46, Hadith 7 (319), accessed 17 March 2014, www.hadithcollection.com.
37. *Fiqh-us-Sunna* vol. 3, Zakaat and Fasting, *Fiqh* 3.093C, accessed 17 March 2014, www.hadithcollection.com.
38. Izutsu, *Creation*, 13.
39. Ibid., 15.
40. Ibid., 16.

classes, to unite man with man, and to make the many one. However, globalization became a dividing and destructive force due to man's failure to experience *fana'*, to purify the self from all the activities of the ego. 'Abd al-Rahman Jami, a famous Iranian poet-philosopher of the fifteenth century, says, "Keep yourself away from your own ego, and set your mind free from the vision of others."[41] Thus a theology of *fana' al-'ana* (the annihilation of egotism) is a necessary theology for the promotion of justice in the age of globalization.

Conclusion

An Islamic theology of migration is most needed in the Muslim world today, for justice is denied to many strangers, Muslims and non-Muslims alike. Not only does the Qur'an provide the foundations for such a theology, but it also challenges us all as Muslims and human beings to have compassion toward the strangers and the vulnerable and to do justice as Muhammad and all the great prophets before him did.

This chapter has attempted to demonstrate the Qur'anic theology of migration and the importance given to strangers and immigrants in the Qur'an and the Islamic teachings in general. From an Islamic perspective, not only are immigrants central in the Muslim community, but they also are *the* community. Immigration theology is a theology of religious pluralism since strangeness has become a symbol of piety, a path to salvation, a mode for purification, and a mirror to see the self in the other. It is important to realize that globalization is a source for further destruction of human dignity and religious values. This chapter has highlighted the role of theology in the age of globalization and how a theology of migration can be used,

41. Ibid., 12.

modified, or reinvented to preserve human dignity and values and face the challenges of the twenty-first century.

8

Gothic "Immigrants" in the Roman Empire

Craig R. Davis

Goths were the first barbarian people to enter the mighty Roman Empire and live to tell the tale. After attacks by horse-borne Huns off the Pontic steppes in 376 ce, bands of Gothic farmers and their families began to appear on the banks of the Danube River, begging for permission to cross over into the protective custody of the Romans. The eastern emperor Valens admitted some of these refugees, mainly to use their young men as recruits for the Roman army and, it was later said, requiring their conversion to his own pre-Nicene form of Christianity—"Arianism"—as the price of admission.[1] Yet each of the incoming groups still crossed the river carrying the totems of its peculiar tribal cult.[2]

---

1. E. A. Thompson, *The Visigoths in the Time of Ulfila* (Oxford: Clarendon, 1966), 78–93.
2. Ibid., 57.

Tribal Identity

Traditionally, Goths shared with other Germanic-speaking peoples a conical conception of tribal identity, dynastic privilege, and divine power. At the apex of this conceptual cone in the not-too-distant past was the supernatural progenitor of the tribe from whom the ruling clan traced its descent down the core of the cone to its present leader at the center of a circular base.[3] This base comprised all the living members of the tribe, who were also understood to have descended from the same divine ancestor, but less clearly and demonstrably so than the royal family, whose members could celebrate their blood-lineal descent from divinity in a series of named generations down to the currently ruling monarch. Some royal pedigrees surviving from a later period are rationalized as a father-to-son succession, but in reality, new kings were often chosen by a system of princely competition, whereby a council of elders or assembly of free warriors chose the most competent leader from a group of dynastic pretenders or, just as often, one such claimant simply eliminated his rivals. In 98 C.E. the Roman historian Tacitus called this ruling patriarch at the center of his tribal kindred a *rex ex nobilitate*, "king on account of his noble pedigree," distinguishing him from a *dux ex virtute*, "war-leader by virtue of his strength," though in practice rulers usually needed both kinds of authority to succeed.[4]

Even so, in Anglo-Saxon England and elsewhere in the Germanic-speaking world, this genealogical theory of tribal identity prevailed. It is fossilized in the Old English title *cyning*, "king," derived from *cyn*, "kindred" *ing*, a patronymic or partitive suffix, meaning "son of," "sprung from," or "belonging to." A Germanic monarch was

---

3. Craig R. Davis, "Cultural Assimilation in the Anglo-Saxon Royal Genealogies," *Anglo-Saxon England* 21 (1992): 23–36.

4. Tacitus, *Germania* 7 (*Cornelii Taciti Opera Minora*, ed. M. Winterbottom and R. M. Ogilvie [Oxford: Clarendon, 1975], 37–62).

understood to be the physical quintessence of his kindred, the purest manifestation of the divine ancestor's seed in the flesh, governing people rather than territory. Every free family under the king's authority, according to Tacitus, had a right to live and farm somewhere within the tribal hegemony and whole tribes could simply pick up and move hundreds of miles to new territories while retaining their essential political cohesion.[5] And as desperate and beleaguered as some of these migrating groups may have been, their kings brought with them a powerful sense of their own divine charisma, a confidence empowered by the genealogical myth of their origins and regularly reinforced by sacrifices, feasts, prayers, funeral obsequies, and other ritual observances designed to promote the tribe's collective solidarity and invoke the continued blessing of its ancestor deity upon his descendants.

These god-sprung kings proved resistant to the gospel message when met by Christian missionaries in their own homelands. The Frisian king Radbod neatly summed up their attitude, saying he would rather burn in hell with his noble ancestors than spend eternity in heaven with a lot of poor people.[6] The Swedish kings, living far to the north in the same place Tacitus had located the *Suiones* a thousand years earlier,[7] did not convert until the very end of the eleventh century.

However, this genealogical construction of tribal identity did not mean that Germanic dynasties proved particularly long-lived. New royal families, along with the tribal polities they constantly reshaped around themselves, came and went with alarming alacrity among the many vicissitudes of migration—splitting, coalescing, reconstituting, disappearing entirely—during each permutation of which the royal

5. Ibid., 26.
6. *Vita Vulframni* (*Monumenta Germaniae Historica: Scriptores Rerum Merovingicarum* 5 [Hannover: Hahn, 1910], 668).
7. Tacitus, *Germania* 45.

genealogies needed to be rescrubbed or invented anew. The early Jutish kings of Kent, for instance, were pirates and mercenary *parvenus*, who had turned on their Roman-British employers in the mid-fifth century. They quickly concocted a pedigree back to the war-god Woden, and only a handful of dubious generations back into the pre-migration mists of time were all that were considered necessary to demonstrate the descent of the new royal family from the deity.[8] And yet their rule was so successful that they sparked a new genealogical fashion among other Germanic warlords in post-Roman Britain. The rulers of Wessex, Mercia, East Anglia, Bernicia, Deira, and Lindsey all picked Woden as their founding ancestor as well.[9] Only the old-fashioned East Saxons held out for an eponymous ethnic progenitor named *Seaxnet*, the tribal god of their kinsmen, the "Old Saxons," on the continent.[10]

Gothic Christian Identity

The Goths who killed Valens at Hadrianople could similarly have thanked "Mars" for their victory, as they sometimes had done in their wandering days outside the empire, according to an *interpretatio Romana*, by hanging their captives and spoils from trees.[11] The fact that they did not do so in this case speaks volumes about their rapid acculturation, first as neighbors in the former Roman province of Dacia north of the Danube, then as immigrants within the empire itself. Far from creating a new national cult of the war-god who had brought them victory like the Anglo-Saxons, the Goths adopted

8. Bede, *Ecclesiastical History* 1.15 and 2.5 (ed. and trans. B. Colgrave and R. Mynors [Oxford: Clarendon, 1969]).
9. Kenneth Sisam, "The Anglo-Saxon Royal Genealogies," *Proceedings of the British Academy* 39 (1953): 287–348.
10. David N. Dumville, "The West Saxon Genealogical Regnal List: Manuscripts and Texts," *Anglia* 104 (1986): 1–32.
11. Thompson, *Visigoths*, 60.

the slain emperor's own non-Trinitarian creed, seemingly speeded in their choice by a new source of ethnic empowerment available to them, the almost completed translation of the Septuagint into the Gothic language by the Arian bishop Wulfila. This was the very first rendering of Christian scripture into a national vernacular, a forty-year project, possibly never completed, which ended with the bishop's death in the early 380s. Wulfila's Arian Bible provided the Goths with a potent narrative of a migrating people of God, supplying them with an expressive liturgy in their own tongue, even as it allowed their kings to keep their antique (though constantly updated) royal genealogies back to the Goths' eponymous ethnic ancestors, now understood to have been merely brave human heroes.[12]

In this sharp curve of cultural assimilation, Goths were aided by learned Catholic clerics like St. Ambrose, who traced the Goths' descent from Magog, son of Japheth, an idea countered by St. Jerome with an alternative suggestion.[13] He saw an even closer consonantal homophony between Latin *Gothi* and Greek *Getai*, the name of a people once living at the mouth of the Danube in the sixth century B.C.E. who, according to Herodotus, were "the bravest and most just of the Thracians."[14] *Getae* thus became the ancient or poetic name of the Goths in Latin, a usage soon popularized by Orosius after the early fifth century.[15] By the middle of the sixth century, Jordanes, an eastern Catholic Goth living in Constantinople, composed *De origine actibusque Getarum*, "On the Origin and Deeds of the Goths," more familiarly known as the *Getica*, in which he further associates these

12. See n. 17, below.

13. Jerome, *Liber hebraicarum quaestionum in Genesim* (*Patrologia Latina* 23 [Paris: Migne, 1865], 983–1060).

14. *The Landmark Herodotus: The Histories* 4.93 (ed. Robert B. Strassler, trans. Andrea L. Purvis [New York: Random House, 2007]).

15. Paul Orosius, *Historiarum adversum paganos Libri VII* 1.16.2 (ed. Carolus Zangemeister [Leipzig: Teubner, 1889]).

supposed ancestral Goths, the *Getae*, with a people called *Goutai* by Ptolemy the Geographer in the second century CE, whose homeland he identifies as *Skandia* in the northern Ocean.[16] Jordanes claims the *Getae* originally came from this *insula Scandza*, "the Scandinavian peninsula," by crossing the Baltic in three ships and migrating thence to the shores of the Black Sea where they appeared years later as *Gothi*.[17]

A context for this migration myth of *Getae* from the north can be found in the long reign of Theoderic, the Ostrogothic king of Italy from 493 to 526, a period of unprecedented prosperity and ethnic amalgamation among various Gothic-speaking groups as they secured their hegemony over the Italian peninsula and its Roman population. At Theoderic's behest the Roman scholar and diplomat Cassiodorus composed a twelve-volume history of the Goths modeled partly on Livy's and Virgil's account of the founding of Rome by migrants from Troy with a nod toward the wanderings of the Israelites to the Promised Land as recounted in the book of Exodus. That history by Cassiodorus is now lost, but was summarized and supplemented by Jordanes, who traces the origin of Theoderic's Amal dynasty back sixteen generations to an ethnic ancestor named *Gaut*,[18] describing the prolonged wars and peregrinations of the *Getae* from Scandinavia to the Black Sea. Both philological and archaeological evidence suggests that proto-Gothic speakers did indeed migrate to the Pontic region, if not from Sweden proper, at least from the southern Baltic shore near the mouth of the Vistula

---

16. *Geographia* 2.11.16 and 2.11.35 (ed. C. F. A. Nobbe, trans. Edward Luther [Hildesheim: Teubner, 1966]).

17. Jordanes, *De origine actibusque Getarum* [= *Getica*] 1, 3, 4, 17, 24 (ed. Theodor Mommsen, *Monumenta Germaniae Historica, Auctores Antiquissimi* 5 [Berlin, 1882, 1961], trans. Charles C. Mierow in *The Gothic History of Jordanes* [Princeton: Princeton University Press, 1915], 9, 16, 25, 94, 121).

18. Ibid., 9 (79).

River. This is the general region where Pliny the Elder in the first century CE, citing Pytheas of Marseilles (c. 300 B.C.E.), places a people he calls *Gutones*.[19] Tacitus explicitly locates a Germanic-speaking people, the *Gotones*, in northern Poland toward the end of the first century CE.[20] The Wielbark culture excavated there has revealed certain distinct continuities in settlement patterns, material artifacts, and funerary practices with the Sîntana de Mures and Cernjachov cultures of Romania and the Ukraine, respectively.[21] In addition, the onomastic consonance of Pytheas/Pliny's *Gutones*, Tacitus's *Gotones*, Ptolemy's *Goutai*, the island of *Got*land, and the modern districts of Väster– and Östergö*t*land in south-central Sweden suggests a general diffusion or cultural influence of the Wielbark "Goths" over the shores and islands of the southern Baltic before the movement of some of them upriver along the familiar amber trade routes to the south and east.

The journey in three ships from the *insula Scandza* during which one was lost is certainly best understood as a dynastic foundation legend promulgated and quite possibly invented at the court of Theoderic in Ravenna with the help of Cassiodorus. It is clearly designed to valorize the distinctiveness and authority of the Amal clan over a winnowed Getic/Gothic nation, a people better known before Theoderic's day for their fissile and quasi-elective system of kingship, whereby a large class of free farmer-warriors chose their kings from a clutch of aristocratic clans on the basis of their leadership in war and commitment to preserving the cohort's ancient privileges.[22] Cassiodorus's Amal origin myth preserved by Jordanes includes many

---

19. Pliny the Elder, *Natural History* 4.13 and 37.11 (ed. W. H. S. Jones and D. E. Eichholz, trans. H. Rackham [Cambridge, MA: Loeb Classical Library, 1938–62], 99–100; 35).

20. Tacitus, *Germania* 44.

21. Peter Heather and John Matthews, *The Goths of the Fourth Century* (Liverpool: Liverpool University Press, 1991), 51–102.

22. Peter Heather, *The Goths* (Malden, MA/Oxford: Blackwell, 1996).

familiar stereotypes from Greco-Roman ethnography, including the image of noble northern savages invigorated by their harsh environment and notable for their ferocity and physical stature, but also kept in a state of moral purity by their distance from the corrupting influence of southern civilization.[23] These fierce, upright *Getae*, however, soon become "nearly as wise as Greeks" under the tutelage of native masters in milder climes,[24] combining, as Cassiodorus puts it in his *Variae*, the *prudentia* of the Romans with the *virtus* of the *gentes*.[25]

This Scandinavian pseudo-history seems to have provided an opportunity for the Goths in Italy to reconstruct a fuller sense of their own ethnic heritage and national identity in their new homeland, just as Virgil had defined for the Augustan age what it meant to be Roman. Cassiodorus had already completed an earlier *Chronicle* in 519, in which he synthesized world history into a sequence of rulers culminating in the union of Goths and Romans.[26] It was thus by adapting familiar *topoi* from the classics of ancient ethnography and employing the techniques of literary ethnogenesis learned from Roman and biblical writers, in combination with whatever vernacular traditions may have been retained of a migration through many lands from the north, that Theoderic's Goths in Italy came to see themselves as a uniquely superior people. Jordanes ends his own history of the Goths by celebrating the birth of a baby boy in March 551 to a defecting Amal princess Matasuentha and Justinian's kinsman Germanus, a child who will unite the dynasties of Amali and

23. James B. Rives, "*Germania*," in *A Companion to Tacitus*, ed. Victoria Emma Pagán (Malden, MA/ Oxford: Blackwell, 2012), 45–61, at 49–55.

24. Jordanes, *Getica* 5 (*Gothic History*, 39).

25. Cassiodorus 3.23.3 (ed. Theodor Mommsen, *Monumenta Germaniae Historica, Auctores Antiquissimi* 12 [Berlin: Weidmann, 1894]).

26. Michael Klaassen, "Cassiodorus' *Chronica*: Text, Chronography and Sources" (Ph.D. diss., University of Pennsylvania, 2010).

Anicii, Goths and Romans—the two noblest nations on earth—into one people.

Theoderic in Italy, while tolerant of Catholics and respectful (at least until the end of his reign) toward the papacy, remained studiously faithful to the new *lex Gothica*, the national version of the Christian faith in his own Gothic tongue. The king discouraged the conversion of Catholics to this creed, as well as intermarriage between Goths and Romans, precisely because he wished to maintain the ethnic distinctiveness of the nation from which his own authority as *rex Gothorum* derived. This new faith co-opted the cult of tribal ancestors as the empowering myth of the Gothic nation, though it is curious that the Christianity the Goths clung to so assiduously was one that stressed the hierarchical relationship between God the Father and God the Son. Gothic freemen just could not get their heads around the abstruse mystery of the Holy Trinity, but they understood very well the proper relationship between fathers and sons, as well as that between kings and their followers modeled upon it, especially the "loyalty down" of a Gothic father to his family or of a Gothic king to his people that inspires their reciprocal "loyalty up" to him. Gothic relationships were both deeply stratified and personally intimate, warmed by ties of blood—real or fictive—but constantly reaffirmed through public vows and formal commitments unto the death. These pledges of personal loyalty, freely chosen and often fulfilled on the field of battle, constituted the core ethos of the Goths. Gothic Arianism came to express this ethnic value in a theologically potent and comprehensible way. The loyal self-sacrifice of the Son to serve the Father for the sake of the people was an ideal all Goths could grasp without hesitation, generating a distinctive expression of the Christian faith that achieved its apogee during the reign of Theoderic in Italy. This new form of "vernacular Christianity" is virtually symbolized by the *Codex Argenteus* preserved in the University Library at Uppsala in Sweden: 118 folios of the New Testament in the Gothic language inscribed in silver ink on purple vellum in Wulfila's invented script combining the Greek alphabet and runic *futhark*. It was produced at the writing office of Theoderic's Arian cathedral of St. Anastasius in Ravenna to enshrine the peculiarly ethnic faith of the Goths.[27]

Gothic Influence

So impressive was this Gothic Arian Christian fusion that the Frankish Catholic emperor Charlemagne later looked to Theoderic as his royal role model. After he had received the title of *emperor* and *augustus* from Pope Leo on Christmas Day 800, Charlemagne headed straight north to Ravenna in the spring. While staying in Rome, the new emperor had ample opportunity to see many imperial images, one of which was the statue of Marcus Aurelius, then in the Lateran and thought at the time to represent the first Christian emperor Constantine. It is now in the Capitoline Museum, the only bronze equestrian statue to have survived from antiquity, showing the emperor calmly riding stirrup-less with his right hand outstretched in a gesture of pacific imperial rule. Charlemagne did not like that one. Instead, he chose to grace his palace at Aachen with a statue he found in front of Theoderic's palace in Ravenna. Around 839, Agnellus writes that

> atop a pyramid of squared stones and mortar, about six cubits high, . . . was a horse of bronze decked in tawny gold, and mounted upon it was King Theoderic who wielded a shield on his left shoulder and with his right arm erect held a spear.[28]

27. Heather and Matthews, *The Goths*, 2; 315–17.
28. *Liber Pontificalis Ecclesiae Ravennatis* 94 (ed. Deborah Mauskopf Deliyannis [Turnhout: Brepols, 2006], trans. Carl I. Hammer, "Recycling Rome and Ravenna: Two Studies in Early-Medieval Reuse," *Saeculum* 56, no. 2 [2005]: 295–325, at 321).

Charlemagne wanted that one. And as Carl Hammer points out, the emperor "did not appropriate the statue as an imperial representation of himself; he retained—unchallenged—[its] original identification" with the Arian king of the Goths,[29] much to the annoyance of Catholic churchmen like Walahfrid Strabo.[30] But there it stood in front of Charlemagne's palace at Aachen under its own name, suggesting that it was Theoderic's character as king, despite his doctrinal confession, that the emperor most admired and with which he wished to associate himself, both in his own eyes and in those of his subjects.

So what exactly did this statue mean to Charlemagne? What was the core quality of the Gothic king's example it embodied for him? We can get some idea from a passage in Fredegar's *Chronicle* composed around 660, describing how Asiatic Huns, here conflated with contemporary Slavic Avars, had driven the Goths back across the Danube into Italy.[31] Theoderic rallies his troops, but an Avar champion takes the field, improbably named Xerxer, who singlehandedly slays two sets of three Gothic warriors sent out against him by the king. Theoderic then charges out to meet the enemy himself, wounds Xerxer with his spear, but then spares his life, taking him captive and offering him many rewards in return for his service. The Avar refuses all blandishments, however, until Theoderic relents, gives him leave to go home and accompanies him with honor to the Danube. After fording the river on his horse, Xerxer turns back and calls out to the Gothic king: "Now that I have been freed from your authority, I know my will is free and that you exercise no power over me; I shall return to you and be the most loyal of

29. Hammer, "Recycling," 318.
30. Michael Herren, "The *De Imagine Tetrici* of Walahfrid Strabo: Edition and Translation," *Journal of Medieval Latin* 1 (1991): 118–39; Hammer, "Recycling," 322–24.
31. *Die Fredegar-Chroniken* 2.57 (ed. Roger Collins [Hannover: Hahnsche, 2007]).

them all."[32] This story, *Frankified* as it is, reflects something of the national character of the Goths as it crystallized around the figure of Theoderic, found portable form in a vernacular legend summarized in Latin by Fredegar, and was embodied physically in the statue of the old king on horseback with shield and spear ready to fight for his people. Four Merovingian monarchs between 511 and 737 were named after the Ostrogothic king, as was Charlemagne's close kinsman, Sheriff Theoderic, who fell against the Avars, and indeed as was the emperor's own last-born son in 807. The Gothic king supplied the Frankish emperor with a model of personal valor and magnanimity toward foes that wins their loyalty, an image of the moral heritage of the Goths that Charlemagne wished to own for himself.

This memory of the Amal Theoderic is not the fruit of an ancient *Traditionskern* "seed of tradition" or continuous sense of Gothic ethnicity borne by the Amal clan from their homeland in the north as implied in the *Getica*.[33] Any Ostrogoth at Theoderic's court over the age of fifty, Peter Heather reminds us, would have remembered the king's messy rise to power over rival Gothic leaders in the Balkans and his personal slaying—murder—of his enemy Odovacar at their reconciliation feast in Ravenna, whatever the king's "later, imperial pretensions."[34] And a decade after Theoderic was dead, the Gothic freemen had no problem at all in deposing his nephew Theodahad, last ruler of the Amal line, in 536, when he failed to take the field against the Byzantine army under Belisarius. They put in his place a military commander, a *dux ex virtute* as Tacitus would have called him, named Wittigis, who said that, even though he did not belong

---

32. Hammer, "Recycling," 324–25.
33. Reinhard Wenskus, *Stammesbildung und Verfassung: Das Werden der frühmittelalterlichen Gentes* (Cologne: Böhlau, 1961), and Herwig Wolfram, *History of the Goths* (Berkeley: University of California Press, 1988).
34. *The Goths*, 239.

to Theoderic's family by blood, he would accept the honor because his devotion to the Goths and deeds of valor on their behalf were of the same quality as those of the old king.[35] The character and career of Theoderic had become the template by which all Gothic leaders would be judged, providing a new tradition of that people manufactured in late antique Italy and appropriated by other nations north of the Alps as a kind of legendary *spolia* preserved in the stories and statue of the old king.

Something of this same appreciation for the Gothic amalgam of ethnic loyalty, Roman prudence, and Christian faith emerges in the wording with which the Anglo-Saxon king Alfred praises Alaric the Visigoth in his rewriting of the fall of Rome at the end of that king's translation into Old English of Orosius's *History against the Pagans*.[36] Alfred claimed descent from the Goths through his mother Osburh, a Jutish princess from the Isle of Wight,[37] but entertained reservations about Theoderic because of his execution of Boethius and his hand in the death of Pope John.[38] Nonetheless, Alfred insisted that the earlier Visigothic king Alaric was not a heretical scourge of God sent to punish Catholic Romans for their sins, as suggested by Orosius, but rather *se cristena cyning ond se mildusta*, "the Christian king and the mildest one," who honored the churches of Rome and gave orders against any deliberate destruction.[39] Alaric for Alfred, like Theoderic for Charlemagne, was a truly Christian king of his people, as remarkable for his kindness, even to enemies, as for his courage in protecting his followers. This legend of the Goths—barbarian

---

35. Ibid., citing Cassiodorus, *Variae* 10.31.
36. Malcolm Godden, "The Anglo-Saxons and the Goths: Rewriting the Sack of Rome," *Anglo-Saxon England* 31 (2002): 47–68.
37. *Asser's Life of King Alfred* 2 (ed. W. H. Stevenson [Oxford: Clarendon, 1904]).
38. *The Old English Boethius: An Edition of the Versions of Boethius's "De Consolatione Philosophiae"* 1 (ed. and trans. Malcolm Godden and Susan Irvine [Oxford: Oxford University Press, 2009]).
39. *The Old English Orosius* 6.38 (ed. Janet Bately [London/New York: Oxford University Press, 1980]).

"immigrants" who had embraced the religion of their Roman "hosts" only to make it uniquely their own—became a model for other Christian Germanic kings and our first example of a distinctly national interpretation of the Christian faith.

9

White Protestant Efforts to Convert Italian Immigrants

The Case of Constantine Panunzio

Linda Mercadante

Protestants—including Methodists, Episcopals, Baptists, and Presbyterians—worked hard to evangelize the hundreds of thousands of Italian immigrants who flooded into the United States from the 1880s until legislation in 1924 severely limited the influx. Their motivations were diverse and often complex. Some felt the immigrants were oppressed by Old World doctrines and attitudes and that Protestantism offered them the best hope of liberation. Some were afraid that Rome had plans to take over America and was purposely sending hordes of migrants here. Many felt that the best hope for everyone lay in the speedy assimilation of these foreigners. They observed that Protestantism had a more democratic polity and more egalitarian theological and social attitudes. Thus, they believed, it was a religion better suited for citizens of a democracy than authoritarian Catholicism and would provide the best route to enculturating the immigrants.

These missionizing Protestants were solidly down the main street of American religion—white, middle-class, and mostly male. It is important to realize that, for the most part, they did not consider these immigrants "white." In fact, not just Italians, but Jews, Greeks, Eastern Europeans, Latinos, and other immigrant groups were classified rather vaguely as an "other" racial category.[1] How much racial identity played a part in American Protestant efforts is unclear, but these home missionaries did feel these efforts as both a civic and religious duty. So, they preached the gospel to the new immigrants, taught them English, helped them adjust, and tried to meet many of their practical needs. Yet in spite of spending many hours and thousands, even millions, of dollars, the success of these home missionaries was disappointing, at least in terms of numbers. Small Italian Protestant congregations rose up like crocuses in the spring and just as quickly faded away. If they had 100 members, they were large. Although by the early 1900s more than 300 Italian missions had been established, only a few decades later all were dead. Even national Italian Roman Catholic parishes, which had many of the same handicaps as the Protestant versions, lasted longer.

The work of these Protestant missionaries was hard, transient, and less than wildly successful. Even in the heavily immigrant city of New York, an area that received significant attention from home missioners, the number of Italian American Protestants remained below 2 percent of the population.[2] So, given all that Protestants tried

1. Among the many works documenting this, a very readable one is Karen Brodkin, *How Jews Became White Folks & What That Says About Race in America* (New Brunswick, NJ: Rutgers University Press, 1999).
2. Frank A. Salamone says it remained this way throughout the 1930s and 1940s; see Salvatore LaGumina, Frank Cavaioli, Salvatore Primeggia, Joseph A. Varacalli, eds., *The Italian American*

to offer the immigrants, why didn't they gain more converts? We can speculate about the many factors that contributed to the resistance of Italian immigrants to the lures of these Protestants. Most obvious was their predominantly Roman Catholic background, however lapsed or cynical about those roots they might be. Even the prejudicial and rejecting attitude of Irish Catholics in America was only enough to keep Italians away from church, but often not enough to make them become Protestants.

To become Protestant, the Italian Catholic immigrant would be entering a faith they had been taught was "of the devil." They would have to give up such important things as patron saints, festas, a rich liturgical life, a sometimes comfortingly authoritarian understanding of religious truth, a clear hierarchical church structure, and a sense of solidarity with other immigrants. Not only that, but the sometimes patronizing and self-righteous attitude of the Protestant home missionaries could not have escaped the notice of these intuitive and intelligent ancestors.

Making the choice even less attractive was the fact that serious estrangement, ostracism, and shame would often be the social results of the decision to convert. For conversion was a giant leap, often causing serious alienation in both practical and emotional ways from family and friends, from inherited doctrines and Old World values. So, for many Italian immigrants, the message of Protestantism was too strange, the changes too dramatic, and the price much too high.

Experience: An Encyclopedia (New York: Garland, 1999), 519. Research shows that even those numbers may have been inflated since the same Italian Americans often frequented multiple Protestant missions. In the book discussed here, Constantine Panunzio, *The Soul of an Immigrant* (New York: Macmillan, 1921; reissued 1924 and 1928; New York: Arno), and in *The New York Times*, 1969, Panunzio says that one Sunday he visited all the Protestant missions in a particular city: "The services at these missions were held at different hours . . . [I] found the same constituency, meager as it was, swelling the ranks of all three. Later, by mere accident, I learned that seventy-five per cent of the membership of one was enrolled on the books of the second, and thirty-five per cent on the books of the third . . ." (240–41).

But some immigrants did convert. And a significant number of them went on to become ordained and to continue the work with Italian immigrants.[3] What factors helped these converts come to terms with this radical break with their roots? How much were they, consciously or unconsciously, inspired by dreams of assimilation, Americanization, or whiteness? On the other hand, how much did Protestant theological ideas truly capture their religious imaginations and help them make this giant leap?

This essay focuses on one convert, Constantine Panunzio, who has given us a graphic narrative of his life journey in *The Soul of an Immigrant*, first published in 1921 and then reissued in 1924. Notice that the second edition came out just when the restrictive immigration laws were being passed. So Panunzio likely did not just want to tell his own story, but to communicate to his adopted America a sense of empathy for the plight of the immigrant. He would thus have a large and important agenda.

Panunzio was born in 1884 to a prominent family in Malfetto, in the province of Bari. His grandmother had great plans for him, to become the incarnation of his famous martyred patriot grandfather. Her plan was to make him "First a priest, then a teacher, and at last a patriotic statesman."[4] But given Constantine's active and adventurous personality, he did not fit well into this scenario. The idea of his becoming a priest was an especially odd goal because his family was fairly blasé about their Catholicism. Indeed his father was downright hostile to the church and even his female relatives only went to

---

3. Colgate Theological Seminary had an entire department, "The Italian Department," dedicated to training for ministry Italian immigrants who had been converted here from Catholicism to Protestantism. For a time it was located in Brooklyn, NY and headed by another prominent immigrant, Dr. Antonio Mangano. The course lasted five years. Lewis Turco, among others, mentions this school; see *The Spiritual Autobiography of Luigi Turco* (Center for Immigration Studies at the University of Minnesota, 1969).

4. Panunzio, *The Soul of an Immigrant*, 12.

146

mass out of duty, he implies. He was never given much religious instruction and the little he had he ignored.

The only indication we have that religious ideas even penetrated his consciousness is when he tells us how he was left alone one day in his grandmother's house and found a book of Bible stories. This is the first and only religious reading he had ever done. He considers this a forbidden book, but becomes enraptured by it. Perhaps Constantine the author is setting us up for his later conversion. He says:

> How such a book ever got into our home I cannot say. I squatted myself down on the floor and devoured some of the chapters. All the while I was conscious of my wickedness in reading such stories. . . . Even so, to me that reading was most sweet. One of the stories was that of the Resurrection of Jesus. It made a deep impression upon my mind.[5]

This book notwithstanding, Constantine continued to show a real lack of enthusiasm for the family plan. Nevertheless, they continued to push him along their well-designed route, all the way to a junior seminary. But he hated everything about it: its smells, its rooms, its harshness, and especially its teachers. Instead, he longed to go to sea and finally, at age thirteen, after subverting their plans many times, he gained his family's permission to sign on with a schooner. After a few years of local excursions, he landed a space on a ship headed for America. He had never intended to emigrate, but just wanted an adventurous life. Once in Boston, however, he becomes fed up with his harsh skipper, jumps ship, and determines to earn enough to book passage back to Italy. This is when his real troubles begin.

Panunzio gives us graphic detail about the scoundrels and scams, prejudice and plights that afflicted immigrants, especially young ones. He is taken advantage of so many times that the reader loses count. Finally, he shows inklings of a religious awakening when he

5. Ibid., 19.

encounters an evangelistic preacher who comes to Staceyville, the rough little town in Maine where he eventually lands. Mixed in with the gospel is this preacher's puritanical attitude toward what he considers social ills such as drinking and dancing.

This is only the second time in the book that the author mentions anything substantive about religious ideas. He says that as he listened to the preacher, something strange gripped his soul, something very real and powerful. "Although neither that experience nor any subsequent one made me very religious, in the strictly Puritan sense of the word, yet for the first time I thought of life in terms of service."[6]

His next encounter with religion is through the kindly family of his new employer. They practically adopt him and, to be with them and please them, he accompanies them to church and participates in their family devotions. Now he feels that he is coming into contact with the best in America. Finally, he says, he had found "a true American home . . . in which are blended order and cleanliness, courtesy and frankness, consideration and ease, simplicity and sturdy morality."[7] From that point on he begins to equate certain values in America with Protestant religion. Eventually, through this family, he is able to enroll in a preparatory school, takes a part-time job helping Italian immigrants through a mission society, and ultimately decides to go to seminary and get ordained.

He spends several years working in American churches, then is sent to work in a mission house among Italian immigrants. At the outbreak of World War I, he spends time with the YMCA overseas, and then serves churches in the Midwest. The book ends there, but we know that subsequently, Panunzio went on to earn his Ph.D. and became a professor in the social sciences. He ultimately ended up

6. Ibid., 134.
7. Ibid., 142.

professor of sociology at UCLA (1931–1952) and authored several books. In 1940 he was honored at the New York World's Fair as a foreign-born citizen who made major contributions to American culture. He died in 1964.

So the first half of Panunzio's career was tied up with American Protestantism and this book is, in effect, a spiritual autobiography as well as an immigrant's tale of hardship. In spite of all this, and given the religious work he had done by the close of the book, I find some things very striking about this conversion story.

The genre of spiritual autobiography in American literature is large, and includes some contributions by Italian immigrant converts and ministers. Most of those from this group focus on the dramatic change in their lives once converted. They praise God, laud Jesus, affirm the centrality of Scripture, repudiate Roman Catholic doctrine and practices, and generally establish their theological credentials for being true believers. For instance, an anonymous writer contributed his testimony to *The Baptist Home Mission Monthly*, in 1909. He relates how he went back to his priest to explain why he can no longer be a Catholic. He tells the priest:

> I did not change my religion, but the religion changed me. It has changed my life and my home, and even my pockets. Where I carried a pack of cards, to-day in the same pocket I have a New Testament. I have become acquainted with God through my Saviour Jesus Christ, and he has made me feel happy. . . . I would like to explain the joy and happiness of my conversion, but it is beyond my power.[8]

Similarly, in 1913, Michael Frasca, writing for *The Assembly Herald*, explains why he is entering the Protestant ministry. After a spiritual experience, he says:

8. Anonymous, "A Young Italian's Story: How the Gospel Transformed a Youthful Gambler and Mischief Maker into an Honest and Happy Member of Society," in *The Baptist Home Mission Monthly* 31 (March 1909): 125.

All doubts were clear, the Roman Catholic Church had degenerated into a worldly political organization, had forgotten her lofty mission, had denied the Redeemer of mankind for a worldly scepter. Therefore, I felt myself no longer bound to her and I embraced the real Christian apostolic church by entering the ministry.[9]

More examples could be cited, but they are all in this vein.[10] Panunzio's, however, is quite different. He rarely, if ever—other than the time he finds the Bible story book—mentions God or Jesus, any particular doctrines of Christianity, or the word "gospel." He never mentions any Protestant ideas we might surmise would be attractive to converts, such as "the priesthood of believers," the idea that no minister need mediate between the believer and God, the idea that God is no respecter of persons and loves all equally, or any of the other central tenets that missionaries likely preached. Nor does he ever overtly compare Roman Catholicism and Protestantism, a common theme among Italian converts.

What does he do instead? He extols the best of America, the virtues of its American ideas, values, and practices. As an intelligent man, a thinker, and the professional intellectual that he was later to become, Panunzio is attracted to American thought. He can make allowances for Americans who don't live up to these ideals and apologizes for immigrants who have never had his good luck to be exposed to these lofty values.

Given this admiration and almost total lack of religious language, one wonders what Panunzio preached from his pulpit during his years in ministry. Although we don't know that, it is clear what

9. Michael Frasca, "Why I Am Entering the Ministry," in *The Assembly Herald* 24 (December 1913): 688.
10. See, for example, Turco's *Spiritual Autobiography*: "In a few months after my conversion God gave me the power to stop smoking, drinking, and unlegal sexual relations. I became very enthusiastic in the work of the church" (4). See also Theodore Abel, "The Story of an Immigrant Minister," in *Protestant Home Missions to Catholic Immigrants* (New York: Institute of Social and Religious Research, 1933).

he admires in America. He identifies seven mental changes in him that occurred thanks to the best in America. This, in effect, is his testimony and his conversion.

1. "The first of these was the gaining of what I might call a mobile and free attitude toward life. . . . [Although Italians come to America, he says] it is not in obedience to a definite attitude toward life but as a matter of necessity, and they are always reluctant to leave the old and approach the new, and eagerly look forward to the time when they can go back. . . . [on the contrary, here] The mental outlook is one of adventure and free movement."[11]

2. "My next change was in the matter of my attitude toward the customs. . . . [In the old country] we seldom thought in terms of right or wrong of the deed, but rather the customary or non-customary. . . . I find that here the individual is left pretty much to his own judgment and that his first consideration is not custom so much as whether a thing is right or convenient or advantageous."[12]

3. "Not unlike this was the change which took place in my thought-life regarding the opinions of others. . . . [In the old country, we] were continually worrying over what this or that person had said or might say."[13]

4. "Another striking change which has taken place in my way of looking at life . . . is my conception of real as contrasted with what I might call inherited worth. . . . As I learned more and more of the simple unostentatiousness of American life, I came to love it, and I realized that it was after all the very highest attitude to take toward life. They place value here on a man's

11. Panunzio, *The Soul of an Immigrant*, 279–80.
12. Ibid., 280–81.
13. Ibid., 282–83.

own worth and character, be he the descendant of the humblest peasant or of the highest lord. [And here too] the people also emphasize progression in worth, not what a man has been, not even what he now is, but what he aims to be."[14]

5. "This leads me to the next distinctly American characteristic of life which I have come to adopt as a part of my philosophy and practice. I refer to the practicability of American ways . . . not the less idealistic, but rather a practical idealism." He found Italy to be idealistic, but in his experience people folded in the face of realities rather than getting on with it.[15]

6. "Here self-reliance and independence are cardinal virtues." "Poverty and pauperism are frowned upon . . . dependence in any walk of life is contrary to the highest form of thought and conduct in America. . . ."[16]

7. "Above all, these years in America have taught me the power and value of optimism. Here again the contrast between the old and the new is very striking. Our tendency was toward somber pessimism. . . . Added to this was the morbidness of our religious teachings."[17]

All this made him eager to naturalize and put up with many hardships in the process. And even when he was offered a chance, finally, to return to Italy and assume an important position, his new American identity triumphed and he went back to America and to pastoring after the war. Yet the ideas just listed above are not antithetical to the Protestantism that Panunzio likely encountered. In fact, these ideas could easily have been linked up with concomitant Protestant

14. Ibid., 284–86.
15. Ibid., 288.
16. Ibid., 289.
17. Ibid., 290–91.

theological doctrine. Yet, for all his religious education and time in church work, Panunzio never makes such connections.

For example, the Protestant belief in "sanctification," that is, growth in holiness, could be linked easily with his adopted American value of progression in worth. His admiration for the American idea that the worth of each individual is not based on heritage, could easily be linked with the doctrine that God judges the heart not the pedigree. Panunzio's attraction to American optimism could be likened to the Christian focus on hope in this life and the next. And clearly, the American value of self-reliance and independence has distinct similarities to the Protestant focus on each person making their own choice for God and salvation (in theological terms, Arminianism). One only has to review seminary curriculum through the years to realize that Panunzio heard these ideas while at Boston University Divinity School and likely many other places, for they are the heart of American Protestantism.

So what kind of conversion was this? Frankly, we cannot know the depth of Panunzio's conversion, the motivations and circumstances that made him enter the ministry, the content of his sermons, or how he understood his religious work. It would be tempting to say that perhaps the assimilationist ideas of his mentors got in the way of any religious concepts they may have wanted to communicate to him. But Panunzio was seminary trained and in those days, even more than now, theology, doctrine, and Bible were core elements of the education of a minister. Why Panunzio sought to explain his conversion in terms of American rather than Christian values may have been a strategy or judgment-call by this intelligent man. He was clearly writing to explain immigrants to long-time Americans and was writing during the height of anti-immigrant attitudes that led to the restrictive legislation of 1924.

But consider this: perhaps it was easier for Panunzio to maintain his hard-won optimism by retaining his cherished American principles and divorcing them from Christian theology. For it is possible that Panunzio had become disillusioned with the American church. There may be something like this between the lines, which Panunzio only hints at when he describes his difficulties in finding or keeping employment in what he considers "American" churches, that is, those outside of the immigrant mission or service posts. It is possible that Panunzio may have eventually left the ministry after too many experiences of prejudice against him as a foreigner. For, the book makes clear that his problems continued even after he was a good English speaker, a highly educated professional, and a committed citizen.

Some religious people might ask if Panunzio had ever really converted. They might ask whether he used the church as a way to become more American. Some may wonder if his mentors communicated assimilation more than theology. Perhaps his inherited disinterest in religion never left him. In my opinion, even answering these in the affirmative would not condemn Panunzio and his path. For this immigrant worked hard for his new homeland and contributed much, as his award at the 1940 World's Fair demonstrates. But no matter what the answers might be, it is clear that Panunzio's story of conversion is very different from the other Italian immigrants who converted to Protestantism and chose to tell about it.[18]

---

18. This chapter originally appeared in "My Conversion and Aspiration: A Comparative Case Study, Constantio Panuzio," in Italian Americana at the University of Rhode Island (Summer 2008).

10

Journeying before God with a Divided Heart

Theological Virtues in Light of the Postcolonial Migrations of Latvian Lutherans

Kristine Suna-Koro

There is hardly any doubt that today migration is among the topmost political, economic, and cultural problems across virtually all continents.[1] New and mostly dreadful headlines about capsized African migrant boats in the Mediterranean, about terrified and violated Central American children on the southern border of the United States, and about exhausted Syrian refugees—to name just the most obvious examples among countless others—populate the

1. I am grateful to Xavier University, Cincinnati, for supporting the research for this essay through the faculty development fellowship. With gratitude and joy I dedicate this chapter to my indefatigable friends at the Lutheran Immigration and Refugee Service (LIRS) as they have been carrying out the ministry of service, justice, and compassion among vulnerable migrants and refugees in the United States of America for over seventy-five years.

breaking news. What might not appear so self-evident is that migration is also a hallmark theological challenge of our time.

Theology is always already contextual, indeed uncannily so, despite the habitual tendencies to avoid this reality within the dominant versions of modern Western Christianity. Theological imagination and spirituality during every era of Christian history have struggled with peculiar, culturally and sociopolitically specific, challenges that have shaped the most profound questions, answers, upheavals, and breakthroughs in doctrine and practice. Today, in the era of a postcolonial and very convoluted globalization, the multifactorial problem of migration with its enormous toll of human suffering and previously unseen cultural hybridity emerges as the signature social reality that tests and contests the fundamental facets of Christian life, thought, worship, and mission. Migration is one of today's pivotal lenses through which the theological and ethical integrity of the Christian worldview and spiritual practice can be discerned *coram Deo* and *coram hominibus*. Hence, today, the theological dispositions and interpersonal responses to migration and, most importantly, the recognition of migrants as human persons created in the image of God, candidly gauge the veracity of Christian discipleship as rooted in the virtues of faith, hope, and love.

In what follows I will, first, reflect on some of the historical conundrums that contemporary global migration has spawned for Christian life and thought through the migration history of Latvian Lutherans in North America; second, I will offer a brief constructive reflection on migration focusing on two theological virtues, faith and love, from my perspective as a diasporic Latvian-American Lutheran theologian.

To the "New World":

The Early History of Latvian Lutheran Migration in North America (1880s–1930s)

Nestled on the southern rim of the Baltic Sea, between Scandinavia and the Slavic lands to the southeast, and neighbored by Lithuania and Estonia, today Latvia is an independent country of approximately 2 million inhabitants. They speak one of the remaining two living Baltic languages: Latvian. In its current post-Soviet era, Latvia is part of the geopolitical and cultural constellation known as "Eastern Europe." After several centuries of colonial subjugation and serfdom under both "core" and "subaltern" European and Eurasian imperial formations (medieval Latin Christian, German, Polish, Swedish, Czarist Russian, and Soviet), Latvia regained its sovereignty in 1991 during the collapse of the Soviet empire. Prior to the liberation of the whole "second world" when the hated Iron Curtain was torn down literally and culturally in the late 1980s, the colonial history of Latvia was positively interrupted only once.

Amidst the post–World War I bedlam and, as a result of the victory in the Latvian War of Liberation (*Brīvības Cīņas*) against the Russian Bolsheviks and the predominantly German West Russian Volunteer Army, Latvia emerged as a remarkably successful independent nation-state from 1918 to 1940 only to be invaded and colonized once again by the Stalinist Soviet empire in 1940 and then again by Nazi Germany in 1941.

But Latvian migration to the New World started even before the tumultuous and fateful events in the twentieth century. The story of the oldest Latvian Lutheran congregation in North America—the church that I served as a pastor some years ago—serves as a good illustration.

The first Latvians arrived in Philadelphia alongside other Eastern European immigrant groups during the Great Migration era in the 1880s. The newcomers desired to find freedom from the political, cultural, and economic exploitation that Latvia endured under the colonial rule of Czar Alexander III and his Russification policies in tandem with colonial oppression by the Baltic German nobility and its predominantly German-speaking Lutheran clergy.[2] Initially, in circumstances of unprecedented religious freedom and in light of their uninspiring religious experiences in the homeland, few immigrants hastened to get involved in institutionalized religious activities. However, with the active leadership of Davids Križe (1860–1953) who arrived in 1890, a new collaboration with a local Missouri Synod German church was initiated. As a result, a Latvian-speaking immigrant congregation was established in 1893: the Latvian (*Lettish*) Evangelical Lutheran Church of St. John in Philadelphia. As immigration grew, Latvian Lutheran churches were also established in hotbeds of Latvian migrants: Boston (1894), Baltimore (1896), and New York (1896). In the early twentieth century, Latvian Lutheran churches were founded in Cleveland, Chicago, and in what is now Alberta, Canada. These congregations among the Latvians who had spread out across the country were the fruits of the pioneering pastor of the Philadelphians, Rev. Ansis Rebane.[3]

A new wave of immigrants arrived in America after the Czarist regime in collaboration with the German colonial nobility crushed the 1905 Revolution. These immigrants were predominantly left-leaning political refugees.[4] Moderate numbers of Latvian immigrants

---

2. *85 Gadu Atceres Izdevums Filadelfijas Latviešu Ev. Lut. Sv. Jāņa Draudzei* (Commemorative Edition on the Occasion of 85th Anniversary of the Latvian Ev. Luth. Church of St. John), ed. Arnis Mikus (Philadelphia, 1978), n.p. I thank Dace Gulbis for assistance in obtaining a copy of this rare publication.
3. Ibid.

continued to arrive in North America and Brazil until the late 1920s when the stream of immigrants from Latvia practically ceased. During this period, the expected "melting pot" process of assimilation intertwined with a shrinking yet resilient desire to preserve the Latvian ethnic/national identity within an increasingly bilingual community. There was a chronic lack of Latvian-speaking pastors. Eventually, starting in 1937, even the church council minutes in Philadelphia were written in English.[5] This situation, however, would change dramatically right after World War II.

Under the Shadow of Totalitarianism and War: A Forced Exodus (1944–1950s)

As the Soviet forces advanced upon Latvia again in 1944, thousands of Latvians had to leave their homeland. Roughly 200 thousand were forced to leave by the Nazi authorities in late 1944.[6] Among those was the Archbishop of the Lutheran Church in Latvia, Teodors Grinbergs (1870–1962). Most fled due to the fear that the Stalinist terror of 1941 would be repeated under the new Soviet occupation. This, regrettably, was exactly what happened. The second Soviet occupation brought back an even more intensive terror, with widespread arrests, executions, torture, and mass deportations. One hundred thirty to one hundred fifty thousand Latvians found themselves as refugees, Displaced Persons (DPs), and POWs in various Western European countries at the end of World War II.[7] As the war ended, Latvia had lost at least 17 percent of its pre-war population to death in combat, the Holocaust, slave labor,

---

4. Daina Bleiere, Ilgvars Butulis, Inesis Feldmanis, Aivars Stranga, and Antonijs Zunda, *Latvijas vēsture: 20.gadsimts* (History of Latvia the 20th century) (Rīga: Jumava, 2015), 58–59.
5. Ibid.
6. Ilgvars Butulis and Antonijs Zunda, *Latvijas vēsture* (History of Latvia) (Rīga: Jumava, 2010), 148.
7. Bleiere et al., *Latvijas vēsture: 20. gadsimts*, 383.

concentration camps, and forced migration.[8] Starting in 1947, thousands of Latvian refugees arrived in the USA and Canada from the DP camps in Germany.

In 1945, one out of every six Lutherans in the world was a refugee or a DP.[9] In this context, American Lutheran leaders joined other faith communities in their common appeal to President Harry Truman to expand refugee resettlement. The intensity of migration grew significantly after the Displaced Persons Act was passed in 1948. For Latvians, this legislation opened the door for the greatest wave of migration to North America. This wave of immigrants was determined to survive, to remain hopeful, and to be ready to return to a free and restored Latvia one day, with their cultural/ethnic identity as pristine as possible. That was no easy task, as the Latvian Lutheran community soon discovered. The words of the archbishop of the exiled Latvians, Teodors Grinbergs, captured the core of the Latvian diasporic predicament: "Our enemies want to destroy us; our friends want to assimilate us; but we want to live."[10]

From Exiles to Reluctant Natives (1950s–1990s)

The Latvian diaspora in North America grew exponentially during the early 1950s when thousands of Latvian refugees were resettled in the United States and Canada. The Lutheran churches in particular became centers of passionate efforts to preserve and transmit the Latvian cultural tradition in a framework of what the majority of

---

8. Ibid. The demographic estimates vary on this subject. Some historical research suggests that Latvia lost 600–700,000 people in 1940–1945, that is, nearly 30 percent of the population. Ibid., 377.

9. Ralston Deffenbaugh, "Ethical Decision Points in the History of the Lutheran Immigration and Refugee Service," *Journal of Lutheran Ethics*, December 2008, accessed 22 May 2009, www.elca.org/What-We-Believe/Social-Issues/Journal-of-Lutheran-Ethics/Issues/December2008.

10. Quoted in Fritz Traugott Kristbergs, "The Lutheran Church and Latvian National Identity," accessed 1 Dec. 2013, http://www.baznica.ca/church/history/Latvian Church History.pdf http://www.baznica.ca/church/history/Latvian Church History.pdf

postwar immigrants called "the exile" (*trimda*) amidst unavoidable cultural and linguistic hybridization.

Gradually and reluctantly, as the five decades (1944–1991) of Soviet occupation dragged on, the children and grandchildren of the former refugees "Americanized" while the diaspora never completely lost hope for the liberation of Latvia. This group of migrants today constitutes the so-called "old diaspora." Resolutely anti-Communist and ardently nationalistic, this diasporic community has been deeply sympathetic to the plight of refugees, especially political refugees. Rooted in its own history of displacement and exile, the Latvian Lutheran community has faithfully supported the ministry of the Lutheran Immigration and Refugee Service (LIRS) with a particular dedication about refugee resettlement.

At the same time, the wartime and occupation traumas remained ever just beneath the surface. Certain strands of the diasporic life, including spiritual practices, became increasingly nostalgic, nativist, self-referential, and self-serving. In this context, one can still occasionally hear lamentations that the Latvians have suffered the worst possible injustices and remain the most unrecognized and betrayed victims of the twentieth-century political power plays.

Without at all discounting the horrors of the colonial and totalitarian oppression and genocidal violence in the twentieth-century history of Latvia, what is theologically and ethically disconcerting is that nowadays, the rather restricted diasporic focus on Latvia and Latvians in charitable and social ministries distances the diaspora from broader social justice concerns. Having become a relatively affluent group in the spectrum of the "new American center,"[11] the Latvian diaspora often disassociates from its own,

---

11. Tony Dokoupil, "Very Anxious: Is America Scared of Diversity?," accessed 1 Dec. 2013, http://www.newsdailytoday.com/very-anxious-is-america-scared-of-diversity-nbcnews-com-blog/.

relatively recent, migrant past. Hence the causes and consequences of contemporary migration, especially economic migration from Central America and other parts of the "third/developing world," are consistently seen with an *a priori* suspicion and apprehension. What makes this disposition rather ironic, however, is the fact that Latvia is currently experiencing its highest wave of economic emigration—ever!

After the Iron Curtain: The New Wave and Its Undercurrents (2000–2014)

In the aftermath of the Soviet occupation, some "old diaspora" members repatriated to Latvia as they had vowed for decades. Yet the aging majority and their descendants stayed put in North America despite patriotic dreams and promises in decades past. In the meantime, a new exodus from postcolonial and post-Soviet Latvia is underway as the country is trying to find its sea legs in the brave new world of ruthless global capitalism. Emigration has grown steadily since Latvia's entry into the European Union in 2004 but especially after the devastating 2008 "great recession," with record numbers of unemployed. Although precise numbers are hard to obtain, researchers believe that at least 213,000 people emigrated from Latvia in the first decade of the twenty-first century.[12]

According to the Ministry of Foreign Affairs estimates for 2011, there are approximately 96,000 persons of Latvian origin in the USA and roughly 26,000 in Canada.[13] Some of the "new wave" Latvian migrants fall into the category that American political discourse labels

12. "Ārvalstīs dzīvojošie latvieši uz mājām ik gadus atsūta 350 miljonus latu," accessed 18 Dec. 2013, http://www.delfi.lv/news/national/politics/arvalstis-dzivojosie-latviesi-uz-majam-ik-gadus-atsuta-350-miljonus-latu.d?id=42903426#ixzz2ns93JkeX. Latvia annually receives approximately 350 million Latvian Lats (now equaling 498 million Euros) in remittances from the worldwide diasporic communities.
13. Ibid.

as "illegal" or "undocumented." That, among other cultural reasons, is a source of friction between the "old" and "new" diaspora. Disagreements about essential cultural values, traditions, orthography, pronunciation, and religious and political views present a challenge to shaping "an inclusive community" that would welcome a broad spectrum of Latvians, with their historically and culturally diverse perspectives on Latvian identity and way of life.[14]

Currently the worldwide Latvian diaspora is estimated to be 350–400 thousand, with the majority currently residing in the UK, Ireland, and Russia. Belgian analysts have assessed that from 2008 to 2012 alone, Latvia lost 8.5 percent of its population due to emigration. That includes 19 percent of Latvians under the age of twenty-five.[15]

In light of these astounding numbers, the issue of migration for Latvians is currently a source of particularly acute ambiguity, fear, despair, frustration, and resentment. As people seeking economic survival and well-being for their families continue to emigrate, the fear of even poorer "foreigners" and "strangers" from Africa and Asia is growing exponentially in the homeland amidst concerns about the survival of the Latvian cultural identity and language. The racial undertones of the increasingly shrill debates on migration policy are hard to ignore, as is the fear of Muslim immigration in particular. Occasionally, the emigrants are perceived as traitors who betray their nation and culture in both homeland and the lands of the "old" diaspora. The need to emigrate for economic reasons is also often seen as shameful while political exile is assumed to have, as it were,

14. See Ilze Garoza's recent analysis of the Latvian schools (mostly associated with Latvian Lutheran churches) in North America, "Latviešu skolas Amerikā—ceļš uz iekļaujošu latviešu kopienu," accessed 23 Nov. 2013, http://www.latvianusa.com/content/view/940/1/.

15. "Pēdējo četru gadu laikā no Latvijas emigrējis katrs piektais jaunietis," *Kas jauns. Lv,* accessed 15 Dec. 2013, http://www.kasjauns.lv/lv/zinas/120531/pedejo-cetru-gadu-laika-no-latvijas-emigrejis-katrs-piektais-jaunietis.

an aura of gallantry and patriotism. Perhaps this is why many Latvian migrants see themselves as economic refugees and, with considerable resentment, hold the government's economic policies and corruption accountable for their heartbreaking resolution to emigrate.

Thus, the current Latvian sociocultural and psycho-spiritual *Zeitgeist* can be most aptly described as a rather paradoxical, perhaps ironic, state of living, with a divided heart when it comes to the painful topic of migration both in homeland and in diaspora. At present, every Latvian family has someone living in diaspora. Despite generating huge numbers of economic migrants and knowing intimately the dangers and ordeals of both political exile and economic migration, the attitudes toward other migrants, refugees, and asylum seekers both in homeland and in diaspora are deeply ambiguous and apprehensive. At times, they are straightforwardly racist and xenophobic. A similar attitude toward undocumented Central American migrants is rather common among the "old" North American Latvian diaspora, whose members do not hesitate to use undocumented labor, exploitatively employing Latvian nannies and housekeepers with the same questionable or (non)legal status.

It is as if their own ambiguity and frequently heartbreaking experiences are not capable of resonating with similar experiences and aspirations of the cultural, racial, and religious "others" on the undersides of the global circuit of neoliberal economic exploitation, with whom the Latvian migrants actually share more than they are usually willing to admit. Here the migrant heart is deeply divided, perhaps, ultimately and reluctantly against itself. Obviously, this is a complex and fascinating psycho-social phenomenon with intricate roots in (post)colonial trauma that I cannot address in full here due to the limitations of space. Suffice it to say that the familiar and often excruciating experience of exile and migration does not automatically engender solidarity and compassion toward other refugees and migrants. Sometimes it is precisely the pain of one's own uprootedness and the fear about one's own personal and communal survival that ingrains a sense of scarcity, endangerment, and permanent wounds despite apparent economic and professional success.

Such an outlook, generated precisely through the traumas of displacement, violence, and oppression, seems to absolve obsessive concerns for survival that issue in self-imposed isolation. It is as if the trials and tribulations of forced migration have wounded and thus distorted the soul of the community. Consequently, the community ventures dangerously close to becoming *incurvatus in se*, to use the Lutheran notion of painful entrapment of life and thought in one's own limited and distorted sense of reality and identity. In a rather lamentable way, the enduring experience of scarcity, the sense of unending woundedness and victimhood, and the deeply buried resentful ambivalence about being made into an "orphan people" by the modern colonial empires (*bāreņu tauta*, as the popular Latvian poet Māra Zālīte put it during the peak struggles of the Third Reawakening in 1988) come together in a truly infernal gridlock of unredeemed pain that precludes empathy and solidarity with equally long-suffering "others."

This state of affairs has a strong resonance with the socio-spiritual disposition that H. Richard Niebuhr described and decried in his analysis of the history of American "denominationalism." A similar dynamic also obtains in the context of American migration history. Groups of religiously neglected poor have historically tried to fashion a type of religious practice and community that corresponds to their distinctive needs. Yet as these groups of newcomers and underdogs "rise in economic scale under the influence of religious discipline" to eventually live "in the midst of a freshly acquired cultural respectability," they tend to "neglect the new poor succeeding them on the lower plane."[16] It is this dynamic that peculiarly characterizes the socio-spiritual landscape of the American history of migration. It continues to influence the contemporary attitudes of "natives" toward migrants and migration policies.

The experiences of deprivation and displacement, and the resulting psycho-spiritual gridlocks, are not unique to postcolonial migrant Latvians. They do show, however, the terrible and often invisible price that forced displacement can exact from the sinned-against who are relegated to the undersides of history, agency, and dignity and who then find it hard not to proliferate the same attitudes toward others. The fact that, historically speaking, all Americans except the Native American nations are colonizers and/or migrants and refugees is often beyond the conscious awareness of those who might themselves be just a generation or two removed from their own migrant ancestors.

It is in this context—among others—that a meaningful and faithful theological vision on migration, *coram Deo* and *coram hominibus*, is to unfold. What becomes of faith and love in light of lives steeped in migrant experience and yet lived before God with divided hearts? In the concluding part of the essay I offer a few reflections on the theological virtues in the context of migration from a Lutheran perspective.

Migration and Theological Virtues

Faith as Daring Confidence

For Lutherans, an effective relation between the principle of justification by faith and everyday living has habitually been a somewhat "neuralgic problem"[17] according to Eric Gritsch. Historically, Guillermo Hansen argues, the Lutheran tradition has

---

16. H. Richard Niebuhr, *The Social Sources of Denominationalism* (New York: Meridian, 1959), 28.

been "plagued" by "the dualistic hiatus between justification by faith and social justice."[18] Cynthia Moe-Lobeda warns that much European and Euro-American Lutheranism has pervasively misread Luther's sociohistorically limited yet passionate concern for justice, even while she acknowledges and struggles with Martin Luther's deep ambivalence and inconsistencies regarding the connection of justification, justice, and just who ought to be recognized as the neighbor that Luther so adamantly advised his followers to love. As a result, Moe-Lobeda observes, "Lutheranism has tended to claim the comfort of justification by faith alone, while eschewing its radical ethical implications. This predicament of moral passivity has countless social structural and theological roots."[19]

These merited critiques of the Lutheran tradition encourage a circumspect approach to the theological challenges migration presents today. The locus of enunciation for my brief reflections here is the American—and Latvian, seemingly incommensurable as these geopolitical realities may appear!—context of being the destinations and "host" societies of the global migration flows. Even though I am a migrant, a hyphenated and naturalized American, it is obvious that today we live in a remarkably different world than in the aftermath of World War II when one out of every six Lutherans in the world was a refugee or DP. Lutherans—"natives" and diasporas alike—are mostly to be found among the host communities. Hence the most "neuralgic" theological questions are, I believe, those that spring up among the host communities. Granted, some communities, like Latvia, might also live with an existentially divided heart as they

---

17. Eric W. Gritsch, "Lutheran Theology and Everyday Life," in *The Gift of Grace: The Future of Lutheran Theology*, ed. Niels Henrik Gregersen, Bo Holm, Ted Peters, and Peter Widmann (Minneapolis: Fortress Press, 2004), 264–65.

18. Guillermo Hansen, "Reconciliation and Forgiveness: A Response to Ambrose Moyo," in *The Gift of Grace*, 159.

19. Cynthia D. Moe-Lobeda, *Healing a Broken World: Globalization and God* (Minneapolis: Fortress Press, 2002), 165.

hover in anxious and ambivalent spaces in what used to be called the "second world," and simultaneously produce outgoing flows of migration. In these historical circumstances, how could we perceive the quickening and transformative operation of faith?

Taking heed from Luther, faith is a verb: faith is a work of God, through the Holy Spirit, "a living, busy, active, mighty thing" percolating in us and bringing a radical transformation.[20] Faith makes us no less than "altogether different men (*sic*)," and it is a confidence in God's grace so sure, living, and daring that the "believer would stake his (*sic*) life on it a thousand times."[21] If this grace is anything more than purely abstract, forensic, poetic, theoretical, and rhetorical alone, then it facilitates a bold leap toward divine generosity having the last and decisive word. As things now stand, often economic reasons inculcate in us the existential sense of scarcity and the seemingly unquestionable assumptions that only ruthless competition for natural resources, power, and goods can allow us to flourish. In this worldview of zero-sum game, of push and shove, migrants are perceived to take away from us what limited goods are available, be they purely economic or cultural. Here otherness is not just otherness; it is always already strangeness, endangerment, and competition.

Now, faith as a divinely enabled virtuous disposition and as a living and daring vitality can indwell and reorient lives trapped in experiences of woundedness, imaginaries of scarcity, and projections of fear. It can open toward the divine generosity of grace that is always and everywhere enough for all. Of course, in the neocolonial world of globalized capitalism, this view can only be a matter of faith at its most countercultural and counter-instinctual level. Here

---

20. Martin Luther, "Preface to the Epistle of St. Paul to the Romans (1522, Revised 1546)," in *Martin Luther's Basic Theological Writings*, 3rd edition, ed. William R. Russell (Minneapolis: Fortress Press, 2012), 79.
21. Ibid.

Luther's "altogether different" should probably be taken almost literally.

Faith is a living and daring confidence in God's grace: and for this sort of disposition and comportment *coram Deo* there is a fitting counterpart, *coram hominibus*—something that has always been quite an allergic theme in Lutheran circles. Namely, this faith is doing good works incessantly, even "before the question is asked"; and "whoever does not do such works, however, is an unbeliever."[22] Notwithstanding Luther's own racial, social, and religious prejudices as to who counts as "our neighbor" and thus a God-given recipient of such works, his words are self-critical and afflictively inclusive. It is "impossible to separate works from faith," yet is also impossible to do good and minister to "everyone."[23] Among the people most in need of ministry—so as to be given what African American theologians call "somebodiness"—are today's migrants and refugees. These are estranged and made strange by wars, impoverishment, religious violence, gender-based abuses, and cultural prejudice.

Moreover, as the Judeo-Christian tradition has reiterated, despite its own colonizing and crusading delusions, the Most High, from Exodus to Matthew 25, has a particular concern for the trinity of vulnerability: orphans, widows, and strangers. Perhaps here is a ground for an often-overlooked solidarity: after all, precisely those who see themselves as living so redemptively close to God acquire a spiritual awareness that they are, in truth, also strangers, foreigners, sojourners, and exiles in this world (1 Pet. 2:11)! In the words of Carmelo Santos, "The Lutheran understanding of grace opens up a space where we can be honest with ourselves about our sin and our brokenness and the concrete expression of such sinfulness and brokenness in the form of unconscious prejudice. . . ."[24]

22. Ibid.
23. Ibid.

Love: Embodied Eschatology for the Groaning and Afflicted

Migration may feel like affliction to those who are forced to migrate but increasingly also for those who now host the millions of migrants and refugees. The burdens as well as the blessings of migration are shared, even though unevenly and often unwillingly. As it escalates, migration is a defining facet of the present postcolonial world—a world seemingly in an ever-accelerating transition toward a future that no one can predict, and many fear, but we all together, migrants or not, will have to share.

The historical reasons for the current phenomenon of global migration are intrinsically rooted in modern Western colonialism and the economic interdependence that underpinned globalization long before jet travel and Twitter. For many in the West it is still hard to fathom that there is a marked connection between their own colonial histories and mass migration today. But history cannot be undone even if it can be silenced, distorted, or avoided.

The Lutheran tradition holds that human afflictions and lament are seen by God for what they truly are. And God "cannot disregard the voices and the groaning of the afflicted."[25] Precisely amidst these voices, faith acquires a realistic and truly incarnate touch as it crosses the threshold toward another equally inconvenient and countercultural virtue: love.

Luther did not indulge in mapping out elaborate eschatological visions of paradise.[26] What matters is rather the efficacy of the double helix of faith and love (yes, works!). Faith becomes incarnate in love;

---

24. Carmelo Santos, "Exploring the Role of Unconscious Bias in the Immigration Debate and the Transformative Power of the Church," *Journal of Lutheran Ethics* (20 December 2013). http://www.elca.org/JLE/Articles/27.

25. Martin Luther, "Genesis 21:17," in *Luther's Works, Vol. 4*, ed. Jaroslav Pelikan and Helmut T. Lehmann (St. Louis: Concordia, 1986), 57.

26. Hans-Martin Barth, *The Theology of Martin Luther: A Critical Assessment* (Minneapolis: Fortress Press, 2013), esp. ch. 14.

and love becomes incarnate in actions vis-à-vis our neighbors and not just in our pious imagination. The love in question here is the love, as it were, in trenches; as Luther argues:

> Here faith is truly active through love . . . it finds expression in works of the freest service, cheerfully and lovingly done . . . I will therefore give myself as a Christ to my neighbor, just as Christ offered himself to me. . . .[27] The command to love your neighbor is equal to the greatest commandment to love God, and that what you do or fail to do for your neighbor means doing the same to God. If you wish to serve Christ and to wait on him, very well, you have your sick neighbor close at hand.[28]

The point here is not that Luther's double helix of faith and love is ferociously honest about the most strenuous spiritual and ethical virtues and practices of Christian spirituality. The point is to contextualize Luther's own acutely contextual understanding of love.

What does this love mean vis-à-vis migrants and refugees? Cherishing Luther's passionate advocacy for *imitatio Christi* through enacted love toward our neighbors, the individualistic slant[29] of Luther's vision of love must be transcended. It must be deepened and enlarged through a belated theological recognition that the personal converges with the social, the cultural, and the political. This is especially true today when the sinned-against in our world include the vast majority of migrants. The double helix of faith and love becomes incarnate and thus a true *imitatio Christi* only when woven into this intricate and enduring poly-helix of created life in all its constitutive dimensions and not in the splendid isolation of disembodied conscience, spirituality, or doctrinal rhetoric.

27. Martin Luther, "The Freedom of a Christian," in *Martin Luther's Basic Theological Writings*, trans. Timothy Lull (Minneapolis: Fortress Press, 1989), 617, 619.
28. Martin Luther, "Whether One May Flee from a Deadly Plague," in *Martin Luther's Basic Theological Writings*, 747.
29. Barth, *The Theology of Martin Luther*, 391.

Migration, especially where it is lived and endured as structurally enforced affliction, challenges all and any Christian words about love of God and neighbor. Lutheranism has to be acutely aware that historically it has "been part of systems and structures that have favored certain ethnicities over others"[30] in very problematic, indeed, racist, ways. In a Lutheran context, it also challenges its whole theological edifice and its historically characteristic passivity toward the social dimensions of economic and cultural justice. As Moe-Lobeda summarizes,

> The moral passivity of many Lutheran communities stems also from the theological tendency to disassociate salvation from public moral life. Key elements of that disconnect include the bifurcation of the person as justified individual and the person as historical social being, the dissociation of social righteousness and righteousness before God, the failure to take seriously the social justice effects of justification, and the disconnection of Jesus Christ savior from Jesus Christ the transformer of the moral life.[31]

Conclusion

To conclude: the everyday life, at least as it is lived in the global consumerist "first" world, is invisibly yet by now inescapably dependent on the labor of unappreciated, exploited, and vilified migrants. For many of those who are forced to migrate, through legal or illegitimate channels, entering the same political and economic system—callous and hypocritical as it—is often the only viable means of survival.

Living by faith, Lutheran faith communities stand before God and fellow humans—created in the image of God as equally responsive

---

30. Kirsi Stjerna, "Demons of Violence: Searching for Theological Responses with Luther," *Journal of Lutheran Ethics* 13, no. 7 (November 2013): 7, accessed 20 Nov. 2013, http://www.elca.org/JLE/Articles/19.
31. Moe-Lobeda, *Healing a Broken World*, 166.

and equally responsible. But many communities and individuals also stand under the shadow of the historical Lutheran ambivalence on social justice. This occurs even while particular Lutheran bishops and prominent theologians, as well as ministries such as the Lutheran Immigration and Refugee Service and its partners, boldly serve and advocate for the most vulnerable among migrants and refugees. And so today, under the shadow of ambivalent history and in the challenging milieu of migration, the virtue of faith must boomerang back to its uncomfortably practical and frequently unheeded counterpart of love. Love, as well as justice, is not exclusively a matter of privatized pious interiority. Nor is the love of stranger somehow a matter of "externals" (*cooperatio in externis*) as certain anachronistic theological inertias continue to intimate. Precisely as a *theological* virtue, love is irrevocably a matter of intratrinitarian and incarnational relations; but equally, and analogically, it is also a matter of (theo)politics, (theo)economics, and even ecclesiastical politics and doctrinal integrity!

Amidst competing truth claims, goals, and values, we all, migrants and "natives," desire the same thing: to recall the words of the archbishop of Latvian exiles and refugees, Teodors Grinbergs, we all want to live. But living together in the world increasingly polarized by scarcity, uncertainty, and competition will be disheartening without discerning what it means to live together in love.

PART III

First Americans and First Immigrants

11

Native American Hospitality and Generosity

Old Symbols of American Welcome

Randy Woodley

"The worst thing that can be said about a Navaho is to say, He acts as if he has no relatives."[1]

Native Americans like to joke about any immigration policy after 1491 being "too little, too late." In spite of jokes that attempt to subvert the painful colonial history between white settlers and America's host peoples, immigration policies promising mythical opportunities, equality, and freedom for all reveal a double standard when confronted with the historical realities. One of those realities was brought home to me recently on a family visit to New York City, where we viewed America's foremost symbol of welcome to foreigners, the Statue of Liberty, with its famous inscription:

---

1. F. R. Kluckhohn and F. L. Strodtbeck, *Variations in Value Orientations* (Evanston, IL: Row, Peterson, 1961), 320.

The New Colossus

Not like the brazen giant of Greek fame,
With conquering limbs astride from land to land;
Here at our sea-washed, sunset gates shall stand
A mighty woman with a torch, whose flame
Is the imprisoned lightning, and her name
Mother of Exiles. From her beacon-hand
Glows world-wide welcome; her mild eyes command
The air-bridged harbor that twin cities frame.
"Keep, ancient lands, your storied pomp!" cries she
With silent lips. "Give me your tired, your poor,
Your huddled masses yearning to breathe free,
The wretched refuse of your teeming shore.
Send these, the homeless, tempest-tost to me,
I lift my lamp beside the golden door!"

Symbols and heritage sites such as the Statue of Liberty are powerful markers that sustain our national myths. National symbols serve to point the masses to the values a nation considers important to its future, even if they are invented from a dubious past. In the case of the Statue of Liberty, the myth of welcoming the stranger to America upholds false notions of unequaled opportunity, social equality, and personal freedom. This is not to disregard the millions of immigrants who have found citizenship in America, but it is a correction to the myth. In order for the myth to reflect the historic reality more accurately, a final line should have been added to the poem: "If they can become white."

America, the nation-state, came into existence as a result of illegitimate claims by Western Europeans on already-occupied land.[2] Part of the strategy of attempted genocide, calculated at many different levels, sought to caricaturize Native Americans as

---

2. North American population estimates at the time of first contact were over 100 million. In 1491 more people lived in the Americas than in Europe; see Charles C. Mann, "1491," *The Atlantic*, (March 2002), accessed 18 May 2014, http://www.theatlantic.com/magazine/archive/2002/03/1491/302445/.

undignified savages who were not using the land (according to European notions of land use). The new colonies ignored Native American claims to the land, and they enacted policies of genocide and forced cultural assimilation.[3] America's host tribes were eventually enslaved to work the land that was stolen from them,[4] and later, after an approximately 90 percent population loss, mainly caused by disease, the American aboriginals were replaced by West Africans.[5] Similar to the Native American–West African exchange, exploitation of underpaid labor still continues in America today. Official and unofficial structures promote policies and practices used to exploit the "less desirable" ethnic populations such as African Americans in the prison-industrial complex, Latino migrant workers, Latino and Asian sweatshop workers, and Native American and other minorities serving in the military. The historical reality of these efforts has created a settler-state based on white supremacy. Such assertions are difficult to hear because they buck the prevailing myth. The choice between myth and reality are made clear by Robert Jensen:

> It can be difficult for white Americans to recognize that white supremacy is the rot at the core of the project and always has been. The country's formation, economic expansion, and imperial endeavors are inextricably intertwined with racism. White society's version of U.S.

3. Two examples of illegitimate European dominance include the papal decree *Inter Caetera*, the bull of 1493 issued by Pope Alexander VI stating, "any Christian king, prince or nation could 'discover' and assume dominion over lands previously known to non-Christians but unknown to Christians" (Steven T. Newcomb, *Pagans in the Promised Land: Decoding the Doctrine of Christian Discovery* [Golden, CO: Fulcrum, 2008], 125). Cf. John Winthrop, who made a law annulling any Native claims to the land: "The Indians," he said, "had not 'subdued' the land, and therefore had only a 'natural' right to it, but not a 'civil right.' A 'natural right' did not have legal standing" (Howard Zinn, *History Is a Weapon: A People's History of the United States* [New York: Harper, 2005], 13, 14).

4. Alan Gallay, *The Indian Slave Trade: The Rise of the English Empire in the American South (1670–1717)* (New Haven: Yale University Press, 2002).

5. Charles C. Mann notes that "more than fifty of the first colonial villages in New England were located on Indian villages emptied by disease" (*1491: New Revelations of the Americas before Columbus* [New York: Alfred A. Knopf, 2005], 56).

history is weighed down by narcissistic fantasies of innocence, entangled in a self-serving web of stories of nobility. Those denials of the past are critical to those who cannot honestly confront the present.[6]

Two Choices

The path to becoming culturally and/or racially white is only an option for certain ethnic groups. Those who cannot or will not take the path to American Whiteness are considered to be the "other" (see e.g., Said, Levinas, Buber, et al.). Americans have a seemingly innate sense of awareness of the kinds of peoples the nation considers "outsiders," "outliers," "oriental," and "other." It should be stated that the roles of the "other" are not all the same. Cherokee scholar and activist Andrea Smith notes:

> . . . white supremacy is constituted by separate and distinct, but still interrelated, logics. I would argue that the three primary logics of white supremacy in the US context include: (1) slaveability/anti-black racism, which anchors capitalism; (2) genocide, which anchors colonialism; and (3) orientalism, which anchors war.[7]

While Smith makes an effective argument for each case, my point is to use the larger category of the "other" to include all those who cannot or will not assimilate into the white-supremacist nation-state we call America. One of the commonalities is the ability of each group to hold up a national historical mirror that points out the hypocrisy of the national American myth of liberty and justice for all.[8] Without a constant look in the mirror, policies that formulate structures based on white supremacy will continue to exploit the "other" and make fair immigration policies unattainable. Those

6. Robert Jensen, *The Heart of Whiteness* (San Francisco: City Lights, 2005), 29, 30.

7. Andrea Smith, "Indigeneity, Settler Colonialism, White Supremacy," in *Global Dialogue* 12, no. 2 (Summer/Autumn 2010), accessed 17 May 2014, http://www.worlddialogue.org/content.php?id=488.

8. See Ronald Takaki, *A Different Mirror: A History of Multicultural America* (New York: Back Bay Books, 1993).

outside the favor of empire can even become complicit in supporting international trade agreements and immigration policies that prop up the illegitimate nation-state. In the case of U.S. aboriginals, these policies also work against long-established Indigenous notions of sovereignty. Protecting borders and building walls on Indigenous lands, like on the lands of the Tohono O'odham or Lipan Apache, go against long-held Native American values of hospitality as well as the values of those Indigenous peoples on the other side of the border.

In protest of Arizona's SB 1070 law, Native American activists occupied the Border Patrol office on 21 May 2010. Included in their record of occupation was the following:

> On this day people who are indigenous to Arizona join with migrants who are indigenous to other parts of the Western Hemisphere in demanding a return to [the] traditional indigenous value of freedom of movement for all people. Prior to the colonization by European nations (Spaniards, English, French) and the establishment of the [E]uropean settler state known as the United States and the artificial borders it and other [E]uropean inspired nation states have imposed; indigenous people migrated, traveled and traded with each other without regard to artificial black lines drawn on maps. U.S. immigration policies dehumanize and criminalize people simply because [of] which side of these artificial lines they were born on. White settlers whose ancestors have only been here at most for a few hundred years have imposed these policies of terror and death on "immigrants" whose ancestors have lived in this hemisphere for tens of thousands of years, from time immemorial.[9]

The protestors demanded:

> An end to border militarization
> The immediate repeal of SB1070 and 287g
> An end to all racial profiling and the criminalization of our communities
> No ethnic cleansing or cultural genocide

9. Andrea Smith, "Indigeneity, Settler Colonialism, White Supremacy," in *Racial Formation in the Twenty-first Century*, ed. Daniel HoSang, Oneka LaBennett, and Laura Pulido (Berkeley: University of California Press, 2012), 86.

No border patrol encroachment/sweeps on sovereign native land
No deportations
No raids
No ID-verification
No checkpoints
Yes to immediate and unconditional regularization ("legalization") of all people
Yes to human rights
Yes to dignity
Yes to respect
Yes to respecting Indigenous People[']s inherent right of migration.[10]

As Smith points out, "the occupiers' statement indicates they identify the problem not as migration, but the nation-state and its reliance on control and ownership of territory."[11]

Another Model

The historic precedence of hospitality in America has direct implications concerning America's current immigration concerns. America before the arrival of Western European immigrants was far more diverse and perhaps far more tolerant than it has been since.[12] Hospitality to strangers has always been a widespread value among America's First Nations and part of what I refer to as Native American Harmony Way constructs. Native American values concerning hospitality are in essence parallel to the hospitality injunctions in the Hebrew Scriptures that promote the hospitality ethic of shalom.[13] There are numerous historic examples of America's indigenes extending at least an initial welcome to white settlers. Anthropologist Carl Starkloff notes the historic practice of hospitality among Native

10. Ibid.
11. Ibid., 87.
12. By "confronting the present," I am not presenting North American Native values as pristine or utopian but simply sharing another established American way of looking at immigration.
13. Randy S. Woodley, *Shalom and the Community of Creation: An Indigenous Vision* (Grand Rapids: Eerdmans, 2012), 1–24.

Americans. On reading the various accounts and monographs by explorers and anthropologists, what strikes one is the almost universal hospitality shown by Indian tribes, especially to their white visitors. It is quite remarkable, as described in David Bushnell's writings about explorers and missionaries among

> the Siouan, Algonquian, and Caddoan tribes west of the Mississippi. . . . There are practically no examples of inhospitality or harsh treatment rendered to Whites. On the contrary, the tribal leaders went out of their way to receive these visitors as special guests. There seems to have been a conviction among the Indians, at least until the middle of the 19th century, that they and the newcomers could share the land equally, even if the land was sometimes thought to be the tribe's sacred inheritance.[14]

Starkloff goes on to say that among Native Americans today, "Generosity . . . is practiced . . . almost to excess."[15]

In many places throughout Indian Country, I have observed what are considered by Euro-Americans to be exceptional acts of hospitality and generosity that are practiced normatively by First Nations every day. My own experience is reflected below:

> Many years ago I moved to Western Oklahoma but I had no relatives there. Libby, the woman who would soon become my adopted mother, had lost a son to cancer the year prior and the Creator had shown her that at the right time, another son would arrive. I became that expected son. I was adopted by her family, and later by another family, as a son. A few months later I was also adopted as a nephew by a Kiowa/Comanche couple and then as a brother into a Cheyenne family. Many years later, I became a brother to an Arapahoe man. In my own tradition, I have adopted an elder brother and I affectionately refer to young men and women learning from me as nephew or niece. The formal and informal adoption process among Native Americans is an extension of a deep and profound sense of hospitality to others that dates back into time immemorial.[16]

14. Carl F. Starkloff, *The People of the Center: American Indian Religion and Christianity* (New York: Crossroad, 1974), 88, 89.
15. Ibid., 89.

The making of relatives is the generous act of giving people a place and sense of belonging in a strange land. My experience has been that no one stays a stranger long among Native Americans. If there were some way to magnify the First Nations spirit of hospitality to a national level, I think we would produce more lenient immigration policies.

America's Hospitable History

The movement among America's Indigenous peoples is always extending the borders of relationships to those with no or little means and little bearing in the new land. This is especially true concerning strangers. The mythic vision of "bloodthirsty" Indians waiting to ambush the passerby is perhaps not completely unfounded in every single case, but it was actually quite rare. Instead, history is replete with examples of Native American people welcoming the stranger, sharing their resources, helping them to get established, and protecting them during perilous times.

Beginning with the first encounters, Indigenous men and women welcomed Columbus and his sailors at the shores of their home in the Caribbean. The Arawaks greeted them with food and gifts. Columbus records this in his log:

> They . . . brought us parrots and balls of cotton and spears and many other things, which they exchanged for the glass beads and hawks' bells. They willingly traded everything they owned. . . . They were well-built, with good bodies and handsome features. . . . They do not bear arms, and do not know them, for I showed them a sword, they took it by the edge and cut themselves out of ignorance. They have no iron. Their spears are made of cane. . . . They would make fine servants. . . . With fifty men we could subjugate them all and make them do whatever we want.[17]

16. Woodley, *Shalom and the Community of Creation*, 154.
17. Zinn, *A People's History*, 3

The Arawaks of the Bahama Islands were much like the Indigenes on the mainland, who, as noted by European observers again and again, were known for their hospitality and their generosity. The Indians, Columbus reported, "are so naive and so free with their possessions that no one who has not witnessed them would believe it. When you ask for something they have, they never say no. To the contrary, they offer to share with anyone."[18] Columbus noted:

> And of all the infinite universe of humanity, these people are the most guileless, the most devoid of wickedness and duplicity, the most obedient and faithful to their native masters and to the Spanish Christians whom they serve. They are by nature the most humble, patient, and peaceable, holding no grudges, free from embroilments, neither excitable nor quarrelsome. These people are the most devoid of rancors, hatreds, or desire for vengeance of any people in the world. . . . They are also poor people, for they not only possess little but have no desire to possess worldly goods. For this reason they are not arrogant, embittered, or greedy. They are very clean in their persons, with alert, intelligent minds, docile and open to doctrine, very apt to receive our holy Catholic faith, to be endowed with virtuous customs, and to behave in a godly fashion. . . . Some of the secular Spaniards who have been here for many years say that the goodness of the Indians is undeniable and that if this gifted people could be brought to know the one true God they would be the most fortunate people in the world.[19]

Perhaps the second most notable case of welcome from America's First Nations occurred in seventeenth-century New England where the Plymouth colony found eventual welcome, first by Samoset and then by Tisquantum (Squanto), whose village had been wiped out by disease. In spite of the hardship of losing his family and friends to diseases brought by the newcomers, Tisquantum welcomed them and taught them the technology needed to survive, and even thrive,

18. Ibid.
19. Bartolomé de Las Casas, *The Devastation of the Indies: A Brief Account of the Devastation of the Indies* (Baltimore: Johns Hopkins University Press, 1992), 28, 29.

in what they understood as a hostile environment. During the early years, New England Native Americans were often a continual help to the pilgrims.

Example of Giving Today

Without knowledge of the words contained in the Christian Scriptures, the Indigenous peoples of America acted out the scriptural injunction to be hospitable to the stranger. Constant visiting among friends and relatives was and is still a hallmark of Native American communities. No matter the economic state of the host, no guest ever goes away hungry from an Indian home. At pow wows and other Indigenous American social functions, complete strangers are often given special honor and gifts. But values of hospitality and generosity may be waning, according to Dakota Sioux pastor Fern Cloud.

How are strangers treated? One of our seven rites is the making of a relative. We really believe that in our way of *wo' dakota*, no one should ever be alone. Someone would take you into their family and adopt you. But today, after having that generosity burned so many times, we are not as open as we once were. We need to tap into this again and make others our family, sharing kinship, living together, and supporting each other.[20]

Reverend Cloud connects hospitality and generosity to the Dakota Harmony Way construct, to the insistence that no one should be alone. Alone, people have no protection. Alone, people have no fellowship. Alone, the tribe or clan does not exist, and harmony cannot exist either. Hospitality and generosity are the natural economy in Indigenous community. A few years ago I was dealing with Native American Harmony Way constructs for my Ph.D. dissertation. When Native American respondents had to describe

---

20. Randy Woodley, *"The Harmony Way": Integrating Indigenous Values within Native North American Theology and Mission* (Ph.D. dissertation, Asbury Theological Seminary, 2010), 274.

186

their understanding of "The Harmony Way" without any prompts, about one-third of them made a direct reference to either generosity or hospitality.

One young man specifically connected generosity to the hospitality he saw in his home growing up. He said he remembered watching his parents sending all visitors away from their home with food, water, and some money. The same person mentioned that his parents always gave what was dear to them, rather than something they valued little, and because of his parents' example, he continues those traditions today.

> I was taught that by my mom and dad. At their funerals people talked about them and I could see how they were valued and the things we were taught were valued. Like when an elder comes over, you get up and get them what they need and when a middle-aged person came you treat them a little different. And no one ever left our home without some food and water and a little money to help them on their way . . . and we were taught to give our best not some old hand-me-down thing we don't want anymore.[21]

Generosity of spirit is shown in this way. Indian people are taught not just to share, but to give their best.

As mentioned earlier, as part of an extended family, I was adopted as a son by an elderly Kiowa couple. I was taught by my Kiowa father that any gift you give from your heart is a good gift. He also taught me that among the Kiowa, if someone compliments you on a piece of jewelry, a hat, or some other object you value then it is your obligation to give it to them, without begrudging the act. Gifts among Native Americans are an act of the heart, regardless of their monetary value. The practice is an exercise in nonmaterialism. Some might call Native American hospitality and generosity radical

---

21. Ibid., 234.

when what a guest desires becomes more important than the material possessions of the host.

It is a cultural norm throughout the United States and Canada for Native Americans to have "Give-aways." Native Americans in the Northwest had a similar practice called a "Potlatch." I have observed Give-ways in many places, with only slight variations. Basically, a Give-away is a formal public ceremony where an individual or family gives away any number of items to others. The Give-away items may be expensive or not; they may be personally valuable or not. I have seen horses, saddles, rifles, baskets, blankets, and many other gifts given. The gifts may even include sacred items such as drums or Eagle feathers. The gifts may be given to strangers, friends, elders, those in need, or other honored guests, and so on, but they are usually not supposed to be given to one's own relatives.

The one thing that all Give-aways have in common is that they are given by, and not to, the person who is being honored. The idea is that it is the privilege of the person being honored to give things away. The honored person shows generosity by sharing his or her honor with others in this way, thereby spreading the honor around. Give-aways are routinely done at certain times in Native American culture. These include a dancer's first-time entry into the pow wow arena; the making of a new chief; when a person is given an Indian name; and other celebratory occasions. My wife and I had a Give-away at our wedding and at my ordination into Christian ministry among other times. Although the Give-away is a formalized method of generosity, the spirit of generosity of the formal ceremony pervades Native American communities even today.

One of the respondents on my dissertation survey described giving in this way: "Give away the best that you have, do not let anyone know you are giving your best away."[22] Prior to reading this

22. Ibid., 235.

statement I had not stopped to remind myself that there is also a quiet, almost secretive way in which Native Americans express generosity. Give-aways are always done in public but I can recall numerous times I have observed and practiced the alternative, very private side to individual generosity among Native Americans.

There is a place in the Indian community for public ceremony and there is a place for subtler giving, and this characteristic differs from tribe to tribe. I have seen people give without any recognition, by leaving a gift in my home after a visit. More often I have seen straightforward and unencumbered giving when a person simply extends their hand with a gift and expects nothing except perhaps a handshake back. I have also observed occasions when acts of kindness are done for someone in need, especially for elders, and all the while no one would know who did it. I have observed boxes of food being left on a person's porch, cut wood for the winter, and yards cleaned—all without anyone knowing who expressed the generosity. What all these forms of secret or quiet giving have in common is simple generosity from the heart, without fanfare or expectation.

Hospitality and the Future of Borders

The problem of America the nation-state is not its immigrants but white supremacy and the corresponding values that prop up hostile and egregious policies that keep others out. From an Indigenous American perspective, these policies of unwelcome defy millennia-old values of hospitality; they erode the sovereignty of Indigenous peoples; and they perpetuate a historic bias toward white supremacy.

This bias was penned in 1899 by Rudyard Kipling in a now-infamous poem reflecting the imperial-mission. Titled "The White Man's Burden," the poem points out the expectation, almost obligation, of the white race to enlighten the rest of the world through a bestowal of the "gifts" of white civilization. Others today are challenging the myth of white superiority:

> Here's where that discussion of history leads: Conversational accounts of U.S. history tend to treat racism as a stain on an otherwise healthy—some would say divinely inspired—society. The United States, according to this mythology, was born out of a desire for freedom and would become both the model of, and vehicle for, freedom around the world. The treatment of non-white peoples was an aberration that would come to be fixed in time, as white people understood their non-white brothers and sisters to be deserving of that same freedom.[23]

The challenge of American immigration policies goes right to the heart of the neoliberal agenda (e.g., the North American Free Trade Agreement [NAFTA]) and to the core of conservative corporatism. For immigration to become more just in America, these socioeconomic standards must continue to be challenged. Cooperatives and alternative communities must serve as examples to the wider public that the historic "American Way" is not the best way to live in the twenty-first century. Solidarity and consensus must be advanced among such groups at the grassroots level as we work together on eroding current unjust immigration policies and enact new policies that provide both security and a spirit of hospitality. Americans must be reminded that welcoming the stranger is nothing new to America, but a long-held value. Sharing our natural resources should not be privatized. Blessings that come from the earth, such as food and water, should not be commodified and kept away from foreigners, but should be used in creative, more cooperative ways.

The Cherokee concept of redistribution of wealth was in direct opposition to the individualistic materialism found in dominant American cultural values. Remarkably, the Cherokees, even after removal from their homelands, were able to retain their communal

---

23. Jensen, *The Heart of Whiteness*, 29.

values. Widely known as their critic, Senator Henry Dawes, after touring Indian Territory in 1887, described the Cherokees in the following way:

> The head chief told us that there was not a family in the whole nation that had not a home of its own. There is not a pauper in that nation, and the nation does not owe a dollar. It built its own capitol . . . and built its schools and hospitals. Yet the defect of the system was apparent. They have got as far as they can go, because they hold their land in common. . . . There is no selfishness, which is at the bottom of civilization. Till these people will consent to give up their lands, and divide them among their citizens so that each can own the land he cultivates, they will not make much progress.[24]

The Cherokee cultural understanding of sharing and generosity reflected similarities to other Native North American nations. Native American and Western worldviews concerning individualism and materialism are in stark contrast. Among America's Indigenous peoples, the land produces abundance for the purpose of sharing with the community. In the white settler worldview, natural resources are seen in terms of exploitation and the increase of individual wealth, as commodities to be consumed. Precolonial Native American patterns of thinking about the land developed over tens of thousands of years and millions of experiences, creating a sense of harmony between the people and the land. This balance maintained the health of both land and people until the onslaught of European colonialism.[25] To most Western minds land was, and often still is, seen simply as inanimate space that is commodifiable in every sense. To America's First Nations, the land is a living gift from the Creator, belonging to everyone—not just those who are able to hoard it through unjust laws

24. Scott L. Malcomson, *One Drop of Blood: American Misadventures of Race* (Darby, PA: Diane Publishing, 2000), 15.

25. Our Native values of sharing were more similar to the Christians in the New Testament, 2 Cor. 8:15, "So that the one who has much, doesn't have too much; and the one who has little, doesn't have too little" (NLT).

and unfounded values. If we can achieve such a goal, perhaps what the artist George Catlin said in the past may be said about our future:

> All history goes to prove that when first visited by civilized people, the American Indians have been found friendly and hospitable—from the days of Christopher Columbus to the Lewis and Clark expedition. . . . And so also have a great many travelers, including myself: Nowhere to my knowledge, have they stolen a six-pence worth of my property, though in their country there are no laws to punish for theft. I have visited 48 different tribes, and feel authorized to say that the North American Indian in his native state is honest, hospitable, faithful, brave, . . . and an honorable and religious human being.[26]

---

26. George Catlin, *Letters and Notes on the Manners, Customs, and Conditions of North American Indians*, Vol. I (Mineola, NY: Dover, 1973), 28.

12

A Shared Narrative

Ray Aldred

In order to have a conversation in our world we have to loosen our grip on certainty and embrace pluralism. But, commitment to pluralism is not itself the goal but part of the process.[1] This is no less the case in Canada, and it presents some difficulties for the ongoing evolution of the peoples who live in Canada, particularly because of the continuing wave of newcomers hoping to make Canada their home. In this process there are indigenous perspectives on newcomers to Canada that we can embrace to help us on a journey toward becoming relatives. There are in particular several things that have helped my family—the Cree, Métis, Mohawk, Scottish,

---

1. Robert Kane, "Seeking Certainty," in *Undergrad Philosophy Conference* (Calgary, AB: University of Calgary Press, 2008).

English, French, and many others—embrace the changing faces in the community.

In 1990, Reginald Bibby, in *Mosaic Madness*, highlighted the danger of making mere pluralism the goal. He pointed out that in Canada all we do is coexist. He was hoping to form a unifying vision for Canada.[2] Concerned with the extreme individualism and the regionalism in Canada, he sought to articulate something more than a vision of multiculturalism to underwrite ethnic enclaves that merely exist but do not function with any kind of shared voice.[3]

Amartya Sen points out in *Identity and Violence* that forcing individuals into the rigid singularity of ethnic identity increases the chance of violent confrontation.[4] There is a need for a pluralism of identity that would allow for a more robust national identity, as growing tribalism, according to Sen, poses a dangerous alternative. Tribalism is a form of identity aimed at entrenching particular ethnic views, which must fight to defend themselves. This violent confrontation is the result of new "tribalisms," forgetting the liberal ideal of the enhancement of the individual in the midst of many groups. Sen echoes Bibby's concern that identity in a modern liberal state continues to be a challenge. However, pluralism is both a challenge and a necessity.

There are at least three needs and three related resources indigenous to Turtle Island[5] that provide a source for reflection on the journey to proper relatedness. First, there is the need to develop

---

2. Reginald Wayne Bibby, *Mosaic Madness: The Poverty and Potential of Life in Canada* (Toronto: Stoddart, 1990).

3. Perhaps the current debate in Quebec as to what constitutes Québecois values is an example of this kind of thinking. In this current debate, it seems the focus is upon the bare minimum needed to coexist. One group is seeking to make its own existence the goal, which seldom results in a positive outcome.

4. Amartya Sen, *Identity and Violence: The Illusion of Destiny* Issues of our Times (New York: W. W. Norton, 2006).

5. Editor's note: According to various indigenous groups, Turtle Island is the true name of North America.

a shared narrative, and the historic treaty-making process provides a way forward. Second, in keeping with the imperative to enhance freedom and loosen the grip of certainty, there is a need to develop a shared spirituality of unity and diversity. Indigenous spirituality offers hope here. I think particularly of its pan-Amerindian expressions, because they are premised on a lived expression of spirituality embracing the provisional nature of our life as part of the land. Finally, there is a need for partnership that respects the land. The circle of relationships between First Peoples and immigrant cultures over the history of Turtle Island provides models of alliances[6] that point in a direction for the future. Treaty implies the notion of becoming relatives—people who share narratives:

> O Grandfather, Wakan-Tanka, behold us! Here we shall make relatives and peace; it is your will that this be done. With this sweet grass which is Yours, I am now making smoke, which will rise to You. In everything that we do, You are first, and this our sacred Mother Earth is second, and next to Her are the four quarters. By making this rite we shall carry out Thy will upon this earth, and we shall make a peace that will last to the end of time. The smoke from this sweet grass will be upon everything in the universe. It is good![7]

The peoples of Turtle Island have long understood the importance of relationships. The quote above, taken from the *Hunkapi: The Making of Relatives* ceremony, expresses the elements necessary for a community to exist and prosper. The Creator, the land, and two different peoples become relatives, so that there is peace upon the land and the universe. This ceremony does something, and by involving the entire universe attempts to provide a living narrative from which to move forward.

6. Lynne Davis, *Alliances: Re/Envisioning Indigenous and Non-Indigenous Relationships* (Toronto: University of Toronto Press, 2010).

7. Black Elk, Joseph Epes Brown, and Michael F. Steltenkamp, *The Sacred Pipe: Black Elk's Account of the Seven Rites of the Oglala Sioux* (New York: MJF Books, 1996), 103.

Moving forward in a good way that respects the creator and all creation (including people) is also mirrored in the treaty-making process of much of Canada. Another ceremony echoes this quest for harmonious relationships. In the sweet-grass ceremony of the Plains Cree of Canada, the braid of sweet grass represents three groups. One strand of the braid represents the First Nations, the people the Creator put first upon this land called Turtle Island. The second strand represents the newcomers to Canada, all those people whose original relationship is traced back through their ancestors to another place upon the earth. Finally, the third strand represents the Creator. This ceremony recalls the Treaty, the covenant originally made between the newcomers and the First Nations: a covenant or a treaty in which we promised to live in a harmonious way upon this place and the Creator would hold us to this promise. With the continued immigration of peoples to Turtle Island, the treaty can continue to be a place of shared narrative that moves us toward harmonious relationships, which is the basis for a society surviving and thriving.

The western indigenous people assumed that in the treaty, the crown of England had entered into kinship relationship. J. R. Miller writes that in 1874 Kakishaway, one of the signers of Treaty 4, "greeted Governor General Lord Lorne as his brother-in-law." Lord Lorne was married to Queen Victoria's daughter, while Kakishaway was related to the Queen through treaty.[8] These treaties were seen as covenants made between the First Nations and the crown under the oversight of the Creator. And, like all good stories, the treaties were to be renewed on a yearly basis in order to remind people that they

---

8. J. R. Miller, "Compact, Contract, Covenant: The Evolution of Indian Treaty-Making," in *New Histories for Old: Changing Perspectives on Canada's Native Pasts*, ed. Theodore Binnema and Susan Neylan (Vancouver: University of British Columbia Press, 2007), 84.

were continuing the narrative or promise to live in the land in a good way.

This is instructive for today. There continues to be a need for a shared narrative that includes both those who have called Canada home for a long time and for those who have come to this land more recently. There continues to be a need for a shared narrative that is not based upon overcoming an enemy or making the other the enemy. There is a need for shared narrative that seeks to provide a living testimony of overcoming animosity to reach for something better. The historic treaty-making process is the best place to turn because it offers a shared perspective that has its roots in both people groups.

One cannot turn to mainstream media as a source of shared narrative. The media can perhaps help to maintain a shared narrative, but as Noam Chomsky has pointed out, the media will tend to maintain the status quo.[9] The media alone is not a force to overcome negative stereotypes without some source from outside of itself. For example, when the Idle No More movement was spreading across Canada and the United States, the media did not always give prominent space until there was a considerable number of people engaged in the movement. The Idle No More movement gained momentum and was maintained by grassroots support through social media. Mainstream media cannot generate a movement of its own. It is governed by and relies on marketers' clever machinations that entice the populace to support its views. It is not truly broad-based.

There is a need for shared narrative. Treaty was entered into both by the First Nations and the newcomers and was to be maintained by their descendants. It was based upon the people occupying or living in relationship with the lands of Canada. The treaty process, although

---

9. *Manufacturing Consent: Noam Chomsky and the Media*, dir. Mark Achbar and Peter Wintonick, Zeitgeist Video, 1993, video recording.

distinctively First Nations in protocol and approach, was not foreign to the newcomers to the land. It has evolved as it has needed to evolve and continues to be the basis of the First Nations' interaction with the Canadian government. There is a need, however, to honor the treaty or continue to enact the narrative of the treaty in order to enter into and live out the intent of the treaty relationship.

A shared narrative is key in the ongoing development of an identity that is indigenous to Canada: an identity that takes seriously the relationship with the land as well as the relationship with the host people and the original founding newcomers, French and English. Without a shared identity there is little basis for moving beyond tolerating one another. It is difficult to develop a shared identity without a shared memory. Treaty offers the place where we can hear the story of peoples agreeing to live in good relationships. Canada and First Nations have had some especially difficult moments in their relationship, including residential schools and mishandled land claims. These have occurred when the intent of the treaty has been ignored. It is my hope that the treaty relationship would point toward a shared narrative that provides a shared memory for all who make Canada their home. This in turn would lead to a shared vision of what it means to live in Canada, which would provide a basis for a principled response in the light of changing global dynamics. The treaty has functioned in this way in the past, and it can function in this way in the future. Of course, there needs to be a reenvisioning of what this all means. Treaty, however, could serve as a resource for developing this shared narrative.

In all of this, the First Nations' perspective on the treaty as an ongoing covenant is key if it is to serve as an ongoing basis for sharing of the land, as well as the basis for a shared identity. This will be exceedingly difficult for the federal government, for it continues to advocate that treaty is part of the past and should be viewed as a contract. As contract, the terms could be met and the contract set aside.[10] Yet despite this, there continues to be a living relationship between First Nations, Inuit, Métis, and the federal government. What has made the relationship sustainable is the treaty—even though the federal government too often tries to reduce treaty to contract.

The concept of treaty offers a holistic approach to the ongoing development of identity with regard to what it means to live a virtuous life in Canada. In saying it is holistic I mean that treaty offers enough space for both First Nations and settlers to thrive upon Turtle Island. It provides space for the indigenous people, whose identities are respected. It provides for the newcomers to live in the land. It acknowledges that the land will be there longer than any one generation and needs to be cared for. It also points toward its evolving character as relationships evolve and shift. Finally, it is based upon a spirituality that aims at proper relatedness. This relationship and spiritualty are captured by the protocol that was part of the signing of the treaty as well as its ongoing significance.

First Nations Spirituality

Jacqueline Ottmann points out that First Nations spirituality resists formal definition.[11] Part of the reason for this resistance is the diversity of First Nations. Also, First Nations assume spirituality as intrinsic to life and thus without definition. I would add that First Nations spirituality is provisional and embraces the mystery of living in relationship. Spirituality is a gift from the Creator and is simply a way of life; it is culturally located and necessary for healing. First

---

10. Miller, *New Histories*, 67.

11. Jacqueline Ottmann, *First Nations Leadership and Spirituality within the Royal Commission on Aboriginal Peoples: A Saskatchewan Perspective* (MA Thesis, University of Saskatchewan, 2002), 98.

Nations spirituality provides room for the ongoing development of relationship with the other in virtue of its provisional nature. This spirituality was and is central to the treaty relationship and provides a spirituality large enough to allow for the other.

For example, in the Cree language the word used for God is *Manitou.* However, there is no one-to-one correspondence between the English word God and *Manitou.* The Cree term derives its meaning from the context and experience of people and refers to the all-encompassing mystery.[12] Mystery does not mean something beyond the real world, but a concept of spirituality that tries to account for the reality of our human perception. Mystery is part of the perception and experience. There is always openness to further understanding.

First Nations protocol surrounding the treaty negotiations illustrates the openness of First Nations spirituality. The First Nations practiced their traditional ceremonies and spirituality as a way toward finding agreement with the newcomers by making treaty.[13] The practice of protocol is seen as a way to respect one another before continuing to find agreement on how to live in a good way on the land. Spirituality was a defining part of the treaty. The First Nations assumed that treaty would be a relationship between the two that would alter their identity and spirituality. In part, this was what inclined some First Nations leaders to enter into the agreement for residential schools, even while it was apparent that the government continually sought to force an agreement on First Nations that would remove First Nations from the land. First Nations leaders, however, understood the need for the development of spirituality and identity

---

12. Earle H. Waugh, "Religious Issues in the Alberta Elders' Cree Dictionary," *Numen* 48, no. 4 (2001): 474.

13. Europeans for their part were not unfamiliar with the concept of treaty, but the protocol used in the numbered treaties were from the First Nations, making this treaty indigenous to North America. See Miller, *New Histories*, 84.

that continued to honor the land but also honored the newcomers.[14] This included vocational training, which First Nations leaders saw of value. They were ambivalent toward Christianity,[15] but part of this ambivalence was due to the unwillingness of European denominations to accept First Nations spiritual practices. On the other hand, First Nations treaty negotiations by the time of the numbered treaties sought to honor both spiritualities.

When negotiating the treaties, First Nations were using a model of treaty indigenous to Canada's ongoing identity as a land that hosted many different nations. The land was the context or reality undergirding the history of the life of the First Nations and their ongoing relationship with settlers. The Creator provided the land for all creatures, including people. This point was part of the European negotiations during the numbered[16] treaties.[17] First Nations acknowledged that the land welcomes all, and so the spirituality of the First Nations—because it is tied to land or environment[18]—has an open, receiving stance toward the "other." In turn this gives evidence of a spirituality that is provisional but aimed at affirming harmonious relationships.

This idea is not completely foreign to Christian theology. Dietrich Bonhoeffer, in keeping with Lutheran theology, points out the need to be completely immersed in the reality of the world.[19] It was in

---

14. Government of Canada, "Looking Forward, Looking Back," in *Royal Commission on Aboriginal Peoples* (Ottawa, ON: Government of Canada, 1996), accessed 29 May 2014, http://www.collectionscanada.gc.ca/webarchives/20071124125216/http://www.ainc-inac.gc.ca/ch/rcap/sg/sg1_e.html#0.

15. See J. R. Miller, "The State, the Church, and Residential Schools in Canada," in *Religion and Public Life: Historical and Comparative Perspectives*, ed. Marguerite Van Die (Toronto: University of Toronto Press, 2001).

16. Treaties 1–11 were to provide access to the land of First Nations by settlers. See *Royal Commission on Aboriginal Peoples*, 161–78.

17. J. R. Miller, "Compact, Contract, Covenant: The Evolution of Indian Treaty-Making," in *New Histories for Old: Changing Perspectives on Canada's Native Pasts*, ed. Theodore Binnema and Susan Neylan (Vancouver: University of British Columbia Press, 2007), 84.

18. Waugh, "Religious Issues," 470.

this context of creation that one lived for the "other." The "other" is a boundary that makes revelation a necessity. We cannot enter into relationship unless our spirituality allows for an open vulnerability. Bonhoeffer writes that we must become vulnerable so we can be strong for the "other."[20] This affirms the First Nations concept of treaty as a basis for a relationship and spirituality based upon a locative identity and shared memory upon Turtle Island.

Shared Narrative and Partnership on the Land

If the land is not healthy, then how can we be?[21]

A shared memory and identity are based upon a shared narrative and partnership, all leading to partnership that embraces care for the land. The land is the soul of our Cree[22] people and in order to ensure the well-being of our grandchildren, we must care for the land. Care for the land includes the caring for all relationships. This includes the identity of the "other."

The Cypress Hills in Saskatchewan exemplify how this care and concern for the "other" was built into the fabric of the spirituality of the land. The Cypress Hills, located at the borders of Saskatchewan, Alberta, and Montana, were and are sacred to the tribal groups of the northern plains. As such, this area was considered international territory.[23] It was a place for all to heal and rest. It was a place of safety for all. This location is an example of a meeting place for sharing land and stories. A shared narrative that respects the land uses proper relatedness to regard all of the land as sacred and a safe place for all

19. Dietrich Bonhoeffer, *Dietrich Bonhoeffer Works, Volume 8: Letters and Papers from Prison*, ed. John W. De Gruchy (Minneapolis: Fortress Press, 2010), 137.
20. Ibid., 160–61.
21. Naomi Adelson, *"Being Alive Well": Health and the Politics of Cree Well-Being* (Toronto: University of Toronto Press, 2000), 3.
22. Doug Cuthand, *Askiwina: A Cree World* (Regina, SK: Coteau Books, 2007).
23. Ibid., 12–15.

human beings. This proper relatedness includes the relations between all things and so the communal identity of all. The only thing not tolerated are those groups that desire to dominate all others.

This was and is the basis of the treaty. This can be the basis for any other group immigrating to Canada. All who come to Turtle Island enter into the treaty relationship that encompasses the newcomers, the First Nations, the land, and the Creator. This is a call for partnership that embraces diversity of identity but shares a narrative.

Canada has seen many types of partnerships or alliances between newcomers and First Peoples.[24] The Canadian federal government has at times practiced a paternalism vis-à-vis First Nations, treating them as wards of the state. Earlier, other models predominated, such as the Two Row Wampum,[25] which focused upon a partnership around shared task. I believe that the desired partnership between First Nations and settlers would aim at making the indigenous agenda primary for all who live upon the land since this agenda recognizes the land as the meeting place.

A partnership that attempted to move the land out of the category of commodity and into the sacred or familial would provide a greater latitude for care for the land. This does not undermine the economic realities of life; rather it seeks to bring greater dialogue around sustainability by extending the planning process to several generations. This is possible from treaty as a shared narrative because as narrative it enlarges identity to the past, present, and future. Also, by including land through an imaginative process in treaty—where the land and creatures are part of the ongoing dialogue—this shared narrative provides greater philosophical resources for a constructive process toward land. At the heart of Cree spirituality is the knowledge

24. Lynne Davis, *Alliances: Re/Envisioning Indigenous and Non-Indigenous Relationships* (Toronto: University of Toronto Press, 2010), 1–12.
25. Miller, *New Histories*, 74.

that we are related to the land. We pray in the fall for a good hunting season, and in the spring we give thanks for a good hunting season. We shall live and die, but the land will remain. We should live in a way that respects this reality. This thinking could be extended to include the need for industrial enterprise. However, it must include all of the groups represented upon the land.

First Peoples have long argued that they want a nation-to-nation partnership. However, what is particular to First Nations conceptions of nation is that nation is made up of relationships. It is primarily the relationships or communal identity of each indigenous nation. This is different from the modern idea of nation-state, which has some benefits. But since it is primarily a Western conception it is limited. The bringing together of these ideas of relationship to land and creation with the advancement of indigenous desires for a healthy Turtle Island could help Canada to finally regard the land as sacred. This would help newcomers move toward becoming indigenous themselves.

This kind of partnership could be based upon a pluralism that acknowledges the communal identity of each group of people. However, this acknowledgment does not locate identity primarily in the past. It makes room for the development of the individual. It does not seek to stifle the cultural development of an individual, but rather seeks to provide the resources for the development of the group as well as the individual. This is based upon a "relational pluralism"[26] that not only acknowledges the individual but also group-to-group relationships. The right to self-define as a group is preserved, but it does not sacrifice the individual, so it preserves the positive aspects of the liberal state. The limitation on the individual is the necessity to consult the "other." If this is set within the context of shared

26. Timothy A. Schouls, *Shifting Boundaries: Aboriginal Identity, Pluralist Theory, and the Politics of Self-Government* (Vancouver: University of British Columbia Press, 2003), 37.

territory, embracing a provisional spirituality that is open to the "other," built upon the indigenous memory and shared narrative of the treaty, it could lead to proper relatedness and could see the newcomer to Turtle Island learn to live as indigenous. This in turn could contribute to a pluralism that affirms the cultures of this country: a pluralism that continues to develop as a mosaic of peoples sharing the land. Perhaps in time, all people in Canada could say, "I am not trying to save my culture, but my culture is saving me."[27]

Conclusion

The historical treaty-making process between the historic newcomers and the First Nations of Canada provides the resources necessary for the flourishing of Turtle Island people. Treaty can function as a shared memory, which could provide the resources to continue to write a new home-grown narrative. This narrative has enough room for indigenous people as well as newcomers. At the heart of this narrative is the recollection that treaty-making and First Nations spirituality show the importance of developing a holistic connection to the land. This is a spirituality rooted in the real material world and so provides new resources to critique the ongoing development of resources in Canada. Finally, as we share this land, a historic pluralism that acknowledged the identity of each group of people allows us to move together as partners on the land. As we move toward proper relatedness, we will find an affirming freedom and equality for all people.

27. Elizabeth Steinhauer, "Personal Conversation" (2013).

13

Immigration

From Borders to Boundaries under First Nations
Tutelage

Allen G. Jorgenson

This paper advances the conviction that insights garnered from the First Nations of the Americas enable Christians to rethink immigration to the end that immigration is understood as a crossing of boundaries rather than borders. By way of prolegomenon, two comments are needed to orient the reader for what follows. The first is autobiographical, and the second theological—although both are properly theological.

In recent years I have learned substantial truths about where I live. Perhaps no truth has been more unsettling than learning that the property I call home was deeded to the Six Nations of the Grand River in the Haldimand Proclamation of 1784.[1] This proclamation

1. Accessed 13 Nov. 2012, http://www.sixnations.ca/LandsResources/HaldProc.htm.

promised the peoples of the Six Nations, and their inheritors, property "six miles deep from each side of the river." This geographical marker includes my house, the church where I worship, the university where I work, and the stores where I shop. When I take the bus to work I am traversing land that was given to people who now live on a fraction of that original property. Insofar as I have to do theology where I am, I am obligated to reckon with the truth that I do theology on aboriginal land.[2] There are, of course, other and equally important reasons for attending to First Nations insights that will arise as the paper progresses, but this self-declaration is where I need to begin. This leads me to a second preparatory comment.

The people who dispossessed the First Nations of this land were Christians. They and their ancestors built the churches that grace our community. In the name of Christ they struggled to convert these dispossessed people to the crucified. In the name of Christ they established residential schools to assimilate First Nations. In the name of Christ they traveled across the ocean to further the reach of British, French, and Spanish rule. Their justification for this exercise was funded by the fact that they bore the gospel, the good news of the new creation accomplished by the cross. They believed, with utter integrity, that this insight justified their self-understanding as civilized; those they met on these shores did not know of this message, and so were not civilized. In sum, migration and mission were married—even while this may not have been articulated—to the end that expansion of empire and exposition of faith were also wed.

In what follows, I first explore migration as a leitmotif in Scripture and relate it to mission, arguing that Christian migration becomes mission insofar as mission is endemic to Christian identity—in varying modes. In so doing I propose that mission most often is

2. Allen G. Jorgenson, "Empire, Eschatology and Stolen Land," in *Dialogue* 49, no. 4 (Summer 2010): 115–22.

advanced by a theology that under-narrates creation, a common Christian prejudice that refuses to see creation as a peer of redemption and tends to discuss salvation alone as God's *opus proprium*. A robust theology of creation anticipates theological insights from the context that informs the gospel. This paper will look especially at resources found in aboriginal American spirituality as a resource that both critiques and renews Christian theology for the sake of a theology of immigration faithful to the gospel and problematizes an understanding of mission and migration as a crossing of borders. I then propose a new way of viewing mission and migration as a crossing of boundaries.

Migration as a Leitmotif

The Christian tradition is awash in theolog*ies* of migration; some of them far removed from consciousness and therefore dangerous. Migration could be deemed a *leitmotif* in the Bible. Abraham is a wandering Aramean moving toward and within the Promised Land. The children of Israel in Egypt are refugees that await repatriation. Shortly after the division of the united kingdom, Israel becomes a people *in dispersionem*. Likewise, Judah's *exodus/reditus* to and from Babylon marks it as a people that moves. The Newer Testament echoes the predominance of this image, in both realist and symbolic keys. Jesus and his family literally retrace the exodus narrative. The early apostles and disciples are scattered across the ancient world. But of astounding import is the manner in which the theme of immigration is deployed in less literal ways. Christians are deemed foreigners and exiles wherever they are. Jesus himself has been seen as an immigrant par excellence: the Word made flesh sojourns from a "far country." Yet, despite migration's near ubiquity in Scripture, its meaning is equivocal.

The most charitable treatments of immigration in the Bible are those in which the children of Israel are encouraged to make provisions for the well-being and justice of exiles in their midst in light of their experience as immigrants. This pattern of treatment guides the Jerusalem council's acceptance of gentiles in the fledgling Jewish-Christian community. A less charitable treatment presumes the following: the faithful are people of promise whose arrival portends the dissolution of darkness and the eradication of enemies. It is important to underscore that this understanding is so well rehearsed as to be rote, and thus thoroughly insidious. Indeed, this perspective is theologically mapped onto the narrative of Jesus in Christian thought so as to render the redeeming work of the Christ a *creatio ex infernis* such that an unbridgeable chasm separates creation and redemption. The legacy of this posture is known the world over. Yet the terror that too often accompanied Christian mission "gone bad" does not end there. The "people of promise" are not only immigrants who displace indigenous people but they also thereby colonize the character of immigration itself. This is especially evidenced in the Americas wherein the original European immigrants sought to supplant the indigenous inhabitants and then suspect subsequent immigrants of the very activity marking their own colonizing immigration that is now colonizing mission.

Mission, of course, presumes dialogue. At the very least, it includes the task of translation—but usually also the give-and-take of discourse. Admittedly, this dialogue too often becomes monologue, with little time or patience for a Christian hearing of the dialogue partner. This is the sad history of too much—yet not all—of the Christian tradition. Christians too often fail to think through the gift and danger of dialogue. We compromise dialogue by undervaluing silence and listening. We undermine dialogue and insult dialogue partners by threatening to take that which isn't meant to be given and by offering to give what cannot be received.[3] Moreover, dialogue that degenerates into monologue will never know what it can bring to the table insofar as thought only arrives by grace of interchange. It is in my interaction with the "other" that I finally become whom I am. The dialogue that is truly dialogue, for that reason, is holy ground. I ground this assertion in Knut Løgstrup's contention that our desire to enter into relationship with another is evidence of a primordial trust in human life,[4] a trust that is manifestly evident in the fact that our day-to-day existence presumes exactly this trust. Our interactions with both neighbors and strangers presume more trust than distrust. Yet this primordial trust, according to Løgstrup, presupposes that relationality as a human phenomenon posits life itself as a gift; Løgstrup would say a divine gift. In other words, our desire to enter into relationship with another—in my case a Lutheran Christian with aboriginal Americans—reveals that I recognize a potency in this relationship that presumes each has something to bring to the table and demands that I think about what guides, prejudices, and drives our desire for dialogue before entering dialogue proper.

The Christian church has a long history of dialogue, some of it authentic, some not, and much of it a mixed bag. It is my contention that we fail to enter most fully into dialogue when we fail to give adequate theological attention to the first article of the creed. A theology of dialogue begins here because we cannot apprehend what God has given us in salvation without an appreciative apprehension of that which God in Christ saves. Gustaf Wingren notes that creation itself is an *opus proprium* of God.[5] Here, Wingren believes

---

3. Cf. George "Tink" Tinker, *American Indian Liberation: A Theology of Sovereignty* (Maryknoll, NY: Orbis, 2008), 141. Here Tinker implores Christians not to invade aboriginal ceremonies. He also notes elsewhere that Lutheranism is not amenable to aboriginals (90).

4. Knut Ejler Løgstrup, *The Ethical Demand*, trans. Hans Fink (Notre Dame: University of Notre Dame Press, 1997), 8.

that he follows Luther, and provides what he considers to be a correction to the theologies of revelation so predominant in the time period in which he wrote. Wingren wrote that Luther's focus of theological discourse was justification, rather than revelation.[6] He considered the neo-orthodox turn to revelation to be overly invested in epistemic concerns. Wingren was very concerned to assert that creation points to the integrity of being human.[7] The gospel is a resounding "yes" to the body.[8] The body, of course, is but an instance of creation proper. Insofar as God's works of creation, in the thought of Luther, are manifestations of God's face,[9] we are able to ponder the works of God, mindful that the Creator appears in what is created.[10] Wingren proposes that this healthy theology of creation receives its first potent blow in the church via pietism.[11] The Enlightenment clearly contributed to this prejudice, but Wingren is especially concerned with the danger manifest in the sort of Christocentrism in his days that he deemed to marginalize creation.[12] He asserts that there is no obedience to God without a relationship with the world.[13] Joining this insight to Løgstrup's assertion that our interaction with the world is a manifestation of the gift of life allows us to ground our desire for dialogue in the expectation that meeting another is itself a gift and might be an occasion for both self-discovery and divine encounter. Further to this, Wingren reminds us

5. Gustav Wingren, *Creation and Law*, trans. Ross Mackenzie (Philadelphia: Muhlenberg, 1961), 30.
6. Gustav Wingren, *Creation and Gospel: The New Situation in European Theology* (Toronto: Edwin Mellen, 1979), 43.
7. Wingren, *Creation and Law*, 27.
8. Wingren, *Creation and Gospel*, 106.
9. Martin Luther, *Lectures on Genesis*, in *Luther's Works, Volume 1*, ed. Jaroslav Pelikan, trans. George V. Schick (Saint Louis: Concordia, 1958), 11.
10. *LW* 1:15. According to Luther, this is why Adam and Eve worshipped at sunrise. This primordial act of worship becomes idolatry under the tutelage of sin.
11. *Creation and Law*, 42.
12. *Creation and Gospel*, 74.
13. *Creation and Law*, 89.

that a gospel concern for the well-being of our neighbor draws us into conversation with her: we do not know our neighbor's need by reading our Bibles, but by meeting our neighbor.[14] Dialogue, then, is an instance wherein we anticipate meeting our neighbor, our self, and in this mix God, who orchestrates conversation for the sake of our conversion. In what follows, I engage indigenous thinkers and themes in an effort to clarify a Christian understanding of migration and mission.

Indigenous Insights

In considering indigenous thought, the Christian theologian is immediately aware that both the familiar and the strange beckon. This sensation arises as various internalized caricatures of Native American life run up against the vast plethora of indigenous spiritualities and worldviews. Yet, as one surveys aboriginal interests, certain themes emerge with some regularity across traditions and thinkers. One will recognize a number of recurring topics, among which I note: an interest in space that rivals occidental attention to time; a notion of governance that respects dissent and employs ad hoc strategies in leadership; a profound respect for land; compelling narratives that problematize rather than explain evil; balance rather than progress as the goal of life; and an understanding of the interrelationships between the Creator, creation, and humans that are sustained by permeable rather than fixed boundaries.[15] In this essay, I will employ this latter theme in critiquing one of what I

14. *Creation and Gospel*, 116.
15. Cf. Harold Cardinal," *Okimaw Win* and Post-colonial Nation-building," in *Intersecting Voices: Critical Theologies in a Land of Diversity*, ed. Don Schweitzer and Derek Simon (Toronto: Novalis, 2004); Vine Deloria Jr., *God Is Red: A Native View of Religion* (Golden, CO: Fulcrum, 2003); Clara Sue Kidwell, Homer Noley, and George E. Tinker, eds., *A Native American Mythology* (Maryknoll, NY: Orbis, 2001); Rupert Ross, *Dancing with a Ghost: Exploring Aboriginal Identity* (Toronto: Penguin Canada, 2006); George E. Tinker, *Spirit and Resistance: Political Theology and American Indian Liberation* (Minneapolis: Fortress Press, 2004); Tinker,

consider to be many Christian loci that fund oppressive theologies of immigration: the Christian employment of the *missio Dei*.

The aboriginal theme of boundaries especially commends itself for what follows because the Western nation-state uses the border as the means by which we construct the category of immigration. The border is the physical boundary of the state. This category is thoroughly fixed in occidental sensibilities and functions as an often-unacknowledged condition for the possibility of civil life. Of course, the notion of a boundary that defines a nation—a border—that is operative in the Americas has not always and is not even now understood thus. Thomas King, in recounting aboriginal experience in North America, notes that the border doesn't mean much to natives.[16] This doesn't mean that *boundaries* are unimportant to aboriginal thought. They are, in fact, profoundly important, but differently understood. In order to understand how boundaries operate in First Nations thought, my sense is that occidental thinkers need to rescind from the predominant image of markers in the sand that fuels our imagination on this account.

Understanding the role that boundaries function in native thought requires attention to narratives that sketch boundary situations. Perhaps one of the most significant of the characters that recur in many indigenous imaginations is the Trickster. The Trickster is a character who defies categorization: a menacing character, he is neither fish nor fowl; neither good nor bad. Trickster dons many guises and is often found to be upsetting the status quo. Missionaries often identified the Trickster with Satan.[17] Aboriginal Americans identify him as a boundary character. Trickster sometimes seems to

American Indian Liberation; Gerald Vizenor, *Manifest Manners: Narratives on Postindian Survivance* (Lincoln: University of Nebraska Press, 1994).

16. Thomas King, *The Truth About Stories* (Toronto: Anansi, 2003), 102.

17. *Native American Mythology*, 119.

be a semi-divine character, living across generations from primordial time, yet betraying human characteristics, both noble and ignoble.[18] Some aboriginal Christians identify Jesus with the Trickster character.[19] To Western ears this may seem problematic, if not heretical. Yet by refusing to even hear this provocation, Christians might miss a useful insight in this identification. The Trickster problematizes the sharp divisions that Western thought draws between categories such as human, creation, and divine. As a boundary character, Trickster reconfigures the character of boundaries. Boundaries become flexible, permeable, and locations for telling great stories.

In sum, boundaries aren't first about borders but about relationships. For native thought, relationships have always been broadly conceived. First Nations people have relationships with what Westerners call "things" because the category of spirit, or perhaps we might say person, is not as restricted as it is in occidental thought, wherein it is applied to the human alone and analogously applied to the divine. Spirit, person, family: all of these words admit crossing of boundaries and so serve as the necessary condition for relationship, and for that reason the foundation for community. Community is thus seen to be a basic structure of life.[20] Moreover, the category of community is thereby broadly deployed. Not only is community basic to human relationships; and divine-human relationships; and human-creation relationship; and the many permutations that follow from these; but community broadly construed is the lens through which life is viewed. Taiaiake Alfred, for instance, argues that an indigenous renaissance that fails to hold together the categories of

---

18. A fine contemporary portrayal of the Trickster is found in the recent novel by Drew Hayden Taylor, *Motorcycles and Sweetgrass: A Novel* (Toronto: Alfred A. Knopf Canada, 2010).
19. *Native American Mythology*, 122.
20. Joerg Rieger, "God and Power, Prophets, and Native Lands," in *Theology That Matters: Ecology, Economy and God*, ed. Darby Kathleen Ray (Minneapolis: Fortress Press, 2009), 69.

land, culture, and governance in community will fail. The boundaries separating these categories are not borders, but meeting places wherein these partners—land, culture, and governance—are sustained.[21] Legitimate political power in this worldview aims at balance.[22] What, then, does this treatment offer a Lutheran pondering the need to articulate a reframed, if not reformed, theology of immigration?

From Borders to Boundaries

In the first instance, Christians will need to confess that borders rather than boundaries have too often served as the substructure for the architecture of our thought. We might then ponder possibilities both internal to our traditions and given by our interlocutors for reconceiving boundaries and movement across boundaries. Finally, the church would do well to imagine how this reconception might inform the body politic. In what follows, I provide an instance of one Lutheran's attempt to offer an initial foray into this task.

Confession in the context of the Americas begins with an honest appraisal of mission. Such an appraisal, as with most things theological, is littered with gray. I have spent enough time among aboriginal people to have heard stories and testimonies so many and varied that they could be used, in isolation, to justify an unequivocal disavowal of mission, or a glowing endorsement of the same, and any variety of positions in between. In the Canadian context, the government's and churches' formal apologies to First Nations for the treatment of aboriginal children at residential schools has been an important first step in rethinking the relationships between church, state, and First Nations. Clearly, in the main, something has gone

---

21. Taiaiake Alfred, *Peace, Power and Righteousness: An Indigenous Manifesto*, 2nd ed. (Oxford: Oxford University Press, 2009), 25.
22. Alfred, *Peace*, 11–12.

horribly amiss with mission in North America. These wrongs have been properly documented elsewhere.[23] What is especially interesting, however, is that church bodies generally have worked very hard to distance themselves from this history by the way we talk about mission. This can be found at both popular and formal levels.

At a popular level, the employment of the word "missional" seems to evidence a gut-level desire to distance ourselves from the history of mission in North America. I sometimes wonder whether those who attempt to duck the critiques leveled at missionaries by being missional are sufficiently aware of what it is that informs dangerous mission. Here too, I suspect that a variety of responses are warranted. Ecclesial discourse at a more formal level, however, surely is aware of the need to rethink some of the presuppositions of certain understandings of mission. This is evidenced in an increasing use of the term *missio Dei* for mission. *Missio Dei* has become a popular concept in ecumenical circles as a way to reframe the older theme of Christian mission. It has much to recommend its utility: the phrase suggests that mission belongs to God rather than humans. Moreover, as utilized in most theological discourse, it generally presumes that God's mission concerns not only redemption, but creation. Most importantly, many practitioners of mission operating under this paradigm no longer consider themselves responsible for the advancement of the Reign of God. What happens, however, when we consider mission from the perspective of aboriginal thought? In the first instance, it will become apparent that it is impossible to divorce *missio Dei* from mission as understood for millennia. The history of residential schools, misappropriation of land, and the legacy of governmental policies aimed at eradicating whole nations will not allow us to escape the legacy of mission by the use of *missio*

---

23. Cf. http://www.trc.ca/websites/trcinstitution/index.php?p=580, accessed 27 May 2012, for a report regarding the residential school tragedy titled "They Came for the Children."

Dei. Moreover, the history of indigenous Americans allows us to see that mission and migration were experienced hand in hand in the encounters of indigenous inhabitants with the European immigrants. European immigrants and their ancestors might imagine that migration and mission are two distinct realities. The First Nations know otherwise.

In sum, mission and migration coexist, despite Christian theology's desire to establish a border between the two. But we might ask ourselves: What happens if we allow the border between mission and migration to become a boundary? What resources from Scripture might better enable us to revisit the relationship between immigration and movement under the tutelage of boundaries? Here I propose that we consider carefully the book of Ruth, where we find plenty of movement, an exemplary immigrant, and boundaries as a bonus.

The book of Ruth is a beloved biblical narrative. It remains a favorite for weddings, and as a novella, fuels the imaginations of its readers as we find ourselves drawn into the narrative. The text depicts Ruth as an exemplar of covenant love, who crosses boundaries in order to secure a future for herself and her mother-in-law. Yet Ruth is not the only character of import in this story. Naomi, too, demonstrates a kind of tenacity that is often overlooked by readers because of their fascination with the Ruth-Boaz connection. Readers do well to remember that Naomi was an immigrant twice over: perhaps the second instance of being an immigrant the more trying one. There is no harder task than coming home after having been away long enough to forge a new identity. Naomi crossed both borders and boundaries and invites us to rethink movement and migration in light of her experience. Familiar space is reconfigured in light of her visits afar.

Too often, the mission work of the church has failed to learn this lesson from Naomi; or perhaps it is better to say that this reality has rarely been confessed and embraced. The truth of the matter is that when Christians engage in mission they can only do that by moving across boundaries into other lands. Sometimes, like Naomi, they return to their home country, with guests in tow. Sometimes they remain afar. Sometime they live at the border; but in either event the encounter, the experience, the exercise of being a foreigner in a strange land makes home foreign.

Practitioners of comparative theology have this experience. They know something of the dislocation that happens when they have spent some time with Trickster, learning anew that boundaries are places of death and resurrection; places of clarity and confusion; places both external and internal. But above all the experience of moving to the edge alters our worldview: sometimes for good and sometimes for ill. For some, time at the boundary becomes a moment when the world is apprehended as evil and dangerous and boundaries morph into borders. For others, being at the boundary occasions not a morphing of boundary into a border, but a morphing of the one at the boundary. For these, boundaries offer conversion and in converting those migrating through the boundary, their apprehension of boundaries itself is converted.

Boundaries are now seen to be opportunities: places of growth where the body touches the world; where the body politic engages the neighbor; where the outside comes in as surely as what is inside goes out.[24] This latter point gives us some leverage for theology to inform the church's place in the world and the world's place in the church, insofar as we who go into the world bring both its needs

---

24. Cf. Mary (Joy) Philips, "The Space Between: The Church as Prophetic Pest/Parasite," in *Being the Church in the Midst of Empire—Trinitarian Reflections*, ed. Karen L. Bloomquist (Minneapolis: Lutheran University Press, 2007), 99.

and its resources into our communities in prayer and at the altar. A good place to begin to explore our experiences of boundaries is to remember the nature of the first wave of immigrants in the Americas in recorded history.

Philosopher John Ralston Saul explores the first contact in an altogether different key.[25] He explores the history of European contact with First Nations by underscoring the manner in which Europeans would not have lasted the first winter aside from the good graces of their aboriginal hosts. It is good for us to spend some time with this thought. When Europe came to the First Nations, the First Nations were numerically superior, culturally sophisticated, and scientifically advanced: they knew what one had to do to survive in a climate and conditions that were unfamiliar to the Europeans. They had technologies appropriate to their context: those who were superior made space for dependent immigrants. They did this, Saul asserts, because the primordial experience of the boundary for First Nations is the circle. The people exist as a circle, with everyone at the boundary: with everyone constituting the boundary. When others—when Europeans—approached the body politic, the indigenous response was to widen the circle; to broaden the boundary; to embrace the other. Saul traces how in certain parts of the Americas a place in the circle was embraced as exactly that—a place in the circle; yet the sad legacy of the first immigrants is one of returning hospitality with hostility; of replacing sacred circles with circled wagons; of turning boundaries into borders under the tutelage of that fiction we call security. Those at the margins can inspire us with their insight, wisdom, and courage. We could do worse than listen to the following sagacity:

Shalom is always tested on the margins of a society and revealed by

---

25. John Ralston Saul, *A Fair Country: Telling Truths about Canada* (Toronto: Viking Canada, 2008).

how the poor, oppressed, disempowered, and needy are treated. . . . A society concerned with shalom will care for the most marginalized among them. God has a special concern for the poor and needy, because how we treat them reveals our hearts, regardless of the rhetoric we employ to make ourselves sound just.[26]

At the edge we are invited to imagine how we think about limits: Are they boundaries or borders? And if they are borders, is the "security" they purport to establish consonant with the gospel?

Conclusion

Perhaps what the church, synagogue, mosque, and temple first need to do today is to unmask security as a fiction. This is especially pressing in light of the fact that boundaries are constitutive of existence and, moreover, *often* negotiated with grace, as Løgstrup proposes. It is only certain boundaries that we struggle to ossify as borders. It might be that the path forward in the body politic will be for religious communities to model habits of thought and practice that explore boundaries recognizing their permeability, their pliability, and their possibility. Such a task entails first a willingness for religious communities to talk with one another, then to talk across the boundary of religious thought, and finally to talk truthfully of the price to be paid when entitlement, rather than gratitude, shapes our way into the world.

26. Randy Woodley, *Shalom and the Community of Creation: An Indigenous Vision* (Grand Rapids: Eerdmans, 2012), 15.

PART IV

Current Immigration Issues

14

———

Lutheran Thought, Civil Disobedience, and the New Sanctuary Movement

Laura E. Alexander

Introduction

In 2006, Elvira Arellano, an undocumented immigrant from Mexico, was named one of *Time* magazine's "People Who Mattered." The mother of a young son gained national attention when she invoked the Christian tradition of sanctuary by sheltering inside Adalberto United Methodist Church in Chicago to protest her deportation and separation from her son, who is a U.S. citizen.[1] In the same year,

---

1. Wendy Cole, "Elvira Arellano," *Time*, 25 Dec. 2006, available at http://content.time.com/time/specials/packages/article/0,28804,2019341_2017328_2017183,00.html, accessed 15 March 2014. A note on terminology: there are several different ways of referring to immigrants who

Cardinal Roger Mahony, then archbishop of Los Angeles, publicly protested H.R.4437, the "Border Protection, Anti-terrorism, and Illegal Immigration Control Act." The bill, which passed in the U.S. House of Representatives but failed to pass in the Senate, would seemingly have made it a crime to assist an undocumented immigrant in any way, including through works of charity often performed by religious organizations. Mahony indicated that he would direct clergy and laity in his archdiocese to ignore its provisions if it became law. This same bill, and the debate it provoked, also played a role in inspiring immigrants and pro-immigrant activists to march in huge protests in several cities, even as the U.S. government moved toward ever-greater fortification of the U.S.-Mexico border and attempted to increase penalties for undocumented immigrants and employers who hired undocumented workers.

Inspired by Mahony's and others' acts of resistance, and reflecting pro-immigrant activists' worry over H.R. 4437 and similar legislation, a group of interfaith congregations, clergy, and activists founded the New Sanctuary Movement in January 2007. This movement drew upon the legacy of the Sanctuary Movement from the 1980s, when churches provided sanctuary to refugees who were denied asylum by the United States government after fleeing massacres in Guatemala, El Salvador, and Nicaragua.[2] For the New Sanctuary Movement, the issue at hand was the deportation of undocumented immigrants away from their families and, for those who were brought to the U.S. as children, from the only home

do not have proper legal documentation to enter or remain in the United States. I will use the phrase "undocumented immigrants."

2. For a historical and sociological discussion of the Sanctuary Movement, see Christian Smith's *Resisting Reagan: The U.S. Central America Peace Movement* (Chicago: University of Chicago Press, 1996).

they had ever known.[3] The movement convened as an interfaith organization in January 2007, with the following goals:

> to take a united, public, moral stand for immigrant rights; to protect immigrants against hate, workplace discrimination and unjust deportation; and to reveal the actual suffering of immigrant workers and families under current and proposed legislation to the religious community and the general public.[4]

The goals of the organization included awareness raising and advocacy, but the most visible and controversial aspect of the movement's work was undoubtedly its provision of "sanctuary" to a few individuals or families who were living in the U.S. without authorization. Though sanctuary did not always mean hosting immigrants physically inside places of worship, religious organizations did provide economic and spiritual support to undocumented immigrants who agreed to make their stories public in order to highlight their experiences and draw attention to the movement's advocacy efforts.

The national umbrella organization of the New Sanctuary Movement does not have as strong a voice today,[5] but interfaith coalitions in several cities still use the name of sanctuary as they continue to advocate for immigration reform. For observers and advocates—whether they approve or disapprove of the work of the movement—the name and idea of sanctuary remains controversial

3. For further information about the New Sanctuary Movement, see Grace Yukich, *One Family Under God: Immigration Politics and Progressive Religion in America* (New York: Oxford University Press, 2013). Information can also be found through the New Sanctuary Movement organizations in several cities, including Philadelphia (www.sanctuaryphiladelphia.org), New York (www.newsanctuarynyc.org), Boston (www.bostonnewsanctuary.org), Chicago (www.crln.org / Chicago-New-Sanctuary), and others.

4. This information was found on the website of the New Sanctuary Movement, at www.newsanctuarymovement.org, in March 2008. The website is no longer functional as of October 2013, although local chapters of the movement retain and continue to update their websites; see footnote 3.

5. The organization maintains a low-visibility presence on social media such as Facebook, mainly to aggregate information and calls to action initiated by local New Sanctuary groups.

due to the connection between providing sanctuary and committing civil disobedience. For the most part, groups that provide sanctuary do not break laws, but by publicly helping those who have entered or remained illegally in the United States, they commit a certain kind of civil disobedience.[6]

Why use the name of sanctuary to protest immigration policies? The primary reason seems to lie in the movement's desire to take a "public stand" and "to reveal the actual suffering of immigrant workers and families." And the notion of sanctuary does get attention: Arellano's story, as noted, ran in a national news magazine, and it was the focus of several pieces in the *Chicago Tribune* and other media outlets.[7] The New Sanctuary Movement uses the publicity generated by its name and its provision of sanctuary as a platform for telling immigrants' stories, as well as for publicizing its advocacy and the changes it hopes to see in immigration policies. Given the history of "sanctuary movements" in the United States, providing sanctuary has connotations of standing (and possibly suffering) with immigrants who are suffering, drawing attention to the personal and relational sides of debates over immigration policy.

Retelling Immigrant Stories: Competing Moral Obligations as a Source of Suffering

The New Sanctuary Movement's primary concern is to alleviate the suffering of immigrant families, which can take multiple forms.

---

6. It is important to note that living in the U.S. as an undocumented immigrant is a civil, not a criminal violation, although crossing the border illegally is a criminal misdemeanor (but not all undocumented immigrants cross borders illegally; for instance, some overstay visas). The Supreme Court's ruling on Arizona's S.B.1070 noted that, "as a general rule, it is not a crime for a removable alien to remain present in the United States." Arizona *v.* United States, 132 S. Ct. 2492 (2012), Section 6.

7. An Internet search for "Elvira Arellano" turns up numerous hits, including several that are new as of March 2014. The *Chicago Tribune* website that features articles about Arellano can be found at http://articles.chicagotribune.com/keyword/elvira-arellano, accessed 15 March 2014.

In addition to suffering economic and emotional hardships, undocumented immigrants also suffer moral and sometimes spiritual conflicts between competing obligations: to family, to their religious beliefs and communities, and to the law. Examining the moral choices which confront all people, but which immigrants face particularly acutely under our current system of laws, brings clarity to questions of immigration policy. It does this by challenging us to articulate what sort of political community best helps its members—immigrants as well as native-born citizens—fulfill their basic moral obligations.

The New Sanctuary Movement provides a rich source of material for this analysis by publicizing the narratives of the families they work with. Consider the story of a woman named Liliana, highlighted by the national New Sanctuary Movement in 2007, which demonstrates how family ties can be a strong pull for immigrants who enter and remain in the U.S. illegally:

> Liliana has lived in the U.S. for 9 years. She has three children, including an infant. All of her children and her husband are U.S. citizens. Her parents are permanent residents and her brothers and sisters are all citizens or residents. . . . When Liliana's family came legally to the U.S. to be farmworkers in Oxnard, Liliana stayed behind to complete high school. After graduating, Liliana was so desperate to rejoin her family that instead of waiting many years (as a result of the case backlog in an underfunded immigration system), she bought a false birth certificate and tried to come to the U.S. She was caught at the border with the fake birth certificate and was turned back. Years later, Liliana's husband tried to petition for her, only to find out that her purchase of the false birth certificate incurred an automatic felony charge—falsely claiming to be a U.S. citizen—which carries a lifetime bar to immigration. She now faces a deportation order.[8]

---

8. New Sanctuary Movement, *Sanctuary: National Newsletter of the New Sanctuary Movement*: 4, http://www.newsanctuarymovement.org/graphics/newsletter/Sanctuary-Color.pdf, accessed March 2008 (no longer available online).

Another family's story, displayed on the website of the New Sanctuary Coalition of New York City, highlights connections between political persecution, religious belief, asylum policies, and undocumented immigration:

> Joe and Linda are wonderful parents to three U.S. citizen children. They entered the country seeking political asylum and have been here for over 10 years, working hard, paying taxes, and establishing their place in the community. They now live under the constant threat of deportation and separation from their children, who cannot return to China with them for fear of religious and political persecution.[9]

These two accounts begin to expose some of the diverse and sometimes contradictory obligations, from family ties to religion to legal issues to economic concerns, that shape immigrants' moral choices about whether to immigrate, where to live, and how to be with and provide for their families.

Here I explore these conflicting obligations by drawing upon ethical thought from my own Lutheran tradition. The question of whether and how to work for change within a given political system can be especially thorny for Lutheran individuals and institutions. Lutheran political thought has been described as "quietist"—a stereotype, but one with some real basis in the tradition—because it seems to obligate Christians to follow without question the laws of the land in which they live, unless those laws explicitly demand renunciation of Christian faith.[10] Those who feel any sort of kinship

---

9. See http://www.newsanctuarynyc.org/families.html for the passage quoted, and http://www.newsanctuarynyc.org/joe.html for a fuller account, both accessed 15 March 2014.
10. See Eric W. Gritsch and Robert W. Jenson, *Lutheranism: The Theological Movement and Its Confessional Writings* (Philadelphia: Fortress Press, 1976), p. 208, for one discussion of "the need to overcome Lutheranism's political quietism and cynicism," as well as Craig L. Nessan's article "Reappropriating Luther's Two Kingdoms," *Lutheran Quarterly* 19 (2005): 302–11, which attempts to rehabilitate Luther's notion of the "two kingdoms," in part as a response to the charge of quietism. In Luther's well-known tract *Temporal Authority: To What Extent It Should Be Obeyed*, he argues that "over what is on earth and belongs to the temporal, earthly kingdom, man has authority from God; but whatever belongs to heaven and to the eternal kingdom is

with Lutheran theological thought are confronted with difficult questions and perhaps even more difficult answers, regarding both the New Sanctuary Movement and the Lutheran tradition. This very tension can give rise to theological and ethical insight, when we ask how Lutheran conceptions of human society and the moral obligations humans bear can shed light on the work of a movement whose tactics seem at odds with traditional Lutheran ethical teachings.

Both addressing and building upon this tension, I argue that Lutheran thought provides valuable theological and ethical resources—to anyone who joins the debate over immigration policy—for understanding the contradictory moral obligations we all, and immigrants especially, face within contemporary legal and economic systems. Martin Luther's recognition that human political communities are shaped by particular "estates" of social existence both elucidates these ethical commitments and shows how they may at times clash. Closer to our time, Dietrich Bonhoeffer's recasting of these "estates" as "mandates" provides an example of how contemporary Lutherans, and others, might apply Luther's original insights in the contemporary age.

Luther on Social and Political Estates, and the Choices Immigrants Make

Luther thought that the organization of social life into different categories of obligations was a theological reality, instituted by God

exclusively under the Lord of heaven." Therefore, a subject's attitude toward a political ruler ought to be this: "I owe you obedience in body and property; command me within the limits of your authority on earth, and I will obey. But if you command me to believe or to get rid of certain books, I will not obey." Thus, while Luther allows for disobedience to political authorities in some circumstances, those circumstances seem to be limited to cases in which a ruler has tried to dictate religious beliefs. Martin Luther, *Temporal Authority: To What Extent It Should Be Obeyed*, in *Luther's Works* 45, ed. Walther I. Brandt (Philadelphia: Muhlenberg, 1962): 111–12.

and thus present in all human communities. In his *Lectures on Genesis*, Luther asserts that God has created three "establishments," semi-distinct categories of identity and obligation, in which human beings are meant to live and move. The first of these is *oeconomia*, or household, which Luther understands to be the "producer" of goods and money as well as children, encompassing both family and economic life; the second is *politia*, which includes the state with its people and rulers; and the third is *ecclesia*, God's church. The church, in Luther's telling, was established for human beings by God prior to either the household or the state.[11] The household or family is next. Both church and household are instituted prior to human sin, so they are fundamental to what the human being on earth is *rightly* created to be. Once human beings sin, however, government (*politia*) comes into existence, since only worldly government can restrain sinful human beings from harming and killing each other. In all of these spheres, human beings have particular roles to play (say, parent or child; ruler or subject; priest or lay believer) and moral obligations that go along with these roles.

Luther's distinctions give us insight into the ethical contradictions undocumented immigrants often face, as highlighted by the narratives above. Liliana, for instance, must choose between obeying the law (complying with her deportation order or, prior to her unauthorized entry, waiting years for a visa) and remaining with her family. She is certainly not the only immigrant who has faced such a choice. Joe and Linda must choose between remaining with

11. Martin Luther, *Lectures on Genesis: Chapter 2*, in *Luther's Works* 1, ed. Jaroslav Pelikan (Saint Louis: Concordia, 1958), 103–4. Luther uses the term "estates" when he connects these "establishments" to individual vocation in his exegesis of Psalm 82: *Psalm 82*, trans. C. M. Jacobs, in *Luther's Works* 13, ed. Jaroslav Pelikan (Saint Louis: Concordia, 1956), 71, as well as in the title of *On the Estate of Marriage* (Martin Luther, *On the Estate of Marriage*, in *Luther's Works* 45). See also Oswald Bayer, *Martin Luther's Theology: A Contemporary Interpretation* (Grand Rapids: Eerdmans, 2008).

their children and obeying the law, and, just as significantly, facing religious persecution if they return to their country of origin. Such examples are theologically significant, and troubling. Luther says very clearly that human beings are ordained by God to live in families and to take care of their spouses and children, as well as that no human law should induce religious believers to betray their faith.[12] For Liliana's parents and others who immigrate to put food on the table, economic realities, combined with laws that give rise to long waiting periods for family reunification, can force parents to choose between caring for their children economically and caring for them physically. Here the household estate of which Luther spoke has broken down, and the spheres of responsibility ordained by God for humanity exist in tension and even direct conflict. And for those who cannot practice their religion in their place of origin, the choice to migrate is even clearer, since Luther plainly asserts that when religious belief is threatened, God must be obeyed rather than human laws.[13]

The stories above are only two examples out of millions in which the family and religion, understood by Luther as more fundamental than politics to the ordering of human life, are broken apart under the current system of laws. When a person who has committed no violation but to reside in the United States without authorization must choose between obeying immigration laws and upholding her

---

12. *On the Estate of Marriage* states: "God himself instituted [the estate of marriage], brought husband and wife together, and ordained that they should beget children and care for them. . . . The estate of marriage and everything that goes with it in the way of conduct, works, and suffering is pleasing to God" (*Estate of Marriage* 38). In *Temporal Authority*, Luther several times asserts that religious belief ought to be free from political or legal compulsion, as cited in footnote 10 as well as here: "The temporal government has laws which extend no further than to life and property and external affairs on earth, for God cannot and will not permit anyone but himself to rule over the soul. Therefore, when the temporal authority presumes to prescribe laws for the soul, it encroaches upon God's government and only misleads souls and destroys them" (Martin Luther, *Temporal Authority: To What Extent It Should Be Obeyed*, in *Luther's Works* 45, p. 105).

13. See footnotes 10 and 12, above.

moral obligations in some other sphere, whether as a religious believer or as a parent, spouse, or child, then something in our ordering of the estates needs repair.

Economic Migration and Bonhoeffer's "Mandates"

Some who hear these stories may find it easier to understand Joe and Linda's fear of religious persecution than Liliana's family's story of economic migration. For religious people especially, it often seems clear that people who immigrate in order to practice religion freely should be allowed and even helped to do so, but it is not so clear how citizens of a relatively wealthy nation should think about economic immigration. We can make some evaluation of cases like these using Luther's discussion of estates, but the terms in which Luther discusses family and economic life are not clearly differentiated.[14] The work of Dietrich Bonhoeffer is more helpful for guiding a Lutheran interpretation of contemporary social, political, and especially economic issues as they apply to immigration.

Like Luther, Bonhoeffer thinks that God orders human lives through universally valid sets of obligations, but he envisions *four* "mandates": work, family, government, and church.[15] In the contemporary world, work or economic life is not tied as closely to family life as Luther envisioned, and thus "economy" in the sense of practices of labor, investment, and trade deserves examination as a fourth estate, or mandate.[16] This allows us to speak more clearly of the ways in which economic obligations intersect, but sometimes also

---

14. In his exegesis of Genesis, Luther speaks of the "household government" as encompassing both labor to raise food from the ground and the raising of children, and he understands the two kinds of labor to be closely linked. See *Lectures on Genesis: Chapter Two*, 102–4.
15. Dietrich Bonhoeffer, *Ethics*, ed. Eberhard Bethge, trans. Neville Horton Smith (New York: Simon & Schuster, 1995): 204–10.
16. Bonhoeffer himself claims that this taxonomy is more biblical than the traditional Lutheran taxonomy of household, government, church. See *Ethics*, 325.

conflict, with family, political, or religious obligations. Bonhoeffer, inspired by Luther's insights, cautions against allowing one of the mandates to encroach upon the others—say, political authorities dictating family life, or the church trying to act as a political ruler. Such encroachment, he says, leads to a troubling imbalance in human social and moral life, and religious people and communities must resist it as morally wrong.[17]

These two ideas—that economic life is a separate sphere of activity and obligation, and that none of the mandates ought to encroach upon the others—are shared by many citizens, and certainly many religious believers. Furthermore, many worry that the concerns and obligations of economic life have seemingly triumphed over all our other concerns and obligations. When the policies that drive the global economy force some immigrants to move away from their families, or bring their families across borders illegally, in order to gain even a basic living, not only has economic life been separated from family life, but economic concerns actually break family life apart. In such cases, the policies that structure communal life require alteration, so that people can fulfill their family, economic, *and* political obligations—namely, to care for family members; to contribute productive labor and gain wages that can support themselves and their families; and to obey the laws of the land.

The New Sanctuary Movement thus draws attention to the theologically and ethically troublesome pressures of contemporary economic and political life, which become especially clear in the lives of undocumented immigrants. Lutheran theological and ethical thinking provides concepts through which we can fruitfully analyze and begin to respond to such pressures, especially in the lives of

17. *Ethics*, 293–96, 339–47. "The commandment of Jesus Christ does not provide the basis for any kind of domination of the Church over the government, of the government over the family, or of culture over government or Church, of for any other relation of overlordship which may be thought of in this connection" (293).

those who must clearly choose between obeying laws and fulfilling their family and economic obligations. Beginning our policy debates with the question "Will these laws allow people to fulfill all of their fundamental human moral obligations?" may lead to very different laws than we currently have. We must comprehend all the factors that cause human suffering and think clearly about how to shape a communal political life—a life together, one that makes it possible both for those who are born in the community and for those who migrate into it to fulfill their basic needs as well as, crucially, their basic moral obligations.

Conclusion

The Lutheran tradition of affirming the moral obligations that weigh on all human beings helps to clarify why immigration policies in the contemporary United States are in need of repair. Current policies force migrants to make choices between their moral obligations—and often force them to choose to fulfill less-fundamental obligations over more-fundamental ones. The work of the New Sanctuary Movement brings these issues to light so that political debates may take into account the stories of migrants who must make such choices. Insofar as the movement's public provision of sanctuary helps make such stories more widely known, it offers a challenge to traditional Lutheran thinking, which teaches that laws ought to be obeyed in nearly all cases.

Lutheran tradition, on the other hand, provides a lens through which to view these stories that emphasizes the impact of immigration policies on our moral as well as our economic and political lives. The work of the New Sanctuary Movement and the thought of Luther and Bonhoeffer in some ways challenge each other, but taken together they shed light on the problems – and some possible solutions – of contemporary immigration and contemporary life, sharing in the hope that all people will be able to attend most fruitfully to *all* the moral obligations that define human life in this world.

15

The Morning After

The Role of Faith-Based Groups Post–Immigration Reform

Alan A. Aja

On April 23, 2010, Arizona Governor Jan Brewer signed one of the most draconian pieces of state-level immigration legislation in U.S. history. The "Support Our Law Enforcement and Safe Neighborhoods Act," or Senate Bill (S.B.) 1070, created a state public policy designed to deter, in the lawmaker's words, the "unlawful entry and presence of 'aliens' and economic activity by persons unlawfully present in the U.S."[1] Among its many provisions, the bill created penalties for sheltering, hiring, aiding, or transporting

---

1. See section "Intent" of S.B. 1070. Quotation marks around the term "alien" are my emphasis, denoting a derogatory legal term used by the U.S. government to describe persons without citizenship status. Instead I use the terms "undocumented" or "unauthorized" interchangeably throughout, a more humanistic way of describing immigrants who may have overstayed their visas for legitimate reasons (as do tourists, businesspeople, and students), or were forced to disobey the laws of the nation–state in order to provide for themselves or their families.

undocumented immigrants, while legally empowering state and local officials to circumvent the federal government's role in enforcing immigration laws.[2] Most disturbingly, the bill extended powers to local law enforcement and state agency officials to determine one's immigration status upon any "contact" (e.g., lawful stop), if there is "reasonable suspicion" they are unauthorized to be in the country. This measure by default encourages racial profiling, compromising basic civil liberties of groups of color, specifically Latinos, Middle Easterners/Arab Americans, and some Asian groups like Filipinos.

While Arizona's "papers-please!" legislation set off a firestorm of public debate over its underlying intentions, various faith-based communities acting on their shared religious call to "welcome the stranger" were actively at the helm of civil and legal actions against the measure.[3] Jewish, Christian, and Muslim scriptures are full of admonitions and mandates to be compassionate to the "stranger" and to treat them justly.[4] Sarah and Abraham were given the mission to "be a blessing to all nations" (Gen. 22:18). For Christians, Jesus' mandate to "love God and your neighbor" as defined in the parable of the Good Samaritan serves as a guidepost for the religious call to action in defense of those who are different or "strangers" in this land.[5] For Muslims, the Qur'an calls "those who believed and adopted exile and fought for the Faith, with their property and their persons,

2. See Article 8, Section B of S.B. 1070, State of Arizona, 49th Legislature, Second Regular Session, 2010.

3. See The Permanent Mission of the Holy See in Geneva, Caritas Internationalis, the International Catholic Migration Commission, and Jesuit Refugee Service, "Welcoming the Stranger: Affirmations for Faith Leaders," *Pax Christi International*, accessed 25 March 2014, http://www.paxchristi.net/news/welcoming-stranger-affirmations-faith-leaders/2719#sthash.cwYhBctt.dpbs.

4. Among many: Do not mistreat an alien [immigrant] or oppress him, for you were aliens in Egypt; Do not oppress an alien; you yourselves know how it feels to be aliens [immigrants], because you were aliens [immigrants] in Egypt (Exod. 22:21, 23:9). Also see Deut. 10:18-19 and Prov. 31:8-9.

5. Here I use "strangers" ironically, given that many of today's Latin American immigrants are descendants of indigenous peoples who were in the Americas long before the inception of the United States, only to be brutally colonized by European arrivals and whose future generations

in the cause of Allah, as well as those who gave [them] asylum and aid—these are [all] friends and protectors, one of another" (Al Anfal, 8:72).

Thus, subsequent to the bill's passing, a multiethnic coalition of clergy, unions, students, and families organized marches and rallies against the legislation, joined by representatives of prominent national organizations. Some religious groups, with support from the National Council of La Raza (NCLR) among other organizations, called for an economic boycott of the state—invoking the spirit and direct action campaigns of the late Cesar Chavez and the United Farm Workers.[6] At the judicial level, the National Coalition of Latino Clergy and Christian Leaders, an organization made up of representatives from over 30,000 churches, were among a long list of organizations and individuals to file lawsuits against the state, arguing that the law violated due process and the most basic Constitutional rights.[7]

Two years later, the Supreme Court yielded a 5–3 decision, ruling that while particular sections of S.B. 1070 violated federal law, the "show-me-your-papers" status checks did not.[8] By this time, the civil rights crisis prompted by S.B. 1070 had already been spreading

were subject to further violent forms of colonization by the United States. In essence, this land is their land.

6. See Randal C. Archibold, "In Wake of Immigration Law, Calls for an Economic Boycott of Arizona," *New York Times*, 26 April 2010. See also Randy Shaw, *Beyond the Fields: Cesar Chavez, the UFW, and the Struggle for Justice in the 21st Century* (Berkeley: University of California Press, 2010), who argues convincingly that the contemporary democratic rights movements, from grassroots campaigns to large-scale electoral politics, are the legacies of Chavez and the UFW.

7. See *NCLCC et al. v. Arizona*, No. 10-00943 (2010). Also, for a list of legal actions filed against B.S. 1070, see the American Immigration Council's "Legal Action Center," http://libguides.law.ucla.edu/content.php?pid=129802&sid=1113370. The plaintiffs argued that the law violated the 1st and 14th amendments and the due process clause.

8. See *Arizona v. United States*, 567 US (2012). This included provisions that made it a state crime to be on Arizona soil without papers, criminalizes undocumented unemployment, and empowers police to arrest individuals without warrant if they suspect they should be deported. For a legal interpretation of the law and its complexities, see Amy Howe, "B.S. 1070: In Plain English," accessed 25 June 2012, http://www.scotus blog.com/2012/06/s-b-1070-in-plain-english/.

across the U.S. Similar legislation had already been adopted in states with growing immigrant communities, including Alabama, Georgia, Kentucky, South Carolina, and others.[9] In Kentucky for example, a coalition of clergy, labor leaders, and civil rights groups organized and protested vehemently against a Kentucky Senate anti-immigrant measure (S.B. 6), disallowing the bill to reach the assembly floor.[10] In Georgia, coalitional opposition was voiced but unsuccessful through the passing of H.B. 87, but immigrant rights advocates followed the examples set by their sisters and brothers in Arizona through methods of civil disobedience and legal action.[11] This included a lawsuit against the state by leaders of faith-based organizations that had long been helping undocumented immigrants find church homes and transporting them to medical offices and grocery stores when in need.[12]

At present, the collective answer to counter the effects of what observers call the "Arizonafication" of U.S. immigration policy is grounded in a multifaceted approach to pass laws that extend basic economic and social rights to millions of immigrants, documented and undocumented alike.[13] Despite the current Congressional

---

9. For a synopsis of similar legislation around the country, see "State Anti-Immigrant Laws," The American Civil Liberties Union, accessed 22 January 2014, https://www.aclu.org/immigrants-rights/state-anti-immigrant-laws.

10. For a good summary of the Kentucky legislation and a cost-based analysis of a similar proposal in North Carolina, see Tzra Mitchell, "Kentucky experience indicates that anti-immigrant bills cost taxpayers and communities," NC Budget and Tax Center, *North Carolina Policy Watch*, 29 April 2013, accessed 3 March 2014, http://pulse.ncpolicywatch.org/2013/04/29/kentucky-experience-indicates-that-anti-immigrant-bills-cost-taxpayers-and-communities/#sthash.mr0TrmVq.dpuf.

11. See Gustavo Valdes, "Georgia Governor Signs Controversial Anti-Illegal Immigration Law," *CNN*, 13 May 2011, accessed 5 March 2014, http://www.cnn.com/2011/us /05/13/georgia.immigration.law/.

12. For a brief discussion of the coalitional efforts behind the Georgia lawsuits, see Azadeh N. Shahshahan and Omar Jadwat's commentary, accessed 12 March 2014, http://www.dailykos.com/story/2011/06/07/983056/-Georgia-Is-Not-a-Show-Me-Your-Papers-State#.

13. For a discussion of "Arizonafication," see Jeff Biggers, "The Arizonafication of America," *New York Times*, 15 October 2012.

impasse and the Obama administration's own interventions, the inevitable passing of Comprehensive Immigration Reform (CIR) may begin to do just that, given that it seeks to create pathways toward citizenship for the millions of immigrants living in America's shadows or waiting for an upgraded status amidst the heavy backlog of case-hearings and decisions.[14]

Yet, no set of policies are without adverse consequences, and considering a post-9/11 political climate based on increased xenophobia, racial profiling, and general harassment of nonwhite populations, there is legitimate concern by religious leaders and immigration reform advocates alike that final versions of CIR are very likely to be punitive in design, heavy on border enforcement and deportations, and weak on issues of economic and civil rights.

Given these likelihoods, I propose the following question: What is next for interfaith and ecumenical communities in this new reality? While it remains unclear whether CIR will pass in the near future or closer to midterm elections, it is evident that the mandate for policy change is driven less by a culture of compassion and inclusion and more out of political fear by both dominant parties (Republicans/ Democrats). While not as anti-immigrant as proposals by the Tea Party and certain right-wing organizations, I argue the bipartisan CIR legislation still violates the interfaith calling of "welcoming the stranger." The forthcoming comprehensive immigration reform

---

14. I am referring to two executive actions taken in recent years by the Obama administration in response to Congressional inaction and pressures by proponents of immigration reform. Deferred Action for Childhood Arrivals (DACA), which went into effect in June 2012, allows undocumented immigrants who entered the country before their 16th birthday to receive a short-term work permit and be exempt from deportation. It does not include pathways to citizenship. The more recent action was a November 20, 2014 executive order that focused on updating border security, shifts deportation priorities to felons and requires undocumented parents of U.S. born children to undergo background checks and other requirements. For more information, see: Kandel, William A. Bjelopera, Jerome P. Bruno, Andorra. Siskin, Alison. *The President's Immigration Accountability Executive Action of November 20, 2014: Overview and Issues.* Congressional Research Service, 4. Also see: https://www.whitehouse.gov/issues/immigration.

package will very likely leave millions of immigrants and their families without the most basic legal and economic rights. Thus I propose that faith-based groups consider a set of bold grassroots initiatives, and local and federal policies to supplement the interfaith calling of "welcoming the stranger."

Brief Background

When the underground networks of refugee support in Tucson, Arizona gave rise to the Sanctuary Movement of the 1980s, it took several years for policymakers to realize that religious congregations had been simultaneously addressing the consequences of an outdated immigration policy while conducting the work of an absent refugee policy.[15] At the time, displaced Central American migrants crossed a brutal Sonoran desert in increasing numbers, driven by war and economic volatility ushered in by U.S. foreign policy and direct intervention.[16] However, instead of succumbing to a hostile political climate that increasingly blamed immigrants of color for the country's economic woes, faith-based groups answered by heeding the call in Exod. 22:21 to "not mistreat or oppress foreigners in any way," collectively providing housing and engaging in direct social services to migrants as they sought work in the U.S.

Eventually policymakers answered, making the Sanctuary Movement a default catalyst for the country's most recent major immigration reform legislation, the Immigration Reform and Control Act (IRCA) of 1986.[17] Unsurprisingly, the act called for more funding for border security while placing the burden on employers

15. For an informative, succinct synopsis of the movement, see "Sanctuary Movement" entry in Miguel De La Torre, ed., *Hispanic Religious Cultures Encyclopedia*, vol. 1 (Santa Barbara: ABC-CLIO, 2008), 498–502.
16. Ibid.
17. The IRCA of 1986 was the first major piece of immigration legislation passed since the 1965 Hart-Cellar Act, better known as the Family Reunification Act, which removed racist national origin quotas and created family- and skill-based preferences (an act further made possible by

through penalties to refrain from hiring undocumented immigrants. It also created pathways toward citizenship for undocumented immigrants already in the country depending on length of residence in the United States and other requirements including payment of filing fees, evidence of "good moral character" (no criminal record), proof of English language competency, and knowledge of American civics.[18]

In hindsight, such policies could be viewed as a success, given that 2.7 million of the 3 million who applied for permanent residency through IRCA received it.[19] But it is the unintended effects of the act that serve as a warning for what may come post–Comprehensive Immigration Reform. For example, the Migration Policy Institute (MPI) notes that 1.3 million people applied for permanent residency through a special agricultural provision of IRCA, when policymakers only projected 250,000 applicants. Furthermore, cut-off dates of entry set by the act marginalized more recent arrivals from mixed-status households who considered the U.S. "home," rightfully not wanting to be separated from loved ones.[20] Thus the demand for regularization of immigrant livelihoods was far greater than policy expectations, and a large pool of immigrants marginalized by IRCA contributed to much of the base of undocumented immigrants still living in uncertainty today.[21]

the faith-based contours and political climate ushered in by the African American–inspired civil rights movement).

18. See Betsy Cooper and Kevin O'Neill, "Lessons from the Immigration Reform and Control Act," no. 3 (August 2005), accessed 22 January 2014, http://www.migrationpolicy.org/.

19. Ibid.

20. Ibid.

21. In addition, the MPI assessed that because resources were diverted to implement IRCA's border-enforcement and employment-regulatory mechanisms from the then-called Immigration and Naturalization Service (INS), creating an underfunded, understaffed agency to deal with the increasing numbers of immigrants applying under family reunification. Ibid. Also see for more information: Hugh Davis Graham, *Collision Course: The Strange Convergence of Affirmative Action and Immigration Policy in America* (New York: Oxford University Press, 2002).

Over twenty-five years later, if the Supreme Court's contradictory ruling on Arizona's S.B. 1070 is any indicator, the political and legal climate will remain hostile toward immigrants of color, and current proposals by lawmakers mirror much of IRCA's punitive contours, if not harsher. The most recent proposal by Congressional Republicans, who currently control the House of Representatives, makes "security" and border enforcement its top priority, while placing pathways toward citizenship on the backburner of policy priority. The Obama administration has increased the size of the border security agencies dramatically and has already deported more immigrants, primarily Mexicans, than the eight years of the Bush administration combined.[22] Furthermore, the proposal includes a visa-tracking system, employment verification measures, an emphasis on high-skilled immigrants, harsh fines, and requirements for Dreamers and undocumented immigrants with no guarantee of due process, permanent residency, or citizenship.[23] As experts have warned, the end product of CIS may further perpetuate the current tragic realities of immigration: more border-crossing deaths, increased immigrant

22. According to journalist Adrian Carrasquillo (see below), the Congressional Hispanic Caucus's (CHC) resolution reads that "an estimated 200,000 deportees in a two-year period were reported to be the parents of U.S. citizens, most of whom were born and raised in the United States" and that "there are more than 5,000 children in the U.S. child welfare system because a parent has been detained or deported, and a majority of those children are U.S. citizens." For more discussion on this resolution and surrounding conflict between CHC and the White House, see Adrian Carrasquillo, "Xavier Becerra and Luis Gutierrez on Deportations and the Search for the Next DREAMers," *Buzzfeed*, 23 March 2014, accessed 25 March 2014, http://www.buzzfeed.com/adriancarrasquillo/xavier-becerra-and-luis-gutierrez-hopeful-after-pressure-on.

23. The term DREAMers stems from the original 2001 bill proposed (and defeated several times) in Congress entitled the Development, Relief and Education for Alien Minors (DREAM) Act. It refers to the thousands of immigrant youth eligible for DACA (see footnote 14). For a critical analysis of the latest Republican immigration reform principles, see Lopez Nativo-Vigil, "Apartheidesque Republican Immigration Principles," *Hermandad Mexicana Humanitarian Foundation*, 7 February 2014, accessed 15 Feb. 2014, http://laprensa-sandiego.org/featured/apartheidesque-republican-immigration-principles-dead-on-arrival/. Also see: http://www.immigrationpolicy.org/just-facts/who-and-where-dreamers-are-revised-estimates.

detention and deportation rates, and, in general, another sizable pool of undocumented immigrants living in the legal and economic shadows of uncertainty.[24]

To remedy these realities, interfaith leaders need to consider nuanced, progressive approaches that begin with the proposition that comprehensive immigration reform is only a demand-side remedy to a supply-side problem. Often missing from the domestic immigration debate is a "world systems" perspective—one that considers the hegemonic structures and purposeful uneven development ushered in by foreign policies of rich countries in the forms of direct military invasion or occupation, along with trade and foreign investment, and how they perpetuate the displacement, eventual exploitation, and disparate treatment of immigrants and their families.[25] We must also be reminded of the segmented structure of U.S. immigration policy: a convoluted, outdated system that gives preferred access to professional immigrants and places family-based applicants secondary at the same time employers rely on pools of exploited migrants (many undocumented) in service, agricultural, and manufacturing sectors who live the day-to-day absence of healthcare and workplace rights.

Given this scenario, the limitations of reform will require bold, complementary initiatives to ensure the most basic economic and

24. Latino policy expert Angelo Falcon recently wrote: "Some are wondering whether the call for 'comprehensive' immigration reform is achievable or desirable given the trade-off it seems to generate between massive border security spending and a path to citizenship. There are others who argue that undocumented Latinos are not all that interested in achieving U.S. citizenship as much as simply becoming legalized in some form that would allow them to work in this country and travel back home safely, even if only temporarily" (Angelo Falcon, "The Fork in the Path to Comprehensive Immigration Reform," *National Institute for Latino Policy*, 25 October 2013, accessed 1 Nov. 2014, http://www.nilpnetwork.org/NiLP_Commentary_-_Immmigration_Reform_2013.pdf).

25. I am applying the often-cited "world systems" perspective as argued by Immanuel Wallerstein in *The Modern World System: Capitalist Agriculture and the Origins of the European World Economy in the Sixteenth Century* (New York: Academic Press, 1974). Also, an excellent read on U.S. trade policy and its impact on migration is David Bacon's "How U.S. Policies Fueled Mexico's Great Migration," *The Nation*, 23 Jan. 2012, accessed 12 Feb. 2014, http://www.thenation.com/article/165438/how-U.S.-policies-fueled-mexicos-great-migration.

social rights for the millions of immigrants who will continue to suffer from the punitive components of CIR. Below, I recommend a brief set of initiatives and policies that faith-based groups could support from the grassroots to the policy level, keeping in mind their limitations and imperfections.[26]

Support Food Sovereignty

In March of 2014, sixteen faith-based bodies and religious organizations from across the country organized to oppose H.R. 3830, the "Bipartisan Congressional Trade Priorities Act." The act, which gives the Executive Branch more authority to choose our trade partners and "fast-track" any trade agreements without committee debate and amendments from Congress, poses a serious threat to democratic participation in legislative matters.[27] In a joint letter to Congress, signatories from the Friends Committee on National Legislation, Church World Service, Presbyterian Peace Fellowship, and other religious organizations wrote that "they are called to meet the needs of the most vulnerable," and that such unilateral, undemocratic actions compromise the interfaith call to "put human dignity and the dignity of God's creation at the heart of any trade policy."[28]

---

26. These recommendations should be viewed cautiously and imperfectly given the unpredictable, incremental context of policymaking and implementation. Also, the current bipartisan trend of "austerity economics" (federal- to state-level budget cuts to basic public goods and social programs) should be acknowledged as a serious but reversible barrier. Some recommendations inspired by myriad initiatives faith-based groups and progressive allies have already been proposed and implemented at some level throughout the United States and abroad, and are only "bold" in the sense in that they challenge the current status quo and are otherwise normal practices in other countries and localities. Other proposals are admittedly ambitious and unorthodox, nevertheless possible and sustainable through broad-based coalitions of support and policy action.
27. See Friends Committee on National Legislation, "16 Faith-Based Organizations Oppose Fast Track Bill," accessed 17 March 2014, http:// fcnl.org / issues / energy / 16_faith_ organizations_ oppose_fast_track_bill.
28. Ibid.

While the bill currently faces stiff opposition from labor unions and other economic justice groups, the coalitional reaction to H.R. 3830 is among many interfaith efforts that represent a growing ecumenical concern and heightened awareness toward the economic and environmental impacts of "economic globalization." Generally defined as the unrestricted movement of goods, services, capital, and people across diminishing national borders, the overarching ideology behind economic globalization is based on a set of "neoliberal" beliefs that "open markets," government deregulation, and increasing privatization of public goods are more efficient methods to produce wealth for all nations.[29] But trade policies like NAFTA (North American Free Trade Agreement) that emanate from these principles, while argued to allow the expedient flows of goods and services into the United States at cheaper prices thus creating economic booms, have been empirically proven to do more harm than good, with long-term adverse environmental and economic effects for rich and poor countries alike.[30]

Alternatively, several faith-based organizations and ally partners have responded by passing resolutions and engaging in direct action to move toward food and economic sovereignty. For example, the *Food Sovereignty Alliance*, a network coalition comprised of faith-based and community-based organizations and research centers from across the world, hold the fundamental belief that people ultimately

---

29. For an excellent discussion on the role of economic globalization, specifically on U.S. immigration, see Saskia Sassen, *Globalization and Its Discontents* (New York: New Press, 1998). Also see Joseph E. Stiglitz's book of the same title, *Globalization and Its Discontents* (New York: W. W. Norton, 2003).

30. Even when acknowledging the benefits, the lack of tariffs, or taxes corporations are absolved from through said trade treaties to encourage fast production and distribution of goods and services, by default deny necessary funding streams for the infrastructure, social programs, and basic public services humans need to sustain their livelihoods and prevent forced migration, especially the middle class and working poor. Also see David Bacon's "How U.S. Policies Fueled Mexico's Great Migration," *The Nation*, 23 January 2012, accessed 12 February 2014, http://www.thenation.com/article/165438/how-U.S.-policies-fueled-mexicos-great-migration.

should have the right to determine their own food and agricultural policies.[31] Rooted in *La Via Campesina* campaign, a transnational movement that represents millions of small- and medium-scale farmers, women's groups, and indigenous communities, "Food Sovereignty" seeks to counter the power and control of "Big Food" (multinational agribusinesses) by engaging in direct "food justice" initiatives that democratize land and resources while undoing the economic conditions that force millions of people into the shadows.[32]

In an illuminating commentary by Agricultural Mission, Inc.'s Stephen Bartlett, a Presbyterian layperson, unapologetically calls faith-based groups to task to confront the monopoly-like concentration of food production while underscoring the impact on immigrants. He writes:

> [T]he control by just three corporations of 80 percent of international grain trade means more than half of all basic grains produced in the world are not destined for human consumption at all. Those grains go to feed cattle, pigs and chickens, often in cruel confinement feedlots known as CAFOs. These are typically hellish places, both for the animals and for the low-paid, often immigrant, workers who toil under increasingly exploitative conditions, afraid to organize under the threat of arrest and deportation in Immigration and Customs Enforcement (ICE) sweeps. . . .[33]

Bartlett's observation further underscores the well-documented reality that small subsistence farmers are often the first to shoulder

31. The alliance's website provides more details of the network organization: http://U.S. foodsovereigntyalliance.org/what-is-food-sovereignty/, accessed 2 April 2014.
32. For more background on *La Via Campesina* movement, see Michael Menser, "Transnational Participatory Democracy in Action: The Case of La Via Campesina," *Journal of Social Philosophy* 39, no. 1 (January 2010): 149-75. Also see, Maria Elena Martinez-Torres and Peter Rosset, "La Via Capesina: The Birth and Evolution of a Transnational Social Movement," *Journal of Peasant Studies* 37, No. 1 (Jan. 2010): 149-75.
33. For a succinct, ecumenically based rationale for food sovereignty, see Stephen Bartlett, "Mass Hunger in the Midst of Record Harvests: Why the World Needs Food Sovereignty," *Response: The Magazine of Women in Mission* (March 2009), accessed 2 April 2014, http://new.gbgm-umc.org/umw/foodfaith/jU.S. tice/foodsovereignty/.

the effects of unequal trade policies ushered in by economic globalization.[34] Multinational corporations and governments collude, often violently, to evict small-scale farmers and bust trade unions in order to create large-scale industries, ultimately creating massive displacement and flows of cross-country and northern cone migration.[35] Food-sovereignty campaigns, programs, and policies reverse those conditions through bottom-up, participatory democratic practices, localizing food sources in ways that empower small farmers (many from indigenous communities), workers (many undocumented), and communities (rich and poor alike) in the United States and abroad.

Agricultural Mission, Inc., a long-time ecumenical ministry with mission to fulfill the "gospel's promises of 'abundant life' for all," is among the many faith-centered groups working to directly confront the structural causes of poverty and injustice through food sovereignty. In addition, the Presbyterian Church (USA), the United Methodist Church, and the United Church of Christ, among others, have also been building awareness among congregations on the importance of food-sovereignty initiatives by passing an array of resolutions, conducting international exchanges, and engaging in direct community-level practices. For example, in 2009, the United Church of Christ passed a resolution supporting food sovereignty while condemning the "nation, merchants, and the rich who profit at the expense of the most vulnerable in their midst" (UCC, 2009). In underscoring the multitude of effects of "big food," the resolution

---

34. In another example, more recently the Presbyterian Church (USA) urged Congress not to pass the Colombia Free Trade Agreement (CFTA) until human rights conditions improved in that country. The Presbyterian Peace Fellowship also organized a fast to build awareness of the legislation and held call-ins to President Obama with hopes to hold off on the bill until it included needed revisions. See Ginna Irby and Jerry Van Marter, "PC (USA) Seeks to Block Free Trade Agreement with Colombia," 18 June 2011, accessed 15 March 2014, http://pres-outlook.org/2011/06/pcU.S. a-seeks-to-block-free-trade-agreement-with-colombia/.

35. Bartlett, "Mass Hunger in the Midst of Record Harvests."

referenced the book of Isaiah, arguing that "true worship involves letting the oppressed go free, housing the homeless poor, and to 'share your bread with hungry . . .' (Isa. 58:6-7)."[36]

One example initiative is undertaken by the Fourth Avenue Presbyterian Church in Bay Ridge, Brooklyn, which has served as the host site for the Bay Ridge CSA. The neighborhood initiative has over 150 members, most of whom are not members of the congregation. The CSA works as a cooperative, in which members collectively support a Hudson Valley farmer who grows and transports a sizable ration of freshly picked vegetables and fruits each Saturday morning for five months of the year, while members volunteer their time to ensure efficient distribution for each family shareholder, not to mention managing the finances and overall administration of the CSA.[37] Other examples from across the country include the Community Farm Alliance (CFA) of Kentucky, which currently supports farmers markets in low-income neighborhoods of Louisville, Kentucky, ensuring locals direct access to affordable, nonmass-produced goods and vegetables. The Detroit Black Community Food Security Network, which runs a seven-acre farm (the largest in the city) empowers the local community through a myriad of programs to engage not only in the planting and eventual distribution of food, but also in the post-consumption phase through waste management.[38]

36. See "The Roles of Church and Government in Addressing Global Food Crisis," Resolution, General Synod (United Church of Christ), 2009, http://www.ucc.org/jU.S. tice/globalization/globalfoodcrisis.html.

37. The Bay Ridge CSA currently makes available 100 shares of vegetables, fifty fruit, and fifty egg shares. Fourth Avenue Presbyterian Church also partners with the local CSA to provide shares for low-income families through a scholarship fund. For full disclosure, I am currently a member of the Bay Ridge CSA and refer to it here given its dedication to food sovereignty.

38. For more on Detroit's important efforts, see http://metrotimes.com/food/features/detroit-black-community-food-security-network-s-growing-determination-1.1562087. See also Ecumenical Ministries of Oregon/Interfaith Network for Earth Concerns, *Food Sovereignty for All Handbook*, accessed 14 April 2014, http.emoregon.org., which provides succinct information, case studies, and recommendations for faith-based communities looking to initiate

Support Municipal ID Cards

In recent bipartisan blueprints for Comprehensive Immigration Reform, policymakers have discussed implementing biometric identification cards that would use fingerprints and biological traits to determine one's immigration status, including permission to work.[39] The proposal, which could become mandatory for all U.S. workers, has been met with a great deal of scrutiny by civil liberty advocates and interfaith groups due to concerns over government surveillance and privacy, financial costs to states, and likelihood of increased denial of due process for immigrants and U.S.-born alike.[40] These concerns are not without merit given the already-draconian REAL ID Act of 2005, which gives unprecedented authority to the Department of Homeland Security to bypass our system of "checks and balances" for border security measures, not to mention the inaccuracies and rejections already embedded in the pilot E-verify system that authorizes immigrants to work.[41]

Alternatively, localities across the country are undertaking their own civic tools to ensure immigrant economic and civic integration independent from federal identification measures, albeit limited in that they do not serve as work permits. In New York City, for

food-sovereignty initiatives among their congregants. This includes guidelines on how to support local community gardens, organize sustainable food kitchens, or create local CSAs (Community Supported Agriculture).

39. For more on the controversial biometric card proposal, see Margaret Hartman, "Immigration Reform Could Lead to Biometric ID Cards for Everyone," *New York Magazine*, 21 Feb. 2013, accessed 15 April 2014, http://nymag.com/daily/intelligencer/2013/02/immigration-reform-could-lead-to-biometric-ids.html. See also Elia Zureik and Karen Hindle, "Governance, Security and Technology: The Case of Biometrics," Studies in Political Economy 73 (Spring/Summer 2004).

40. Ibid, 40.

41. For analyses and critiques of the Real ID act and E-verify system, see for example: http://www.civilrights.org/advocacy/letters/2005/opposition-to-the-real-id-act-of-2005.html and http://www.washingtonpost.com/blogs/wonkblog/wp/2013/06/03/e-verify-is-supposed-to-stop-undocumented-employment-it-could-also-harm-legal-workers/, accessed 15 April 2014.

example, the Bill de Blasio administration has implemented a policy of citywide municipal IDs, making it the largest city in the country to allow all of its residents, regardless of immigration status, to hold an identification card.[42] The popular measure, also implemented in cities like Los Angeles, Princeton, San Francisco, and New Haven, makes it easier for residents to access basic services including library cards and bank accounts; leasing apartments; applying for employment and driver's license (if they choose and are allowed by state law); accessing public and private spaces (like schools) requiring identification; and for children, listing parental contact information, drug allergies, or medical conditions.[43]

In New Haven, the first to start such a program, the city has already issued 12,000 IDs since 2007, and the policy has been attributed to increasing cooperation between local law enforcement and immigrant communities.[44] In San Francisco, which has issued 20,000 cards since the program's implementation in 2009, officials cite its benefits in that undocumented residents without access to bank accounts often carry cash, making them targets for petty crimes. This comes with the evidence that undocumented immigrants are less likely than foreign-born to report crimes given fears of deportation, even though as some experts have found, they may experience crimes at rates similar to or higher than that of the population at large.[45]

---

42. See "NYC Mayor proposes ID cards for undocumented immigrants," *NBC News*, 11 Feb. 2014, accessed 24 March 2014.

43. For a brief analysis of municipal ID card benefits, see Kica Matos in the *New York Times*, 13 Feb. 2014, accessed 24 March 2014, http://www.nytimes.com/roomfordebate/2014/02/13/should-all-immigrants-be-able-to-get-id-cards/identification-cards-integrate-all-residents-into-the-community.

44. Another example of media coverage on municipal ID cards: http://www.cnn.com/2014/02/21/ U.S. /municipal-id-cards-undocumented/.

45. For a scholarly examination of the intersections between local law enforcement and immigration, see Nik Theodore, "Insecure Communities: Latino Perceptions of Police Involvement in Immigration Enforcement," University of Illinois at Chicago, May 2013, accessed 24 March 2014, http://www.policylink.org/atf/cf/{97c6d565-bb43-406d-a6d5-eca3bbf35af0}/INSECURE_COMMUNITIES_REPORT_FINAL_V2.PDF.

Furthermore, such a policy would serve as a complementary initiative to current Friendly Cities campaigns across the country, localities that have passed ordinances protecting the rights of immigrants, regardless of status, from harassment and discrimination by local authorities.

Support Dual Language Programs

In 2001, the Bush administration's No Child Left Behind policy was passed in Congress, taking with it one of the most important pieces of immigrant-support legislation in U.S. history. The Bilingual Education Act of 1968 (Title VI of Elementary and Secondary Education Act) was the first mandate to give immigrants access to education in their primary language (amended in 1988). But when NCLB was passed, it cut funding for English Language Learners (ELLs) and mandated yearly tests in the English language, acts that advocates note violate the antidiscriminatory clauses (Title VI) of the monumental Civil Rights Act of 1964 and subsequent decisions by the Supreme Court (see *Lau v. Nichols*, 1974).[46]

In reality, the incremental dismantling of bilingual education began long before the passing of NCLB, driven by contemporary English-only movements of the 1980s and 1990s and evidenced by state-level pieces of legislation including California's Proposition 227 (June 2, 1998), Arizona's Proposition 203 (Nov. 7, 2000), and Massachusetts' Question 2 (Nov. 5, 2002) among other initiatives. While there was hope among educators that the Obama administration would rectify past policies, critical experts note that the 2009 *Race to the Top* contest, which awards states monies based

46. For an excellent critique of NCLB's impact on the Bilingual Education Act, see James Crawford, "Obituary: The Bilingual Ed Act, 1968-2002," *Rethinking Schools*, www.rethinkingschools.org/restrict.asp?path=archive/16_04/Bil164.shtml, accessed 22 May 2015.

on a weighted set of performance-based reforms they undertake, further threatens the sustainability of dual-language programs (see Wright, 2010). The emphasis on tying teacher performance and closing down schools based on student standardized test scores, which are scientifically invalid and culturally inappropriate methods of assessing student learning, creates the likelihood that concerted energies and funding toward bilingual education programs will continue to dissipate in favor of punitive policy.[47]

But despite an "English-only" political climate, one that leads to English Language Learners being placed in developmentally inappropriate "sink or swim" type immersion programs, some school districts across the country have decided to embrace our multicultural roots by touting the cultural and economic advantages of learning in dual languages. In Illinois, for instance, community- and faith-based immigrant rights groups have emboldened the state legislature to require bilingual programs in public schools, making it the first state in the union to do so. For example, in Urbana, Illinois kindergarteners and first-year students recently began learning in classrooms where instruction is 90 percent in Spanish and 10 percent in English, with hopes to open up classes for Mandarin speakers. The students, by the fourth grade, learn both languages equally.[48] In New York City, a recent report found that 42 percent of children came from homes where English is not the primary language; thus the city responded by opening up twenty-nine new transitional bilingual and dual-language programs in 2013 where English is taught alongside

---

47. For an excellent example scholarly critique of *Race to the Top*'s impact on bilingual education see Wayne Wright, "The Great Divide Between Federal Education Policy and Our National Need for Bilingual Citizens," Speaking in Tongues 4 (Nov. 2010), accessed 15 March 2014, http://speakingintonguesfilm.info/tag/race-to-the-top/.
48. Prior to its demise, NBC Latino published a set of articles on immigrants and language attainment including bilingual education: For example, see: http://nbclatino.com/2012/08/15/will-illinois-lead-the-country-in-bilingual-education/ and http://www.dailyherald.com/article/20140214/news/140219116/print/.

a range of languages representing the city's newcomers including Spanish, Mandarin, French, and Arabic.[49]

Supporting bilingual education programs from the local to state level is essential in building bridges between communities, especially in nontraditional immigrant entry states in the South and Midwest who have been slowly becoming the top destinations for immigrant families. Such models of learning not only prevent segregation by language and country of origin at the facility and curricular level, but also benefit U.S.-born and immigrant alike given the cultural and economic benefits of multilingualism.

A National Jobs Guarantee

In the late 1970s, a coalition of labor leaders, religious groups and minority caucuses helped pass the Full Employment and Balanced Growth Act, better known as the Humphrey-Hawkins Act of 1978. At the time, rising inflation and high unemployment rates represented a downwardly spiraling economy that disproportionately affected the lives of African Americans, Latinos, and vulnerable immigrant communities, requiring appropriate policy response. Passed into law by President Carter in November 1978, the law sought to increase consumer demand by stimulating the private sector with short- and long-term goals of reducing inflation.[50] But embedded within the mandate was a lesser-known clause: if the private sector did not create enough jobs through stimulus spending,

49. See report by NYC's Independent Budget Office demonstrating use of English language at home: "New York City Public School Indicators: Demographics, Resources, Outcomes," May 2013, accessed 31 March 2014, http://www.ibo.nyc.ny.U.S. /iboreports/ 2013educationindicatorsreport.pdf. Also, for a good analysis of bilingual education programs with recommendations on how local public school districts can support bilingualism, see Ashley Clark and Kelsey Oliver, "How NYC's School System Can Keep Your Child Bilingual," *New York International* 20 (September 2103), accessed 24 March 2014, http://nyintl.net/story/ nyc_school_systems_bilingual_dual_language_programs.
50. See Harvey L. Schantz, Richard H. Schmidt, "The Evolution of Humphrey- Hawkins," Policy Studies Journal 8. no. 3 (December 1979): 368-77.

the federal government was responsible for providing that "missing work" through direct job creation.[51]

The 1978 bill was never fully implemented, and nearly thirty years later, unemployment rates remain as high as they were then for African American and Latinos in many urban centers, not to mention that the working poor and middle class continue to suffer the long-term economic effects of the 2007 housing crisis and subsequent "Great Recession." In response, Congressman John Conyers from Michigan introduced a bill in 2011 that seeks to fulfull the original mandate, titled the Humphrey-Hawkins 21st Century Full Employment and Training Act (H.R. 1000). Conyers's proposal, which has started to gain support (including co-sponsors) from a growing number of faith-based and economic justice advocacy groups, would use federal trust funds to grant monies to state and local communities for specific job-creating activities and job-training programs.[52]

While H.R. 1000 is a step forward, faith-based groups could be much bolder by supporting coalitional efforts toward a permanent, federal jobs guarantee. By creating a National Investment Employment Corps in the same vein as the FDR administration's temporary but effective WPA program the Civil Conservation Corps, such an initiative would not only alleviate unemployment but also ensure that work for a livable wage and decent pay is a basic right for all Americans (Darity and Hamilton, 2012). Imagine a permanent job guarantee, which would cost no less than the Bush administration's first bank bailout ($700 billion) and equivalent to federal anti-poverty expenditures, that could be used to improve the

51. See William Darity Jr. and Darrick Hamilton, "Bold Policies for Economic Justice," *Review of Black Political Economy*, 39, no. 1 (March 2012), 79-85.

52. The official text for HR 1000 is found here: http://conyershr1000.org/files/74240401.pdf

country's infrastructure and rebuild/sustain public institutions (see Aja et al., 2013).

While such a program would likely not be extended to undocumented immigrants until they reach permanent residency status, given the high number of "mixed-status" households, a federal jobs program would serve as a permanent source of income for at least one member of the household. This would lessen economic burdens yielded from constant exploitation (unsafe conditions, low wages, lack of access to healthcare, etc.) and job insecurity prominent in the secondary or informal labor markets undocumented workers currently encounter. Moreover, it is likely that a federal job guarantee would over time raise wages for vulnerable workers like undocumented immigrants, given that a national jobs program would also bid up wages in the general economy.[53]

Support Living Wage Laws

While a national job guarantee (discussed above) would set the standard for minimum salaries, until its implementation, efforts to increase the minimum wage beyond the level recently set by the federal government have sprouted throughout the country. According to the Center for Economic and Policy Research, today's minimum wage, if adjusted for worker productivity, should have reached $21.72 an hour in 2012.[54] Even if we used the same estimates of inflation used in 1969, when the minimum wage reached its peak, the minimum wage for 2012 should stand at $10.52, making a

---

53. Alan Aja, Daniel Bustillo, William Darity Jr., and Darrick Hamilton, "Jobs Instead of Austerity: A Bold Policy Proposal for Economic Justice," *Social Research* 80, no. 3 (2013):781-94.
54. For a succinct critical analysis on the minimum wage, see John Schmitt, "The Minimum Wage Is Too Damn Low," Center for Economic and Policy Research, *Issue Brief*, March 2012, accessed 15 March 2014, http://www.cepr.net/documents/publications/min-wage1-2012-03.pdf

current proposal by the Obama administration to increase the wage for federal contractors to $10.10 an hour seem reasonable.

The Obama administration's modest proposal, along with efforts at state and municipal levels around the country, are welcomed by several religious groups including the Interfaith Worker Justice (IWJ), the General Board of Church and Society of the United Methodist Church, and the U.S. Catholic Church, among others.[55] While this is a step toward economic justice, minimum wage calculations use a different set of criteria than those used for a "living wage," which is the minimum income necessary for families to meet a decent standard of living (calculated to be higher than the more arbitrary prevailing wage set by the state or businesses). This bolder approach, which began as a grassroots movement initiated by Baltimore church groups and labor unions in the mid-1990s, takes into account rising food costs, childcare, housing, transportation, and other place-based characteristics in assessing the minimum income necessary to sustain one's livelihood.[56] For example, according to the Living Wage Project calculator, in Atlanta, Georgia, the hourly rate an individual must earn to support their family as sole provider and working full-time is estimated at $19.00 an hour (for one adult, one child arrangement). In the same city, the living wage for one adult with two children rises to $22.63, and for two adults with two children the living wage is estimated at $19.52. These figures are compared to the current state-set minimum wage of $7.25 an hour.[57] In New York, where the cost of living is considerably higher

55. Example efforts include the faith-based organization Interfaith Worker Justice (IWJ), which has been active in organizing communities and religious groups to target specific corporations and state governments through campaigns, rallies, and other direct-action initiatives, accessed 24 March 2014, http://www.kintera.org/site/apps/nlnet/content3.aspx?c= frLJK2PKLqF&b=2952567&ct=12011833&notoc=1.

56. For a condensed report of the living wage campaign origins, see Jon Gerter, New York Times, 15 Jan. 2006, accessed 26 March 2014, http://www.nytimes.com/2006/01/15/magazine/ 15wage.html.

than in Atlanta, the living wage stands at $12.75 for one adult, but rises sharply to $24.69 for one adult with one child and $22.32 for two adults with two children. This is also compared to the state-set minimum wage of $7.25.

According to the National Employment Law Project, more than 120 municipalities across the country have passed local living wage laws since the movement began to spread in the mid-1990s.[58] Most recently, for example, youth representing the United Church of Christ in Greater Seattle have joined other local advocates, including the local Church Council, to place pressure on local officials to raise the minimum wage akin to that of a living wage.[59] In New York City, continued pressure from religious groups and labor unions over the last few years was met with support from Mayor Bill de Blasio. The mayor recently signed an executive order to increase the minimum wage to $13.13 per hour, a proposal largely inspired by "living wage" concepts.[60]

Support Single-Payer Healthcare Models

In 2009, thirty faith-based groups representing Muslim, Christian, Jewish, and Buddhist communities coalesced to ensure grassroots, faith-based participation in the Obama administration's attempt to reform the country's costly and inaccessible healthcare system, citing

---

57. Here I used the Living Wage Calculator provided by MIT's "Living Wage Project" for Atlanta City, Georgia and for New York City, New York County, accessed 31 March 2014, http://livingwage.mit.edu/.

58. For a condensed summary of living wage laws, including links to policy reports and studies, see the National Employment Law Project's "Living Wage" resource page here: http://www.nelp.org/index.php/site/issues/category/living_wage_laws/.

59. See Emily Schappacher, "Young Adults Work to Establish a Living Wage in Seattle," United Church of Christ, 2 April 2014, accessed 3 April 3 2014, http://www.ucc.org/news/young-adults-living-wage-Seattle-04022014.html?utm_source=feedburner&utm_medium=feed&utm_campaign=Feed:UnitedChurchOfChrist (United Church of Christ).

60. See video and press release at: http://www1.nyc.gov/office-of-the-mayor/news/459-14/mayor-de-blasio-signs-executive-order-increase-living-wage-expand-it-thousands-more#/0

a moral priority to ensure "quality, affordable health care for every American family."[61] While coalition members varied in their philosophies and strategies over policy-specific contours of reform, three years later the concerted energies of television ads, prayer rallies, district meetings, and national conference calls were finally answered when the monumental Patient and Affordable Care Act was signed by President Obama in 2012.[62]

The Affordable Care Act is a market-based attempt to extend the availability of healthcare to all Americans by "mandate." Its regulations and provisions include weeding out existing plans that gouge families and offer minimal coverage, allowing young people up to the age of twenty-six to remain under their parents' plans, eliminating "preexisting condition" clauses that providers have often used to deny healthcare coverage, and a host of other necessary changes.[63] But it is no secret that the ACA falls short of equitably providing healthcare for all populations, especially undocumented immigrants.

Contrary to inflammatory rhetoric purveyed by healthcare reform opponents, the current law does not allow undocumented immigrants to access the health insurance exchange, leaving millions of people without basic healthcare rights. Even if undocumented immigrant parents apply for health insurance for their U.S.-born children, who are indeed eligible for Medicaid programs and other forms of public assistance, there are reports in some states that such

61. The list of healthcare reform supporters is available at http://faithforhealth.org/who-we-are.
62. The Pew Research Center provides a plethora of scientific surveys on immigration, healthcare and other economic indicators. On the intersections of healthcare reform and religious support, 8 Oct, 2009, accessed 15 March 2014, http://www.pewforum.org/2009/10/08/religious-groups-weigh-in-on-health-care-reform/.
63. For a discussion of universal single-payer models, living wage ordinances, federal job guarantee proposal and other policies in the context of anti-racist coalition building, see Alan Aja, Daniel Bustillo, and Antwuan Wallace, "Countering Anti-Blackness Through Black-Brown Alliances and Inter-Group Coalitions: Policy Proposals to Break the Silence," *The Journal of Intergroup Relations*, Vol. 35, no. 2 (Winter 2014): 58–87.

attempts have exposed unlawful linkages between local law enforcement, the Social Security Administration, and Homeland Security Administration.[64] While the Obama administration has vowed to protect applicants from illegal collusion between agencies, these fearful scenarios discourage mixed-status families from applying for medical care their children are entitled to out of fear of harassment and deportation.[65]

However, in Vermont, a 2011 bill served to control these scenarios while universally expanding the right to quality healthcare through a publicly financed, single-payer system that would be made available to all state residents, including undocumented immigrants.[66] The attempt, currently on hold as legislators seek to fiscally justify its implementation, is simply a matter of political will and funding priority, while other states also test the idea. In neighboring Maine, legislators have agreed to fund a study questioning the efficacy of a statewide single-payer healthcare model, which advocates argue would streamline the health insurance process.[67] In Pennsylvania, grassroots activists continue to pressure legislators to opt out of the market-based healthcare exchanges created under the Affordable Care Act and turn toward a more universal, single-payer model.[68] But in hindsight state-level single-payer initiatives are simply not

64. For an excellent case example of interagency collusion in the state of Kentucky, see Ellen Sherby and Elmer Zavala, "Unaccounted For: The Affordable Care Act and Undocumented Immigrants," in *Unbound: An Interactive Journal of Christian Social Justice*, Presbyterian Church (USA), accessed 26 March 2014, http://www.justiceunbound.org/carousel/unaccounted-for-the-affordable-care-act-and-undocumented-immigrants/.

65. This should also be viewed within the context of concerted efforts by republicans to halt ACA's provisions for Medicaid expansion in states like Florida and Texas, both states with sizable immigrant populations. See Ricardo Alonso-Zalvidar, "Hispanics on Sidelines: Largest U.S. Minority Group Lags in Signing Up for Health Care Plans," *Star Tribune*, 24 March 2014, accessed 1 April 2014, http://m.startribune.com/business/251983071.html.

66. See Dave Gram, "Vermont lawmakers resolve immigrant health care issue," *Forbes*, 3 May 2011, accessed 3 April 2014, http://www.pnhp.org/news/2011/may/activists-decry-exclusion-of-undocumented-workers-from-vermonts-h202.

67. See "Maine Bill OKs Bill to Study Single-Payer System," *Forbes*, 3 April 2014, accessed 3 April 2014, http://www.healthcare-now.org/maine-house-oks-bill-to-study-single-payer-system.

enough, and that grassroots, inter-faith efforts to make health care a universal right must eventually place their focus at the federal level.

In summary, as religious communities across the country continue to place pressure on policymakers for fair and just immigration reform, a realistic assessment that considers the presently hostile political climate demands heightened awareness and bold responses by faith-based groups to "welcome—and be in solidarity with—the stranger" even in the most unorthodox of ways. During Jesus' time on earth, he broke many traditions and taboos, perhaps most exemplified by the story of his interaction with a member of a marginalized group, the Samaritan woman, in the Gospel of John. This teaches us that when Comprehensive Immigration Reform is finally passed, the moral responsibility to shelter, feed, and empower those who will likely suffer by the policy should in no way cease in effort and action. Given the imminence of continued flows of migration into the United States, and the likelihood that a new pool of undocumented immigrants will not be eligible for provisions of the act, bold local to universal policies and initiatives, however controversial and unorthodox, should remain at the center of any progressive, faith-based policy agenda.

68. For a brief summary of latest trends in single-payer efforts, see Tammy Worth, "The Single-Payer Movement Expands," *Health Care Finance News*, 14 March 2014, accessed 15 March 2014, http://www.healthcare-now.org/the-single-payer-movement-expands.

16

Blending Past and Future

How Whitehead's Metaphysics Speaks to
Immigration Reform

Joseph A. Bracken and Marc A. Pugliese

Clearly many Americans oppose immigration and a more just treatment of immigrants. Change coming from an unexpected direction makes everyone a bit nervous. Fear of change is behind the discrimination, inequities, dehumanization, shaming, and even violence that immigrants suffer.

There is accordingly an implicit clash in minds and hearts between a classical metaphysics wary of change and a process-oriented metaphysics favoring change. Yet, change is inevitable. It is at the base of reality. Although permanence-oriented views of reality dominate us, they are untenable. We must "change" our views on the value of change itself if we are to humanize and embrace immigrants, and to simply view reality accurately.

In 2012 an estimated 40 million foreign-born persons lived in the U.S., 13 percent of the total U.S. population and the largest percentage since 1920.[1] Yet, immigration and the reform of immigration policy are controversial topics today. Immigration policy involves the interplay between the individual who wants to immigrate and two societies, the one the emigrant is leaving and the other society the immigrant wishes to join. As a model for problems the immigrant faces, the interface between a Whiteheadian actual entity and Whiteheadian societies may be of value. Regarding this interface, Whitehead says:

> The causal laws which dominate a social environment are the product of the defining characteristic of that society. But the society is only efficient through its individual members. Thus in a society, the members can only exist by reason of the laws which dominate the society, and the laws only come into being by reason of the analogous characters of the members of that society.[2]

There is a tension between the aspirations of the immigrant and the two societies. One has shaped her and the other will shape her if she succeeds in joining it. Her leaving one society and joining another will also have some impact on the continuing structure and organization of both societies. There is similar creative tension between our own relationships as natives to contemporary American society. We are influenced by our cultural ethos and country's laws, but we also transform them.

---

1. This includes noncitizens and citizens, authorized and unauthorized. Douglas W. Elmendorf, Director, Congressional Budget Office, "A Description of the Immigrant Population—2013 Update," accessed 8 May 2013, https://www.cbo.gov/sites/default/files/cbofiles/attachments/44134_Description_of_Immigrant_Population.pdf.
2. Alfred North Whitehead, *Process and Reality: An Essay in Cosmology*, ed. David Ray Griffin and Donald W. Sherburne (New York: Macmillan, 1929; corr. ed., New York: Free Press, 1978), 90–91 (henceforth "PR"); see also Alfred North Whitehead, *Science and the Modern World* (New York: Macmillan, 1925; reprint, New York: Free Press, 1967), 51 (henceforth "SMW").

Whitehead only offers a conceptual model that could serve as a guide for thinking through some complicated problems in immigration reform. It does not imply that a human being is like a Whiteheadian actual entity and that human societies are like Whiteheadian societies. This is only a model in the abstract useful for understanding the more complicated relation between the individual and society in real life.

Admittedly, metaphysics is suspect—but by no means dying—today. Whitehead himself delineates the limitations of language and metaphysical abstractions as they grope to describe generalities applicable to all experience. Language is an inherently ambiguous metaphor, mutely appealing for an imaginative leap born of intuition.[3] We should not reify abstractions.[4] Speculative philosophy is like the evocative, pregnant, polysemic expressions of poetry. Although necessary and ineluctable, it is always provisional, inevitably doomed to deposition when tried through experience.[5] Metaphysical categories apply analogously but not univocally for analyzing concrete situations in the empirical order.

Thus the relation between the Whiteheadian actual entity and society is an imprecise metaphor that may be of service in thinking through immigration issues. We must keep the metaphorical and symbolic nature of these metaphysical categories ever in mind as we investigate their symbolic value for immigration reform today.

To understand the model we must survey some rudimentary process categories. These are: actual entity, society, and Creativity.

---

3. PR 4.
4. This is the "Fallacy of Misplaced Concreteness," SMW 51; PR 7–8.
5. PR xiii, 1–17; SMW 77–94; and Alfred North Whitehead, *Modes of Thought* (New York: Capricorn, 1958), 7, 68–69 (henceforth "MT"). Therefore Whitehead's technical vocabulary is at once drawn from subjective experience and deliberately experiential and protean.

Actual Entity as Model

For Whitehead, the final and only "real" things are actual entities. Derived from quantum mechanics, relativity theory, and developments in modern philosophy,[6] the actual entity replaces "*primary* substance" in classical philosophy. Any and all "reasons" originate from actual entities[7] as the final and only really existing things.

We are more complex than actual entities. Here, though, we begin to see a possible model to help us think about ourselves. For, from one perspective, human beings actually account for everything "human" in our experience—communities, societies, cultures, languages, the arts, religions, states, economic systems, and so forth.

An actual entity is an *event* of a weaving together of manifold experience from its own unique perspective. It is a process of becoming that actualizes a quantum of space-time, but it does not become within space-time. It is an indivisible whole but abstractly divisible for analysis into causal and spatio-temporal "components."[8] This "becoming" Whitehead dubbed "concrescence."[9]

We, too, contemplate ourselves abstractly as different "parts," but we remain fundamentally irreducible. We are not static "things" but "happenings." Yet we transcend time's flow and space's discreteness. We are each unique, in part due to our own perspective on the world.

Whitehead's ontology also repudiates the distinction between substance and quality. Entities are not independent substances with

6. PR 18, 21–22. Whitehead's reliance on the revolution in contemporary physics strongly commends his metaphysics.

7. The metaphysical term "actual" derives from "to act" as "being of consequence."

8. SMW 125–26; PR 22, 35–36, 77, 73, 85, 219–20; and Alfred North Whitehead, *Adventures of Ideas* (New York: Macmillan, 1933; reprint, New York: Free Press, 1967), 204 (henceforth "AI"). Because actual entities are not in Newtonian absolute space and time—due to relativity—spatio-temporal analysis analyzes an entity's perspective vis-à-vis all other actual entities.

9. PR 26.

only external and accidental relations that are nonessential to their being. Entities are constituted by their "internal relations" to all other entities and likewise they help to constitute other entities. This is the "principle of relativity."[10] The subject–predicate distinction, although useful, is untrue.[11] Contemporary physics belies it. For process thought social–relational ontology replaces older individualistic, substance ontologies.[12]

Whitehead coined the neologism "prehension"[13] to connote the entity's internal relatedness to the world. Prehensions express the concrete facts of an actual entity's relationship to all other entities. They are efficient causes of an entity's internal constitution.[14] Thus an entity arises out of "stubborn fact" and is a "cumulation of the universe, not a stage-play about it."[15] Prehensions are "energy transfers," but because there is no real subject–object distinction they also involve "knowing and feeling." Using subjective terminology, Whitehead speaks of "memory" regarding prehensions.[16] All of reality from the perspective of an actual entity's concrescence impinges on it through internal relations, making it a microcosm of the macrocosm.[17]

Western thought, especially in modernity, has viewed human beings as independently subsisting individuals. The truth is that we are not "islands" independent from everyone and everything else. Our very being is the result of internal relations to everyone—and

10. PR 22.
11. PR xiii–xiv, 138, 167; SMW 94; and MT 151.
12. PR xiii–xiv, 22, 28, 58–60, 137; SMW 17, 25, 72, 84; AI 112; MT 151; CN 20; idem, *An Enquiry into the Principles of Knowledge* (Cambridge: Cambridge University Press, 1922), 2; and idem, *Religion in the Making* (New York: Macmillan, 1926; reprint, New York: New American Library, 1974), 98 (henceforth "RM"). Whitehead is the proximate source of the relational ontologies commonplace in theology today.
13. "Apprehension" wrongly connotes a subject grasping an object.
14. Whitehead delineates different types of prehensions, including conceptual ones.
15. PR 237.
16. PR 120, 239.
17. PR 215; SMW 25; and MT 151.

everything—else. Many religious and philosophical systems have rightly said we are microcosms of the macrocosm.

With contemporary physics Whitehead urged that an actual entity is both objective reality and experiencing subject.[18] He also repudiates the supposition of inert matter known from the outside by a human subject, or the doctrine of "vacuous actuality."[19] Apart from subjectivity there is nothing.[20] The world is composed of subjects experiencing other subject-objects. It is thoroughly intersubjective and panexperiential.[21] Hence his technical terms—"feeling," "aim," "decision," "satisfaction," "intensity," and so on—are drawn from subjective experience.

Actual entities are simultaneously objects. As such, actual entities are the only real causes or reasons.[22] An actual entity's objectivity becomes a fact influencing the becoming of other actual entities. Subjectivity and objectivity are unified, however. The entity's subjectivity is "private," internal to itself. Its objectivity is "public," affecting its environs and the rest of the world. Reality is thus *organic*.

Our objective worlds are the reasons for who we are now. Our personal histories, other people, our social contexts—even the phenomenon of immigration itself—are all aspects of our actual world impacting on who we are, here and now. Our relationship to the facts

18. PR 25–26.
19. PR xiii, 29, 167, 309.
20. "The subjectivist principle is that the whole universe consists of elements disclosed in the analysis of the experience of subjects. Process is the becoming of experience." PR 166. See also PR 167.
21. Whitehead cites Bacon: "It is certain that all bodies, whatsoever, though they have no sense, yet they have perception: when a body is applied to another, there is a kind of election to embrace that which is agreeable, and to exclude or expel that which is ingrate." Quoted in SMW 41. See also Alfred North Whitehead, *Symbolism: Its Meaning and Effect* (New York: Macmillan, 1927; reprint, New York: Fordham University Press, 1985), 10; SMW 141, 194–95; PR xi, 7, 48–51, 67–72, 79–80, 189, 310. On "feeling" as a metaphor, see PR 87, 160–62, 166, 308, 310.
22. "It is a contradiction in terms to assume that some explanatory fact can float into the world out of nonentity. Nonentity is nothingness. Every explanatory fact refers to the decision and to the efficacy of an actual thing." PR 46; cf. PR 23, 40, 43.

of immigration itself and our subjective perceptions of those facts causally impact who we are and our postures toward immigration.

The actual effects of immigration are disputed. Some urge that immigrants expand the United States' productive capacity; stimulate investment; improve competitive advantage; generate net gains through additional taxes; and do not take jobs from citizens.[23] Others contend that immigrants lower wages for young and unskilled native workers; cause federal deficits by consuming more social services; stifle technological growth; decrease international competitiveness; shift resources from licit to underground markets; reallocate wealth from the poorest to the richest; and shrink the middle class.[24] These disparate conclusions probably arise from the specific factors considered and the levels of analysis undertaken. For instance, there are differences in impact on the federal, state, and local levels, and there is disagreement over the size and the best way of measuring the effects on the national level.[25]

23. Slobodan Djajíc, "Illegal Immigration and Resource Allocation," *International Economic Review* 38, no. 1 (1997): 98–99; Giovanni Peri, "The Effect of Immigration on Productivity: Evidence from U.S. States," *Review of Economics and Statistics* 94, no. 1 (2012): 348–58; Giovanni Peri, "Immigration, Labor Markets, and Productivity," *CATO Journal* 32, no. 1 (Winter 2012): 35–53. Gordon H. Hanson, Raymond Robertson, and Antonio Spilimbergo, "Does Border Enforcement Protect U.S. Workers from Illegal Immigration?," *The Review of Economics and Statistics* 84, no. 1 (2002): 73–92; Giovanni Peri and Chad Sparber, "Task Specialization, Immigration, and Wages," *American Economic Journal: Applied Economics* 1, no. 3 (2009): 135–69; Giovanni Peri, "The Effect of Immigrants on U.S. Employment and Productivity," *Federal Reserve Bank of San Francisco Newsletter* 26 (2010): 1; Eduardo Porter, "Illegal Immigrants Are Bolstering Social Security with Billions," *New York Times*, 5 April 2005; Francine J. Lipman, "Taxing Undocumented Immigrants: Separate, Unequal, and Without Representation," *Tax Lawyer* 59, no. 3 (2006): 813–66.

24. George J. Borjas, *Heaven's Door: Immigration Policy and the American Economy* (Princeton: Princeton University Press, 1999); Slobodan Djajíc, "Illegal Immigration and Resource Allocation," *International Economic Review* 38, no. 1 (1997): 98–99; Steven A. Camarota, "The High Cost of Cheap Labor: Illegal Immigration and the Federal Budget" (Washington, DC: Center for Immigration Studies, 2004), accessed 20 May 2014, http://cis.org/High-Cost-of-Cheap-Labor; George J. Borjas, "Native Internal Migration and the Labor Market Impact of Immigration," *Journal of Human Resources* 41, no. 2 (2006): 221–58; Andrew Sum, Paul Harrington, and Ishwar Khatiwada, "The Impact of New Immigrants on Young Native-Born Workers, 2000–2005" (Washington, DC: Center for Immigration Studies, 2006), accessed 20 May 2014, http://cis.org/NewImmigrants-NativeBornWorkers.

Also, the effects of immigration we perceive can differ from others' perspectives. Concomitantly, others' perceptions of immigration's effects can affect us. Popular opinion among Americans, for example, is extreme and clearly negative concerning the government's ability to handle immigration issues with any policy,[26] and media presentations heavily inform our views on immigration.[27]

The relationships of immigrants to their actual worlds likewise influence who they are and what they are doing—immigrating. As with immigration's effects, immigration's causes are controverted. Economic incentives are frequently cited.[28] Varying reasons cited in demographics include: the higher standard of living in the United States; escape from social and political turmoil; and joining family members already living in the U.S.[29] Still other reasons include globalized economies and increased labor mobility; the opportunity to earn and send money home; and family relations: the "immigration multiplier."[30]

25. Congressional Budget Office, "The Impact of Unauthorized Immigrants on the Budgets of State and Local Governments" (Washington, DC: Congress of the United States of America, December 2007), accessed 20 May 2014, http://www.cbo.gov/sites/default/files/cbofiles/ftpdocs/87xx/doc8711/12-6-immigration.pdf.

26. See Francine Segovia and Renatta Defever, "The Polls—Trends: American Public Opinion on Immigrants and Immigration Policy," *Public Opinion Quarterly* 74, no. 2 (2010): 375–94; and Cari Lee Skogberg Eastman, *Shaping the Immigration Debate: Contending Civil Societies on the US–Mexico Border* (Boulder, CO: First Forum Press, 2012), 14.

27. Johanna Dunaway, Regina P. Branton, and Marisa A. Abrajano, "Agenda Setting, Public Opinion, and the Issue of Immigration Reform," *Social Science Quarterly* 91, no. 2 (2010): 359–78; John P. Carvalho, Andrew G. Davis, and Amanda M. Mullins, "The View of the Border: News Framing of the Definition, Causes, and Solutions to Illegal Immigration," *Mass Communication & Society* 14, no. 3 (2011): 292–314.

28. Barry R. Chiswick, "Illegal Immigration and Immigration Control," *The Journal of Economic Perspectives* 2, no. 3 (Summer 1988): 101–15; Rakesh Kochhar, "Survey of Mexican Migrants–Part 3: The Economic Transition to America" (Washington, DC: Pew Hispanic Center, December 6, 2005), accessed 20 May 2014, http://www.pewhispanic.org/2005/12/06/survey-of-mexican-migrants-part-three/.

29. Oliver C. Anderson, *Illegal Immigration: Causes, Methods, and Effects* (New York: Nova Science, 2010).

30. Sei-hill Kim, John P. Carvalho, Andrew G. Davis, and Amanda M. Mullins, "The View of the Border: News Framing of the Definition, Causes, and Solutions to Illegal Immigration," *Mass Communication and Society* 14 (2011): 292–314; Judith Gans, "Illegal Immigration to the

Now, do these causal relationships imply determinism? It may seem so, but it is not the case.[31] Prehensions are efficient causes, but the actual entity transcends them in its subjective freedom, "deciding" its own actuality.[32]

Here Whitehead retrieves classical "final" causality.[33] Each entity has a value-oriented "goal" for its own actuality, an imagining of what it will become.[34] The entity is thus a unit of realized value, aesthetically "intense" insofar as it is set against the backdrop of relevant alternatives.[35]

The entity conceptually values prehensions in a hierarchy of relevance to its value-oriented goal. In an elaborate process[36] guided by its subjective form, the entity rejects some or many causal influences.[37] It more or less values certain causes and negatively devalues others,[38] incorporating negative prehensions to a lesser degree or not at all. This attenuates the causality of its settled past.

The actual entity's decision is a blend of feeling-level prehensions of the past actual world but also of imaginative projections of how its decision here and now could affect what it will be in ways different

United States: Causes and Policy Solutions" (Tucson, AZ: Udall Center for Studies in Public Policy, 2007), 1–4; Gordon Hanson, "The Economics and Policy of Illegal Immigration in the United States" (San Diego: Migration Policy Institute, 2009), accessed May 20, 2014, https://www.migrationpolicy.org/pubs/Hanson-Dec09.pdf; Fred Arnold, "Unanswered Questions about the Immigration Multiplier," *International Migration Review* 23, no. 4 (1989): 889–92; Slobodan Djajíc, "Illegal Immigration and Resource Allocation," *International Economic Review* 38, no. 1 (1997): 98; 186–87.David L. Ortmeyer and Michael A. Quinn, "Coyotes, Migration Duration, and Remittances," *Journal of Developing Areas* 46, no. 2 (Fall 2012): 186–87.

31. PR 88, 93–94, 221–21. How Whitehead transcends the determinism–freedom dialectic is beyond the scope of this paper.
32. PR 42–46, 88, 150, 221–22.
33. Science's success has led to an almost exclusive focus on efficient causality in modernity.
34. This is its "subjective form" (PR 19, 108, 150, 244–45, 244).
35. SMW 93–94, 178; PR 234, 252–55; MT 147, 151.
36. See PR, Part III.
37. PR 23–24, 41–42, 83, 106, 220–35, 237, 345.
38. These are "adversion" and "aversion" (PR 27).

from its settled world. An actual entity can "blindly" ratify an objective past or it can introduce possibilities for a different future.

This balance between memory and imagination plays a key part in the thinking of us all. We should certainly not underestimate how our past impacts us. Years of privilege, prejudice, racism, inhospitality, and injustice are puissant forces, but we can reject them. We can imagine and aim at a new and different future. In aesthetic novelty we can choose equality, color-blindness, warm welcoming, and justice.

Likewise, immigrants feeling the weight of their previously settled worlds can break from those pasts. Leaving a home country is itself an exercise of such freedom. The decision to immigrate makes one an immigrant, just as an actual entity's "decision" determines what it will be. There are seemingly smaller but just as consequential levels. An immigrant's decision to break with the milieu of mutual disdain, fear, and animosity by showing respect, trust, and kindness can create her anew, but transforms others as well.

The imagination of what can be is a powerful impetus for a new future unshackled from the past. Imagining and actualizing such brighter futures requires pro-immigration values. Here lies an obligation to convince others of values that are more moral, but in the long run more satisfying.

Whiteheadian Society as Model

So far we have seen how interrelationality constitutes actual entities. Do actual entities as the final real things imply atomism? Here Whiteheadian "societies" are critical.

The world is replete with macroscopic objects. These are "societies," organically fused consistent organizations of actual entities. Anything perduring across time—particles, waves, molecules, cells—are societies. Societies endure while their member entities come and go. Though unique, actual entities in a society share similarities important for them as a group. They have a shared personal history, and are structured according to a defining characteristic called a "societal form."[39]

Societies, too, are not "simply located." They exist in and are internally related to environments of larger societies up to and including the entire cosmos. All societies mutually interpenetrate one another. An actual entity's prehensions include objectifications of all societies in which it is proximately or remotely situated.[40]

The causal laws dominating a society (its "defining characteristic") become factors in the concrescence of its member entities. Prehending their society's form through societal predecessors, entities exist by reason of the laws dominating their society.[41] The influence is not unidirectional, however. A society's form continues via its ongoing transmission by its members. Its laws come into being only through its members, and their self-constituting decisions over time impact the laws governing the society.[42] Societies can change through novelty introduced by member entities.

We exist in different but analogous "societies." The defining characteristics of our societies bear heavily on our conditioned

39. PR 22–23, 34–35, 55–57, 72, 83–84, 89–111, 129, 192, 198, 244; AI 204. This evokes Aristotelian hylomorphism but is more like a Platonic form.

40. PR 89–93, 97–98, 103, 327.

41. SMW 79; PR 25, 34, 27, 41–42, 58, 89–92, 251–53; AI 203–4. In light of scientific developments since Whitehead, Joseph A. Bracken argues that the societies are: (1) the "fields" of contemporary physical science; (2) equiprimordial with the actual entities; (3) real; and (4) exhibit agency. See Joseph A. Bracken, *The One in the Many: A Contemporary Reconstruction of the God-World Relationship* (Grand Rapids: Eerdmans, 2001), 3–7, 131–34, 148–49; idem, *Christianity and Process Thought: Spirituality for a Changing World* (Philadelphia: Templeton Foundation, 2006), 7, 16–17, 57–58, 107; and idem, *God: Three Who Are One* (Collegeville, MN: Liturgical, 2008), 67–68, 78, 114. In sociology, see Raimo Tuomela, *Social Ontology: Collective Intentionality and Group Agents* (New York: Oxford University Press, 2013).

42. PR 90–91. Bracken draws out the implications of this. See Bracken, *The One in the Many*, 148; idem, *Society and Spirit: A Trinitarian Cosmology* (Selinsgrove, PA: Susquehanna University Press, 1991), 44–45, 149; idem, *The Divine Matrix: Creativity as Link between East and West* (Maryknoll, NY: Orbis, 1995), 62.

identities. Immigrants' societies of origin and America as their new home contribute to their identities, especially *qua* immigrants. Separation from family, or the lack of material resources for themselves and their families, are just some examples of how societies of origin lead them to immigrate. An example of how our society's laws influence immigrants is the Immigration and Nationality Act of 1965, which caused an exponential increase in immigration over the past four decades.[43]

Policies favoring immigration rights correspond to a process-oriented approach to reality wherein the relation of the actual entity to its environment demands ongoing adjustment. How can these adjustments come about? Our choices may seem to have negligible effects. Can individuals ever significantly change our country's laws? Can we effect significant changes in government policies?

Psychology's "Group Identity Model" describes our natural tendency to construct groups that include "insiders" but exclude "outsiders." Research shows that these insider/outsider categories influencing group members are not fixed. Insider/outsider bifurcations can dissipate. Common goals and allocation of resources benefiting all can replace competing interests.[44]

Nor are immigrants fully determined by their social contexts. They also can change their social contexts. Sending money home changes the economies. If our society makes immigration difficult, the choices of immigrants—"legal" or "illegal"—can "substantially" alter that. Their very presence alone precipitates heightened social consciousness, greater hospitality, solidarity, and even policy reform.

43. This act repealed the 1921 Emergency Quota Act, which limited the number of immigrants annually from any given country to 3 percent of the nationals from the same country living in the U.S.
44. See Dayna Bowen Matthew, "Applying Lessons from Social Psychology to Repair the Health Care Safety Net for Undocumented Immigrants," in *The Health Care Safety Net in a Post-Reform World*, ed. Mark A. Hall and Saran Rosenbaum (New Brunswick, NJ: Rutgers University Press, 2012), 91–107.

Whiteheadian Creativity

Another Whiteheadian category relevant to immigration reform is "Creativity." Creativity revolutionizes the perennial Western tenet that permanence and immutability are superior to flux and mutability.

For Whitehead the principle of novelty is one of three ultimate categories of existence. This principle of novelty grounds the ongoing process of a settled past being supplemented by ever-new weavings together of new actual entities. Whitehead calls this grounding of change "underlying" or "substantial" activity, or "Creativity."[45] Creativity is not a determinate, factual substance or entity. Nor is it simply potentiality. It grounds all potentiality and actuality.[46] Creativity is a nonreifiable activity discerned only from its empirical manifestation in the perpetual appearance of new actual entities.[47] Here Whitehead again resorts to poetic intuition, describing Creativity as the "creative urge."[48]

Conclusion

A metaphysical scheme like Whitehead's remains a metaphor "mutely appealing for an imaginative leap." Yet the actual entity's concrescence and its relationship to societies could still have symbolic value for immigration and immigration reform.[49] This by no means implies an exact correspondence between Whiteheadian actual entities and societies on the one hand, and individual immigrants

45. PR 7, 20–21, 31, 57, 81; cf. SMW 70, 165.
46. PR 31; AI 259.
47. PR 31.
48. PR 219, 224, 239.
49. Some urge that symbols themselves are incomprehensible in older static, substantialist terms. But in fact they are relational, dynamic, process-oriented events occurring in intentional fields. See Dario Zadra, "Symbol und Sakrament," in *Christlicher Glaube in moderner Gesellschaft* (Freiburg: Herder, 1982), 28:94–95.

and their societies on the other. Symbolically disclosing aspects of immigration that need our attention, these symbols must be taken "seriously but not literally."[50]

Again, immigration is as old as America itself. The families of those who oppose immigration reform originally settled in the U.S. out of the same need to survive and prosper in a new environment as immigrants today. What if the status quo was preserved? They would not be in America, and America would not be what it is today. Some yearn for "the good old days" with nostalgia for a more fixed and secure past. Others are more future-oriented, excited by new opportunities. History vindicates the latter.

Immigration reform requires change to existing societal structures. For process-relational thought, change is woven into the fabric of reality, and thus inevitable. For process-relational thought, change is not from one reality to another. It is a newly patterned present reality building on a settled past. It is additive, not transitional. The settled past imposes itself upon all successive realities. At the same time change in the appearance of new actualities continuously occurs. New entities are inextricably bound to their past but not determined by it. In our subjective freedom we can add aesthetic value to unavoidable change. There is hope for *positive* change.

To use a Whiteheadian metaphor, we are faced with a decisive question on immigration today: Will we be "low-grade" entities "blindly running,"[51] transmitting the settled past with negligible change? Or will we in a "bid for freedom"[52] set aside parts of the past to introduce robust change constituting an aesthetic achievement? Choosing the former maintains the status quo, perpetuating present

---

50. Reinhold Niebuhr, *The Nature and Destiny of Man, Volume II* (New York: Charles Scribner's Sons, 1943).
51. SMW 79.
52. PR 104.

societal forms. Deciding for the latter breaks from the past, introduces sizable change, and generates aesthetic achievement.

17

Immigration as/and Mental Illness

More Than Metaphor

Ronald W. Baard

In spring of 1916, at the age of eighteen, my grandfather, Francois Alexander Baard, immigrated to the United States from the Netherlands, arriving through Ellis Island in New York before settling in eastern South Dakota as a farm laborer. About a decade later he developed a serious mental illness and subsequently spent most of the remainder of his adult life as a patient in a large state psychiatric hospital in South Dakota. Was his mental illness partly caused by the stress of immigrating to a foreign land at such a young age?

While that is probably true, the purpose of this chapter moves in the other direction. A major intent here is to explore ways in which the experience of mental illness can be understood, metaphorically, as a special kind of "immigration." We know that people who are forced or who choose to immigrate in geographic terms do truly become "strangers in the world" in so many ways; yet in a closely related way, persons afflicted with a mental illness also become "strangers in the world."

My contention is methodological—namely that there is something valuable to be gained by exploring the metaphor that the experience of mental illness is akin to the experience of immigration to a foreign land, with all the concomitant points of disorientation and stress that such experience brings, and yet also producing many profound insights. Mental illness, like immigration, makes a person a "stranger in the world." In becoming a stranger, religious and spiritual resources often provide the greatest kind of comfort, courage, and inspiration. In this regard, we should recall that the root meaning of the word *religion* is "to rebind."

This chapter will unfold in three basic sections. First, by way of background, I will present a brief understanding regarding various (and at points conflicting) views on aspects of mental health and illness related to diagnostic practices in contemporary Western culture. In the second section, I will share a brief case study, regarding what I know about the life and suffering of my paternal grandfather. Here I will tell my grandfather's story in more detail, with a focus on his journey with serious mental illness in terms of an important guiding question—what does his story teach us? In the third section, I will present some multireligious reflections on all of the above, emphasizing again the metaphor and framework of immigration and/ as mental illness, or, if you will, mental illness as "inner migration." Here the larger guiding question will be framed religiously and spiritually, as "Where is God in the experience of the mentally ill?" Finally, I will state some conclusions of a hortatory nature for improving the lives and treatment of mentally ill persons today.

Mental Illness and Diagnostics
in Contemporary Western Culture

There are disadvantages to putting labels on people. This is especially true with respect to persons struggling with mental illness. The disadvantages are multiple; attaching a diagnostic label to such persons has personal, relational, and societal effects that often do more harm than good. Dr. Thomas Szasz, in his classic book titled *The Myth of Mental Illness: Foundations of a Theory of Personal Conduct*, puts it this way:

> Such considerations generate two diametrically opposed points of view about mental illness and psychiatry: according to one, mental illness is like any other illness, and psychiatric treatment, whether voluntary or not, is like any other treatment; according to the other, mental illness is a myth, psychiatric intervention is a type of social action, and involuntary psychiatric therapy is not treatment but torture. This book attempts to demonstrate the fallacy of the former view, and the validity of the latter.[1]

Szasz prefers to use the phrase "problems in living" instead of any medical or diagnostic labels. He maintains that both the persons involved and society as a whole would be better off if his approach was universally adopted. I do sympathize with Dr. Szasz's view, to a degree. I do not believe, however, that we should throw out the medical framework altogether, despite the atmosphere of stigma it often helps create and perpetuate. This medical diagnostic model may bring with it, at times, some very real advantages. Sometimes an accurate mental health diagnosis can actually be a comfort to persons because it makes no attempt to blame or shame anyone, and may render an individual's suffering more understandable and approachable to all involved, including close family members.

---

1. Thomas Szasz, *The Myth of Mental Illness: Foundations of a Theory of Personal Conduct* (New York: Harper, 1974), 12.

Still, words of caution are in order regarding the current environment in Western culture and its diagnostic approach to mental health and illness. In his recent book *Crazy Like Us: The Globalization of the American Psyche*, Ethan Waters argues that we have been "exporting" our Western ideas about what makes for mental health and illness in ways that have been detrimental to other cultures around the globe. We have done this, in part, because our Western homogenized notions tend toward disrespect for regional differences and diversity in other parts of the world.

Behind the promotion of Western ideas of mental health and healing lie a variety of cultural assumptions about human nature itself. Westerners share, for instance, beliefs about what type of life event is likely to make one psychologically traumatized, and we agree that venting emotions is healthier than stoic silence. We are certain that humans are innately fragile and should consider many emotional experiences as illnesses that require professional intervention. We're confident that our biomedical approach to mental illness will reduce stigma for the sufferer and that our drugs are the best that science has to offer. We promise people in other cultures that mental health (and a modern style of self-awareness) can be found by throwing off traditional social roles and engaging in individualistic quests of introspection. These Western ideas about the mind are proving as seductive as fast food and rap music, and we are spreading them with speed and vigor.[2]

While the primary thesis of this chapter is that the experience of mental illness is like an inner immigration of sorts, another interesting extension of the metaphor is that in U.S. culture we are now continuously "migrating" out our central theories about mental health and illness to countries all over the world. Even the notion that

2. Ethan Waters, *Crazy Like Us: The Globalization of the American Psyche* (New York: Free Press, 2010), 4.

stigmas against the mentally ill are being reduced across the globe by extending this universalizing use of the medical model is being challenged:

> When asked to name the sources of mental illness, people from every country studied are increasingly likely to mention "chemical imbalance" or "brain disease" or "genetics" as part of the cause of mental illness. . . . Unfortunately, as mental health professionals and advocates for the mentally ill have been winning this rhetorical and conceptual battle, they've been simultaneously losing the war against stigma. Studies of attitudes in the United States between the 1950s and 1996 have demonstrated that the perception of dangerousness surrounding the mentally ill has steadily increased over this time.[3]

On the practical level, all those who care about the mentally ill, including family members, should be very intentional about developing an ability to communicate professionally with advocates for good mental health from a wide variety of backgrounds (including medical doctors and psychiatrists). Yet, even so, a renewed degree of skepticism toward the medical model perspective is still called for. An approach to diagnostics that is highly interdisciplinary and intercultural, respecting cross-cultural and cross-religious dialogue, is the best practice. Such an approach draws helpful insights from many disciplines and perspectives, while keeping a special emphasis on a unique spiritual and religious vision that lies at the heart of the matter, remembering again that the root meaning of the word *religion* is to rebind that which has been fragmented.

Mental Illness as/and Immigration: A Case Study

In Donald Capps's book titled *Fragile Connections: Memoirs of Mental Illness for Pastoral Care Professionals*, his orienting question about persons with mental illness is "What do the mentally ill and their

---

3. Ibid., 172.

families have to teach ministers about mental illness?"[4] This is a deep listening approach and it stands in contrast with other approaches toward case study work that address the issues from the perspective of what we can do for such persons and families. So, in this section, the focus is on my paternal grandfather's journey with mental illness from the overarching and guiding perspective of what does it teach us? This is the same perspective of Ernst Bruder, who once wrote poignantly in his book *Ministering to Deeply Troubled People*, that "the sanity of the insane has much to offer by way of illuminating the insanity of the sane."[5]

So, to begin, here are the facts of my grandfather's life as I have researched them: Francois Alexander Baard (known in the United States as "Frank") was born on 12 April 1898, in Beetsterzwaag, Friesland Province, Netherlands, the youngest child of a large family of eleven children. Frank had three brothers and seven sisters. Family records show that his parents (Wolter Pieter Baard and Hermina Stall Baard) ran a small business in Sneek, Holland—a tailor shop. Perhaps they moved to Gorredyk, Friesland in the same region in Holland later on in their life together. Frank was given a common school education growing up and also attended a mechanics school. His social life revolved around church. The records also show that his brother Wolter, older than Frank by two years and three months, immigrated to South Dakota in 1914, arriving some two years before his younger brother.

Frank came aboard the steamship *New Amsterdam* from Rotterdam, the Netherlands, disembarking at Ellis Island, New York on 24 May 1916. He was eighteen years old. He soon settled into work as a farm laborer and carpenter near the small town of Harrisburg in Grant

4. Donald Capps, *Fragile Connections: Memoirs of Mental Illness for Pastoral Care Professionals* (St. Louis: Chalice, 2005), 4.
5. Ernst B. Bruder, *Ministering to Deeply Troubled People* (Englewood Cliffs, NJ: Prentice Hall, 1963), 24.

County in eastern South Dakota. The official records that document his life's journey are scant. His U.S. WWI draft registration card shows that he officially registered on 18 September 1918. On 19 May 1920, at the age of twenty-two, he married Hannah Green, the daughter of German immigrant framers in the area, in a service at the Presbyterian Church in Brookings, South Dakota performed by an Evangelical Church minister. Frank and Hannah had one son, named Robert William (my father), born on 22 April 1926. At the time of the birth of his son, Frank was twenty-eight years old.

On 7 December 1927, at age twenty-nine, Frank was admitted to the State Hospital in Yankton, South Dakota. He had been married seven years, and his only son Robert was one year eight months old at the time. While the hospital is not allowed to release medical diagnoses, even of deceased patients, due to confidentiality of patient records, my father told me when I was in college that the diagnosis was "dementia praecox," or what we now call schizophrenia. Frank lived at the State Hospital until his discharge on 1 December 1961, when he was released to the Resthaven Nursing Home in Canova, Miner County, South Dakota.

During his time at the State Hospital, Frank had very few visitors. On one occasion, when my father Robert was a young teenager, some of his relatives—probably his two aunts who were Frank's older sisters—took him to visit his father at the State Hospital. When he visited, Frank was hallucinating about bygone days on the farm; in his mind he was back on the farm, calling out and bringing in the horses from the fields. To invoke the guiding metaphor, he had migrated to another place in his inner world. By his own telling of the story, Robert was frightened by this visit with his mentally ill father, and so he never went back to see him again.

Frank was sixty-three years old at the time of his discharge, and at that time, attempts were made to contact his son, but the letter of notification was sent to the wrong address. The letter was mistakenly sent to Menomonee, Washington, instead of the correct address of Menomonee, Wisconsin, where Robert and his family lived. Thus, the letter was returned (twice) to the State Hospital, and remained forever unclaimed.

Death records obtained from the state of South Dakota show that Frank died on 8 February 1964, at the age of sixty-five years, nine months, and twenty-six days. The cause of death as listed on the death certificate was suicide. No autopsy was performed. His older brother Wolter signed the death certificate as the informant to the county coroner. Thus Frank spent over half of his life in institutions—almost thirty-four years as a patient at the State Hospital, and then another two years and two months at a nursing home in a nearby small town in South Dakota prior to his death.

What does Frank's long journey with schizophrenia have to teach us? How does it inform us? It seems clear at the outset that Frank's case reinforces many points that others have made about the experience of mental illness in Western culture.

First, in the background of Frank's story is the severe stress of the immigration and assimilation process, coupled with the stress of living near the poverty line. These factors most certainly had much to do with the etiology of Frank's mental illness. First-generation immigrants generally show higher rates of mental illness than the rest of the population, because of the difficulties and challenges involved in assimilating into a new culture. Suicide rates are higher than the general population for persons with mental illness because their suffering is both consistent and intense. Thus it is not surprising that Frank's journey ended in taking his own life, for many persons struggling with severe mental illness choose to end their lives and their suffering in this way.

Second, during his life, like so many institutionalized mentally ill persons, Frank's story also reveals that he had very little contact with any family members during the long years he spent at the State Hospital. Mental illness is a complicated phenomenon, and for so many, including close family members, it is a strange and frightening phenomenon as well. So we learn from Frank's case that the inevitable isolation and stigmatization of persons struggling with mental illness has always been severe in our society. Part of the "insanity of the sane" that our society continues to express is in the ways it exacerbates the problems of the mentally ill by keeping them continually isolated from others.

Yet this sense of isolation is also internal, living inside the person who is affected by mental illness. Anton Boisen, sometimes referred to as the grandfather of the clinical pastoral education movement in the United States, and a sufferer of mental illness himself, described this sense of internal isolation in his groundbreaking book, *The Exploration of the Inner World*:

> [T]he real evil in mental disorder is not to be found in the conflict but in the sense of isolation or estrangement. It is the fear and guilt which results from the presence in one's life of that which one is afraid to tell.[6]

If Boisen is right, we can only speculate now, years later, what exactly was present in Frank's life that he was "afraid to tell" which may have contributed to his deep inner isolation, to his own "inner migration" to a strange internal land.

Reflecting further on what we learn from Frank's case, we turn to Brian Grant's insightful book *Schizophrenia: A Source of Social Insight*, where he presents a more positive and even prophetic view

---

6. Anton T. Boisen, *The Exploration of the Inner World: A Study of Mental Disorder and Religious Experience* (Chicago: Willett, Clark & Company, 1936), 264.

that reframes the social "contribution" that persons like Frank offer all of us through their struggles with schizophrenia:

> The schizophrenic's contribution is an irreplaceable one, because the schizophrenic can see and feel the results of society's choices with an intensity that is lost to the rest of the community, and feels enough pain and responsibility to see that these results are made known. . . . Because of the schizophrenic's utterance, the society and its individuals are, in varying degree, freed to live in fuller contact with the reality that surrounds them.[7]

There is much to be affirmed regarding Grant's analysis of schizophrenia. His ideas about the redeeming social value of schizophrenia and his care in pointing out how it can so function lend some hope, dignity, and a new perspective to an often all-too-depressing subject. His work is another step forward in the direction of healing or even removing painful stigmas that our society attaches to persons afflicted with schizophrenia and mental illness in general. These stigmas, Brian Grant would argue, have their roots in an all-too-comfortable medical-model misconception of this phenomenon.

Religiously speaking, perhaps some type of holy truth is being revealed in every instance of schizophrenia. If it can be translated correctly, it has the potential to bring a prophetic word of truth to the society around it. Persons with schizophrenia may have indeed immigrated to a strange land, but it is a land that often brings new insights to the so-called commonsense land we all inhabit together in our society.

So let us now return again to our guiding question and ask: What more does Frank's case have to teach us? Is there some prophetic word to our society that we should interpret from his story? In Frank's case we probably don't have enough information to answer that question more precisely. It is important to note here that in some

---

7. Brian Grant, *Schizophrenia: A Source of Social Insight* (Philadelphia: Westminster, 1975), 171.

other cultures across the globe, we know that in figures like shamans, or lucid dreamers, what we call "psychosis" is viewed respectfully as traveling (or migrating) to other worlds, or even moving between this world and the next world. These persons are seen in the common life of their societies as possessing very special gifts for healing, and the people revere them. The truth is, every life deserves this level of respect.

Multireligious Reflections on the Metaphor of Mental Illness as Immigration

Religious experience as well as mental disorder may involve severe emotional upheaval, and mental disorder as well as religious experience may represent the operation of the healing forces of nature. The conclusion follows that certain types of mental disorder and certain types of religious experience are alike attempts at reorganization. The difference lies in outcome.[8]

There is no question that many forms of mental illness have a religious/spiritual dimension to them. This dimension expresses itself clearly in the agonizing and painful emotional struggles that persons so afflicted endure. In some cases this struggle, which Anton Boisen sees as an attempt to radically reorganize the inner world, takes an acute short-lived expression. In other cases it is stretched out over a long period of time. The pain involved is as real as any physical ailment, and as Boisen points out, its purpose and function is precisely that which we have always associated with physical ailments—namely, healing. And healing, for the religious person, always has deep spiritual connections and dimensions. In using the resources of his own painful life experience to come to this interpretation of mental illness, Anton Boisen has done humanity

8. Boisen, *Exploration*, vii.

a great service. In the contemporary world, we have turned over care of the mentally ill to professionals of the secular healing trades—psychologists, psychiatrists, along with other medical practitioners and social workers. Indeed these professions have taught us and continue to teach us much, and in many ways they have vastly improved conditions for the mentally ill in our contemporary society. Anton Boisen's life and ministry, however, was a testimony to the claim that the religious and spiritual realms still have an important if not central role to play here.

In the Christian tradition, Jesus neither feared nor misunderstood mental illness, but rather took a healing approach toward it. Luke 8:26-39, the story of the Gerasene demoniac, is one of several such encounters of Jesus and a mentally ill person recorded in the gospels. Jesus was not simply interested in the individual's healing, but in the healing of the larger social context; that is, the whole society and social order of his day. In that sense the healing ministry of Jesus always had a systemic and a prophetic edge to it. Persons of Christian faith, by the example of Jesus, are called toward this type of prophetic compassion with respect to those who are mentally ill.

It is not just the Christian tradition, however, that calls us toward service in this arena. The ethical imperative to show compassion toward "strangers in the world" runs across the entire world of lived religious traditions—including all of the five major traditions of Judaism, Islam, Christianity, Buddhism, and Hinduism. The moral of the story is that these particular "immigrants"—meaning all those who suffer from mental illness—need our help, our compassion. We are called by an overarching interfaith and multireligious perspective to overcome our fears and work against societal stigmas in order to be present in compassionate ways to these people.

Conclusions

In conclusion, there is great value to this exploration of the metaphor of immigration and/as mental illness. Persons with mental illness do truly immigrate to a foreign land. For immigrants in this way, the resources of religion, including deep spiritual insights, may offer great comfort or even healing in certain cases. Though healing was not the apparent end result in my grandfather's story, there is still a way in which our careful listening to his tragic story can hold him, along with his tumultuous and multifaceted journey of immigration, in an honest and sincere reverence.

Indeed, all those who have become "strangers in the world" through the suffering of their mental illnesses need both our deep compassion and our respect. Stephen Olsen and Joretta Marshall, writing in an edited volume titled *Ministry with Persons with Mental Illness and Their Families*, suggest four powerful and effective ways for ministers in the Christian tradition to demonstrate this kind of compassion. Representatives of other world religions could do the same:

First, the importance of education about mental illness cannot be overstated. Conversations about schizophrenia belong in religious classes and other places where people gather to think about the meaning of life and connect it to the bigger reality of spirituality.

Second, challenging the stigma of mental illness during sermons or talking about persons whose lives are marked by psychosis with a deep sense of respect becomes part of the public voice of pastoral leaders.

Third, voicing concerns and talking about mental health issues in general from the pulpit, in worship, and in other aspects of a community's life can do a great deal to break the shame and silence that often greet individuals and families who live with this disease.

Finally, it is important that the church be involved in public conversations about healthcare, alternative living spaces for those with schizophrenia, and responding to the needs of those who are slipping through the cracks and ending up on the streets or in jails.[9]

May we listen closely to this guidance, for the benefit of all the "strangers in this world" who struggle with mental illness, and for the good of society as a whole. For we remember again, in closing, that the root meaning of religion is to rebind all that has been fragmented, all that has been broken, and help restore it to wholeness.

9. Robert H. Albers, William H. Meller, and Stephen D. Thurber, eds., *Ministry with Persons with Mental Illness and Their Families* (Minneapolis: Fortress Press, 2012), 79–80.

Afterword

A World Strangely New, as Old as History

Francis X. Clooney, SJ

The urgency of the issues of immigration and the increasing complexity of theology today as an interdisciplinary mode of reflection make *Strangers in This World* a timely volume, and it is impressive in its diversity of authors and perspectives. It is particularly gratifying to see how it grew from conversations at the AAR-Luce seminars in Theologies of Religious Pluralism and Comparative Theology. The volume includes a number of participants from those seminars but, quite nicely, has drawn additional voices into their project.

I need not summarize the essays here, since Alexander Hwang has capably done so at the start. Suffice it to say that we find in these essays many things; each focuses on its own issues, interestingly juxtaposed side by side with others differently related to the migration theme: a mix of histories of arrival and reception, steadfast remembrance and scandalous failures to remember; theories and theologies of reception and hospitality; philosophies of society as static or changing; even mental illness as a kind of lonely migration, welcomed or not, into a strange new land. Similarly, a rich array of related but distinct terms mingle together: refugees, strangers, aliens, exiles; tourism, migration, immigration; migration as chosen and forced; immigration; travel; pilgrimage and the religiously inspired mission; travel compelled by economic, political, or religious pressures; the dynamics of hospitality, proffered and withheld bonds between host and guest.

"The Immigration Question," as Hwang puts it in his introduction, challenges both the immigrant and the actual or potential host communities on religious grounds. This is a very large question indeed; immigration and the severer forms of forced migration and refugee flight are not only complex issues in themselves, but they are tied in with a host of other global opportunities and problems. These essays compel us to consider the wider horizons within which immigration occurs and is studied, pondering issues of law and policies on immigration. And yet there are also subtler psychological issues and attitudes toward what is new, unexpected, or inconvenient, the desire for stability and the prospect of living with long-term uncertainty.

Traditions of human decency may push to the side hesitations and resistances regarding welcoming the stranger, and conservative religious values may hold a society together. But the same traditions and values, not easily adjusted, may make it harder to welcome specific strangers, particularly if they come from very different cultures or religions and carry along their own enduring traditions and values. Conversely, conservative immigrants may fit poorly in societies more liberal and more open than the one they left behind. Immigrants may or may not be ready for the new conditions confronting them upon arrival, and may not be ready for the adjustments that welcoming communities expect of them. From every angle, new questions arise, and these essays reach out in so many of the right directions. They interestingly highlight tradition-specific sources and problematics, ways of thinking through the arrival of the stranger and experiences of exile. Fortunately, the historical sweep is wide: the nearly archetypal sufferings of the people of Israel, Goths coming to the Roman Empire not just to plunder but to stay, Italian immigrants seeking new homes in the Protestant culture of the USA, Buddhists and Hindus finding ways to accommodate new social formations and welcome the stranger. The experience of Israel offers in a sense the quintessential case, forming for many of us the archetypal instance of the stranger and alien, the outsider we welcome because we once were such ourselves. Similarly fundamental is attention to the Native American experience, the original American host and the host ruined and erased by European immigrants ready to forget their own arrival on this continent.

Theology is at stake too: How much should the newcomers be pressured to fit in with already-existing spiritual and moral values? On what spiritual grounds will a community truly be able to welcome newcomers, not merely as visitors, but as neighbors now here to stay? How do basic religious instincts make it possible to envision ideal yet open communities? Practically, collaboration across religious boundaries is of great help for the practical and intellectual tasks related to immigration. And for this collaboration in practice, thinking together is required, as basic values of culture and religion come together. We can also philosophize about the right balancing of the values of continuity and change.

Joseph Bracken and Marc Pugliese intriguingly show us that even a refined and expert line of speculative thinking can be a resource in confronting matters of practical import. Thus, process theology helps us to think through the fundamentals:

> For process-relational thought, change is woven into the fabric of reality, and thus inevitable. For process-relational thought, change is not from one reality to another. It is a newly patterned present reality

building on a settled past. It is additive, not transitional. The settled past imposes itself upon all successive realities. At the same time change in the appearance of new actualities continuously occurs. New entities are inextricably bound to their past but not determined by it.

When faced with a choice between opting (vainly) for as stable a society as possible, or welcoming the new, we can make a real difference: "Choosing the former maintains the status quo, perpetuating present societal forms. Deciding for the latter breaks from the past, introduces sizable change, and generates aesthetic achievement." It will be interesting then to see how other philosophies, in other settings, shape expectations about the nature of society.

The essays are excellent in uncovering resources specific to particular traditions. I can only point to a few examples here of the many ways the essays stimulate our thinking by asking us to be more specific. Native American experiences and dispositions, enduring despite every obstacle, have much to teach us, particularly if we remember where we are coming from and who we are in facing contemporary issues. Randy Woodley reminds us that "[p]recolonial Native American patterns of thinking about the land developed over tens of thousands of years and millions of experiences, creating a sense of harmony between the people and the land. This balance maintained the health of both land and people until the onslaught of European colonialism." Whereas most Westerners saw the land as "inanimate space that is commodifiable in every sense," the First Nations see the land as alive, "a gift from the Creator, belonging to everyone—not just those who are able to hoard it through unjust laws and unfounded values." On every level, the First Nations had other intuitions about how the newcomers were to be received, and the disastrous failure in understanding reverberates through today's misunderstandings as well.

Laura Alexander invites us to explore the theology and politics of the New Sanctuary Movement as an ecumenical Christian initiative grounded specifically in Lutheran tradition. She writes that the movement

> draws attention to the theologically and ethically troublesome pressures of contemporary economic and political life, which become especially clear in the lives of undocumented immigrants. Lutheran theological and ethical thinking provides concepts through which we can fruitfully analyze, and begin to respond to such pressures, especially in the lives of those who must clearly choose between obeying laws and fulfilling their family and economic obligations.

Asking, right at the start of policy debates, "Will these laws allow people to fulfill all of their fundamental human moral obligations?" will lead, Alexander tells us, "to very different laws than we currently have." From the start we must notice "the factors that cause human suffering and think clearly about how to shape a communal political life," as a life together that makes it possible "both for those who are born in the community and for those who enter it as migrants to fulfill their basic needs as well as, crucially, their basic moral obligations."

Drawing on Islamic sources, Hussam Timani highlights "the importance given to strangers and immigrants in the Qur'an and the Islamic teachings in general." From an Islamic perspective, "not only are immigrants central . . . , but they also are *the* community. Immigration theology is a theology of religious pluralism since strangeness has become a symbol of piety, a path to salvation, a mode for purification, and a mirror to see the self in the other."

In perhaps the most directly and necessarily political of the essays, Alan Aja becomes still more specific in urging a faith-grounded response to state and federal government inaction on immigration reform. Aja challenges the reader: "As religious communities across the country continue to place pressure on policymakers for fair and just immigration reform," religious communities may have to be as disruptive as Jesus, the breaker of traditions and taboos. Nor does the challenge end when reform becomes law. Rather, "the moral responsibility to shelter, feed, and empower those who will likely suffer by the policy, should in no way cease in effort and action." Articulating both local and national policies and initiatives, "however controversial and unorthodox," will remain essential to "any progressive, faith-based policy agenda."

Just as going deep into particular traditions matters, crossing back and forth across religious borders is also timely, as comparative theological reflection shows us. Reid Locklin's essay highlights the constructive interreligious study that reconfigures the Christian in light of another tradition's views: "A Hindu-Christian comparative theology of the quarters would locate itself neither in the imagined India of Śaṅkara's *vijaya* nor in its symbolic re-placement by an image like the BMI [body-mind-intellect] Chart. It would emplace itself, instead, in the dynamic movement between them." Subsequent adjustments would arise "in confidence that these particular Hindu and Christian traditions—as migrant, pilgrim traditions emplaced within broader visions of journey and transformation—presume their own thorough transcendence, as a condition of self-discovery." His essay exemplifies the cross-fertilization that the conversation promises, our views of our own theological and social positions changed, enriched, challenged, by what we learn from others. In a sense, comparative theology expects and requires continual intellectual migration, and continual readiness to receive hospitably ideas and practices unasked for and unexpected.

A strength of this book is that it does not present itself as treating its topic with any finality. Given the diversity and breadth found in the essays, it is easy to see how the topic will benefit from further studies that fill it out in every direction. We can easily benefit from essays that highlight the religious challenges immigration poses for those arriving as they decide how smoothly they want to fit in, as "good guests." We can benefit from further distinctions among those traveling in search of improved living conditions and those driven from their homes by violence and in desperation. What happens to those who are sometimes overwhelmed by the immigrant community merits more attention. Still other examples will be required to sketch the terrain outside the North American context. Readers will readily, after all, think of other migrations and receptions: Jews returning to Israel; Turks arriving in Germany; people of several religions fleeing the violence in Iraq and Syria; India, Pakistan, and Bangladesh welcoming, even at great cost, innumerable refugees over the past seventy years; South Asians seeking new homes in Australia or New Zealand; Africans driven from their homelands by the past century's long series of wars. Notably too, none of the essays dwells on that very terrible and archetypal instance of forced migration: the violent transfer of millions as slaves to the Americas.

Strangers in This World is a very good start on a very important conversation, and the editors and contributors are to be commended for their pioneering work, a setting of the questions with a fine balance of depth and breadth. It establishes this important field of interreligious study, cutting widely across the range of possible topics. In their rich complexity, its essays rule out piecemeal and oversimplified approaches inadequate to the intersecting issues that must be dealt with together. The book is sustenance for the reader's own journey, as she travels into this new land where everyone is a stranger, and all of us are just beginning to realize that we've actually been on the road together, for a long time.

Index